The Porter-Deaver Debate
on
Congregational Benevolence

by

W. Curtis Porter and Roy C. Deaver

ISBN-10: 1-58427-187-6

ISBN-13: 978-158427-1871

Guardian of Truth
P.O. Box 9670
Bowling Green, Kentucky 42102
www.truthbooks.net

Table of Contents

Introduction to the Porter-Deaver Debate, Donnie V. Rader . . . . . *v*

First Night

Porter's First Affirmative 7

Deaver's First Negative 18

Porter's Second Affirmative 30

Deaver's Second Negative 42

Second Night

Porter's Third Affirmative. 53

Deaver's Third Negative. 64

Porter's Fourth Affirmative. 77

Deaver's Fourth Negative. 89

Third Night

Deaver's First Affirmative 101

Porter's First Negative 113

Deaver's Second Affirmative 125

Porter's Second Negative 137

Fourth Night

Deaver's Third Affirmative. 149

Porter's Third Negative. 161

Deaver's Fourth Affirmative. 173

Porter's Fourth Negative. 186

Introduction to the Porter - Deaver Debate

This debate between W. Curtis Porter (1897-1960) and Roy C. Deaver (b. 1922) took place in Dumas, TX on October 22-25, 1957.

The proposition for the first two nights was, *"According to the Scriptures, churches of Christ, each acting in its congregational capacity, are adequate to accomplish all of the work of benevolence that God has given the church to do. And they should do this work without delegating it by the contribution of their funds to benevolent organizations"* (W. Curtis Porter affirms, Roy C. Deaver denies). The proposition for the last two nights was *"The Scriptures teach that a church may contribute to Boles Home, Quinlan, Texas"* (Roy C. Deaver affirms, W. Curtis Porter denies).

Both men were able debaters. Both debated other brethren on this issue. Roy Deaver met Earnest Finley (Bunavista, TX, 1957), W. L. Wharton (Joliet, IL, 1961 and Fort Towson, OK, 1963), Charles Holt (Jacksonville, FL, 1963), Ward Hogland (Pensacola, FL, 1977), and J. T. Smith (Gainsboro, TN, 1984). Curtis Porter had debated Guy N. Woods twice before this debate (Indianapolis, IN, 1956 and Paragould, AR, 1957).

The name, W. Curtis Porter, was best known for his outstanding ability on the polemic platform. Brethren from all around called him frequently to help them by meeting a man in debate. He had seventy-seven such debates. His expertise was in answering and responding to arguments and quibbles that his opponents would make. He would often speak of "quibbles that backfire"—meaning the argument or quibble proved to be inconsistent for his opponent.

This publication will make eight of brother Porter's debates that are in print. The others are Porter-Bogard, Porter-Tingley, Porter-Woods, Porter-Waters, Porter-Dugger, Porter-Abercrombie, and Porter-Myers. Brother Porter would have been pleased to see this debate in print. He once told Edgar J. Dye that he was more pleased with this debate (with Roy Deaver) than any of the others he had (at least on this subject).

This work was transcribed from a tape recording by Thomas F. Shropshire many years ago.

The charts that each man used are not printed in the book for the simple reason that we do not have copies of all of them.

I am delighted to see another of W. Curtis Porter's debates made available for the reading public.

Donnie V. Rader
November 20, 2006

Porter's First Affirmative

Brethren Moderators, Brother Deaver, Brothers, and Sisters: I am grateful for the privilege of being here upon this occasion to enter into this discussion that will deal with things in which we are vitally interested and about which we are deeply concerned—matters that pertain to the work of the church for which the Lord Jesus Christ gave his blood. We regret of course, that discussions of this kind are necessary between brethren but when we differ upon matters of this kind certainly it is worth our time to make an honest investigation of those things revealed in the book of God that we may be able to determine just what may be God's will in the matter. And then for Brother Deaver to be my opponent upon this occasion as we enter into this discussion of these vital things. We appreciate your presence and thank you in advance for the attention we are sure you will give us while we endeavor to present to you a number of things during these few hours.

The proposition has been read for your consideration or for your information and it is my duty as is ordinarily the duty of the affirmant to make some definitions of the terms of the proposition. *According to the scriptures, churches of Christ, each acting in its congregational capacity, are adequate to accomplish all of the work of benevolence that God has given the church to do. And they should do this work without delegating it by the contribution of their funds to benevolent organizations.* By the term "scriptures" of course, we mean the word of God—that which we call the Bible; and in particular, as it pertains to this proposition—to this subject tonight—the New Testament scriptures of course. And by the expression "according to the scriptures" I simply mean that it is in harmony with New Testament scriptures of course, and New Testament teaching—according to the teaching of God's book. By the expression "churches of Christ" I mean simply local congregations of the Lord's people as they are found in various sections of the country today. By "benevolent work" I refer to the work of caring for the needy—relieving those who are in distress. I think we all understand the significance of the work of benevolence in that connection, and that each congregation acting in its congregational capacity or as a congregation would act—that these congregations thus acting are adequate or they are able or they are sufficient to accomplish all of the work of benevolence that God has given the church to do. That is, whatever work of benevolence God has assigned the church, the churches acting in their congregational capacity are able or sufficient or adequate to do or to accomplish that work. And they should do this work—that is, the work of benevolence that has already been mentioned—without delegating it or surrendering it by the contribution of their funds—that is, by donating or giving their funds to benevolent organizations. By "benevolent organizations" I mean organizations or associations or societies set up to do the work of benevolence which are human in their origin. And it is my contention that churches are adequate to do the work that God gave them to do without assigning or delegating their work to organizations of this nature. I think that may be sufficient as far as a definition of the terms are concerned to clarify the same, so I want to enter into some things for your consideration at this time.

First, I want to make just a little bit of an analysis of the proposition in addition to the definition that has been given. And for the purpose of that I want to use a chart on the projector screen. My chart "A" please and whoever operates the lights will turn the lights off for us just a moment. We have here the proposition analyzed. The proposition is first copied on the chart, as you see, which I have just read from my notes a few moments ago. Then on the bottom portion of the chart I have listed my position and Brother Deaver's position. On the left hand, my position regarding this proposition is: First, that God has given a work of benevolence to churches. Over on the opposite side, Brother Deaver's position is that God has given a work of benevolence to churches. On that particular point we are perfectly agreed. God has assigned a work of benevolence for churches to do. God has given it some responsibility—some obligation along that line. In the second place, my position is that the churches are adequate to do the work that God gave them to do. And Brother Deaver's position, in the second place, is that the churches are not adequate to do the work that God has assigned. And in the third place, my position is that they should do the work. And Brother Deaver's position in the third place is they should not do the work. And in the next place, my position number four is that they should not surrender or delegate that work to benevolent organizations. Brother

Deaver's position is number four, that they should surrender the work to benevolent organizations. Now friends, to me that is an amazing proposition for a man claiming to be a gospel preacher to sign in the negative. A few years ago if somebody had told you that any gospel preacher beneath the sun could have been induced to sign a proposition like that you would have thought he had about lost his mind. And yet that is the very thing that Brother Deaver has signed the negative of, and that is where he has placed his responsibility in this discussion tonight and tomorrow night.

We both agree that God has given the congregations or churches a work in benevolence to do. But from there on we disagree. I believe—I maintain—I affirm that the churches are adequate to do all the work or to accomplish all the work that God has given the church to do. Brother Deaver says it is not so. He is denying that the churches are adequate to do what God assigned them to do. He is denying the all-sufficiency of the church. And that God gave the church a work to do and yet the church is not able to do it. And furthermore, if they were able, they should not do it anyway, but should surrender that work to benevolent organizations. Could you have ever dreamed a few years ago that any man, claiming to be a gospel preacher, would sign the negative of a proposition like this? Absolutely denying that the church that God gave and the church for which our Lord Jesus Christ died is not adequate to do its work—that is, cannot accomplish the work that God assigned it to do? Well, that is exactly where Brother Deaver stands tonight. And I shall hold him to that as this discussion goes on. And I want you to keep this in mind: that he is saying that, while the churches have a work of benevolence that God has assigned them, they are not adequate to do it. And furthermore, they should not anyway but should surrender that work to benevolent organizations which are human institutions. Now that is the difference between my position tonight and Brother Deaver's position in this debate.

Well, proceeding from that, I want to use now just following that, chart "B" , as we get that matter further before you (and these charts, Brother Deaver, I pass to you). We have here chart "B" which comes up along the same line, the title of which I have placed as "Church or Benevolent Organizations." Now we have both of them involved in the proposition. My proposition speaks of the church or churches of Christ the local congregations—and also, of benevolent organizations. Both of them are in the proposition tonight, over on the left I have the diagram drawn to represent the two—the rectangle at the top representing the church and the rectangle over there at the bottom representing the benevolent organization. Then I have one over here on the right representing the home or the place and clothing with food and medical care and supervision and things of that kind in which care maybe rendered to someone who is in need—the work of benevolence—whatever it may be along that line—it may be of one kind or another. But the work of benevolence is involved and God has assigned a work of benevolence to the church to be done. I believe that that church over there that Jesus Christ built—that he died for, which is of divine origin because it was authorized by the Lord, is governed by the gospel of Jesus Christ and directed by the elders of the congregation, is able and adequate to do the work of benevolence that God has assigned it. That it can meet its obligations with respect to matters of this kind. That the church, the congregation, acting in its congregational capacity, can do that. But Brother Deaver says it cannot—it is not able to do it—it is not adequate to do it. Instead of it doing that, it should delegate that work to benevolent organizations down here which are of human origin, authorized by the state and governed by its charter and directed by a board. And then let that benevolent organization do the work that the church is not able to do. And that is exactly where we stand upon this tonight. Here is my position: The congregation of divine origin can do the work of benevolence that God assigned it. Brother Deaver says the congregation—the church—cannot do that work—is not able to do it—is not adequate to do it—and so it should surrender or delegate that work to a benevolent organization or benevolent organizations, and let them in turn do the work that God gave the church to do. Now the issue out here is not benevolence—it is not whether the church has an obligation along that line. The issue between us, my friends, is this right here—the benevolent organizations that he says the church is to surrender its funds to and let them do the work that God ordained the church to do.

And then I want another chart following that—chart "C". And in connection with this chart I want to call your attention to some things regarding the all-sufficiency of the church. And my proposition tonight is affirming the all-sufficiency of the church. And I believe that God's plans have always been adequate and sufficient—that man has not been able to improve upon them. When God gave to the world the gospel of Jesus Christ, he gave an adequate gospel and the very same gospel that was preached in the first century, needs to be preached today. Man has not been able to improve upon that gospel the Lord gave. It was an adequate gospel for the work designed to be done. Furthermore, when the Lord revealed the plan of salvation as we teach today, we believe that that is an adequate plan. That when men, having heard the gospel of Jesus Christ, believe with all of their hearts, repent of their sins, confess Christ and are baptized for the remission of their sins, they will obtain the salvation of their souls. Man has not been able to improve upon the plan of salvation that God gave. It was an adequate plan. And when God gave the worship to the church, he gave an adequate worship. Those items of worship ordained by the Lord Jesus Christ stand today and need to be practiced today just as they were in the first century, for that plan of Jehovah with regard to worship has never been improved upon by any human being beneath the stars. And furthermore, when God gave the church a work to do and assigned that work to it, we find that when he gave the church this work that the church was adequate to do the work that God assigned it. The church in its worship, in its organization, in its work was an adequate church. And men have not been able to improve upon the church the Lord died for in the long ago.

And I submit to you tonight that if the local congregation is not adequate to do the work that God has assigned the church to do, then the New Testament is not adequate as a guide in religious matters. Why, the only organization which the New Testament authorized to exist to perform the functions of the church is the local congregation. And if that cannot do it—if that congregation is not adequate to do it, then the New Testament is not adequate as a guide—the Lord failed to give us a sufficient revelation—he failed to give us a guide that is sufficient to lead us in the way that we should go. So as the result of it, we have an inadequate church, according to Brother Deaver, that must resort to benevolent organizations to do the work that it is not able itself to do. Therefore, (the church) delegates its work by the contribution of its funds to things of that kind instead of doing the work that God ordained it to do.

And now on this chart here—chart "C"—"The all-sufficiency of the Church. And with respect to the work of the church we agree I think upon the fact that there are, in the main, three fields pertaining to its mission: First, in evangelism, the second in edification—that is self-edification, and the third, benevolence. Regarding the work of evangelism, I believe the church is adequate to do all that God has assigned it do to. In 1 Timothy 3:15, Paul wrote Timothy, instructing him how to behave himself in the house of God which he says is the church of the living God, the pillar and ground of the truth. And in Ephesians 3:10 we have revealed to us the fact also that it was God's will that his wisdom might be known by the church, or that it might be known by the church the manifold wisdom of God. Here we have then revealed to us the work of evangelism that God assigned the church to do. And I believe the local congregations, acting in their congregational capacity, were able to do what God has given the church in the field of evangelism. We start with the church in Jerusalem, the first one established, in the second chapter of Acts. Not long after that there came about a persecution and the church was scattered abroad. We are told in the eighth chapter of Acts that they went everywhere preaching the word. And in Acts 11:19 we learn that some of them went down as far as Antioch. And them that received the word—heard the word and believed the word, accepted it. And also in Acts 11:22,23 that the church in Jerusalem, having heard of it sent Barnabas there. He engaged in the work of exhortation over at Antioch. And so we have another local congregation established as was the local congregation in Jerusalem. And the church was at Antioch, according to Acts 13:1-4. And they came back from that journey as the fourteenth chapter of Acts tells us and reported to the church that sent them out. And then we learn from Acts 16 that they made another trip from the same point—location—and on this trip they went into Philippi according to Acts 16:31-33. And there Paul preached the gospel to the Philippian jailor and the church was established in Philippi. Furthermore, according to Acts 17:1-4, they went on to Thessalonica and there the gospel was preached and men believed it and accepted it and a church was established there. And Paul writing to the Philippian church in Philippians 4:14,16 declared that they had sent once and again to his necessity while in Thessalonica. And then in 1 Thessalonians 1:8, we read as Paul then writes the church in Thessalonica that "from you sounded out the word, not only in Macedonia and Achaia, but in every place your faith toward God is spread abroad." Here we find the church was adequate as local congregations to do the work that God had assigned the church to do. One local congregation and another and another and another, on down the line, and in every case, we have it either individual or congregational work in which many engaged in those days. And therefore the church was adequate to do all that God assigned it to do in the field of evangelism. And I am certain of the fact that they did not do this: The Jerusalem church did not set up a missionary society or missionary organization and delegate its work by the contribution of its funds to that society and let that society establish a church in Antioch, at Philippi, Thessalonica and Achaia and various other places. This was not done. When men did this a hundred years ago or more, they simply expressed their view of the insufficiency of the church. By such an arrangement, they declared that the church was not sufficient; it was not an adequate institution, in the field of evangelism. And therefore they set up a missionary organization to do the work that they did not believe the local congregation could adequately accomplish.

And so in the field of edification we have also an obligation placed. Ephesians 4:16 makes reference to the fact that they are to be built up by such edification, making the increase of the body unto the edifying of itself in love. Here in the church at Ephesus we find that edification was carried on, Ephesians 4:11, 12, in which they were edifying the church or the brethren upon that occasion. And in Corinth in 1 Corinthians 14:12 the same thing. And so each congregation engaged in the work of self edification. And I am certain they did not do this: No church of that time set up a Sunday school society and then delegated their work by the contribution of their funds to that Sunday school society which in turn performed the work of edification the church could not do. No, I think Brother Deaver and I will agree on what we mean by a Sunday school society. We recognize the difference between the Bible classes which we teach today and the organized Sunday school society or association as found among the denominations of the world. And so that kind of thing was not set up. To do so would declare the church as not adequate—something else must be done to do the work the church could not do.

And so in the field of benevolence I believe the same thing to be true. First, there is the Jerusalem church, Acts 6:1-4, that cared for its needy upon that occasion when they were in distress, acting simply as a congregation. And then in Acts 11:27-30 we learn that the disciples at Antioch determined to send relief to brethren in Judea when they heard about their distress over there. And likewise in Romans 15:25, 26 we learn that the churches in Macedonia and Achia had made a certain contribution to the poor saints at Jerusalem. So here we have a congregation taking care of its own needy, simply as a local congregation acting in its congregational capacity. Here we have the church sending to churches that are in distress. Here we have a number of churches sending to Jerusalem which was in distress and in each case the congregation acting in its congregational capacity. But my friends we did not have this (referring to chart)—there is nothing of this kind in God's entire book. The churches of Macedonia and Achia and other places did not organize a benevolent society or an organization and then delegate their work by the contribution of their funds to that society or organization and them send the funds over to Jerusalem to do a work that the church could not do. And furthermore that the church at Antioch did not set up a benevolent society or benevolent organization and delegate its work to that benevolent society by the contribution of its funds and then let this benevolent society do the work of relief among the brethren in Judea. It was not done that way. This, my friends, represents the all-sufficiency of the church—this represents my position tonight (referring to chart). And this represents Brother Deaver's position tonight. Brother Deaver is saying that the church is not adequate to do what God requires it to do—that the church is not sufficient—therefore it cannot do this work. I am wondering if they cannot then, how could they in the days gone by? If today churches are not adequate to do the work of benevolence God gave them to do, why were they so in the first century—or were they? According to my opponent's position, Brother Deaver would have to say that the church must delegate its funds—or its work by the contribution of its funds to a benevolent organization and let that benevolent organization do it. He says it should be done this way. I believe it should be done like it was done in the first century, in the days of the apostles of Jesus Christ. Each congregation acting in its congregational ability or capacity and doing what God wanted it to do as the all-sufficient organization for which Jesus Christ gave his life's blood. All right, let us have the lights back now.

Brother Deaver and I agreed to submit to each other five written questions prior to the discussion each evening, some twenty minutes or so before time to begin and we would write in our answers and hand back the answer to the person who had given the questions then these would be discussed during our session. The questions which I handed Brother Deaver with his answers are these:

1. If the benevolent organizations which provide homes among us are not human organizations, just how would they have to be arranged in order to make human organizations? In other words, what are the component parts of a human organization?

Brother Deaver says, you beg the question. Boles Home is simply a home which is incorporated and different human organizations, he says, have different parts. Now friends, he did not beg the question; he evaded the question. He said I begged the question when I asked that. The question is: If the benevolent organizations which provide homes among us are not human organizations, just how would they have to be arranged in order to make human organizations? He said, "you begged the question, Boles Home is not that." After all, the proposition does not say a thing in the world about Boles Home unless it is a human organization. Unless it is a benevolent organization, there is not a word in the proposition about it. And the proposition, Brother Deaver, says benevolent organizations and that is what I put in the question here that I asked you. You are saying in the proposition that churches should delegate their work to benevolent organizations. Now if we do not have any, you had better get busy and set up some because you say it must be done that way. Or at least—it should be done that way. It should not be done the other. And so if we do not have any such thing as a benevolent organization, it is time for you to start—for you say that the church should delegate their work to benevolent organizations. Now do we have them, Brother Deaver, or don't we? If we do, where are they? If we don't, are you going to set up some? You must because you are saying that; in the propositions you signed, it says very plainly that it should be delegated to benevolent organizations. You are denying that it should be done without that; therefore, that it should be done that way and consequently you must have benevolent organizations to carry on your program, according to this proposition.

Then regarding the second part of it, he said different human organizations have different parts. I asked him what the component parts of a human organization were. He said different human organizations have different parts. Well, I would like to know a few of the parts of some of them, Brother Deaver. Will you tell me a few of the parts of some of them?

2. Will you endorse in the field of evangelism, an organizational set-up for the church like that you actually endorse in the field of benevolence?

His answer is: Legal requirements can be met in both benevolence and evangelism. Well, what are those legal requirements? We want to know something about that. Legal requirements can be met in both benevolence and evangelism. But I did not ask you must legal requirements be met, or whether legal requirements can be met. I asked you, would you endorse, in the field of evangelism an organization or set-up for the church like that you accept and endorse in the field of benevolence? You do, don't you, Brother Deaver? You endorse the benevolent organization in the field of benevolence because you say it should be done that way. Therefore, you are endorsing the benevolent organization. Now I want to know if you will endorse a missionary organization like that for the work of evangelism. Forget about your legal demands; tell me whether or not you will endorse it, will you? Will you tell me? I want to know, Brother Deaver. This audience wants to know. We have a right to know and we shall insist that you answer. That you tell us whether or not you will endorse in the field of evangelism the same kind of organizational set-up you have for the work of benevolence that you are contending for in this discussion tonight.

3. Just what is the function of work in the field of benevolence that God has given the church to do?

His answer is: To properly supply the needs. Well, what are those needs? I want to know what you mean by that. I would agree with that answer. We both agree upon much as you said here. Properly supply the needs; but what do you mean? What does the church do when it supplies the needs? Will you tell me? What do you mean by that? What is the function of the church? What work did God give the church to do? I want to know what it is.

4. Would you endorse as scriptural or oppose as unscriptural a home for orphans or for the aged if placed under the supervision of the elders of a local congregation?

He says: The men who are elders may oversee a home but in their oversight of the home, they do not function as elders. I didn't ask you that. I didn't ask you whether they did or they didn't. I just asked you if you would endorse it if it were so. Would you, Brother Deaver? Would you endorse a thing like that? I didn't ask you whether we have any or not, I just asked if you would endorse something like that. Would you endorse as scriptural or oppose as unscriptural a home for orphans or for the aged if placed under the supervision of the elders of a local congregation—would you endorse it or oppose it? Now tell me, Brother Deaver; you have not told me yet. I don't know. I haven't the faintest idea from what you answered here just what you think about that—whether you will endorse it or oppose it. I want to know.

5. What scripture proves that one church can send a contribution to another church? And he gave Acts 15:22-32. That is the only one in the bunch he did not evade.

Well, we shall proceed now. Do we have a little time left?

Moderator: One minute.

Well, since we have only one minute left, I want to impress upon you again the significance of this question before us tonight. Keep in mind the chart we had there a while ago, chart "A" in which we have there the proposition being discussed and my position with Brother Deaver's position. We both agree in the first place that God has given the work of benevolence to the church. In the second place, I am affirming that the church is adequate to do that work. Brother Deaver says it is not adequate to do that work. In the third place I am affirming that the church should do that work. And Brother Deaver is affirming that the church should not do it if it could. It can't of course, but if it could, it shouldn't anyway because he is saying that it should not do the work. My position is that the work should not be surrendered or delegated to benevolent organizations. His position is in the fourth place, that the work should be delegated to benevolent organizations. That is what he says when he signed the negative of this proposition. When he put his name on the negative side of it that simply means he is denying what is being affirmed. And I am affirming the four points I mentioned, therefore he is denying all of them except we both agree that there is a work given to the church, in the field of benevolence. He is denying that the church can do it—that the church is adequate to do it. The church is not able to do it he says.

Deaver's First Negative

Brethren Moderators, Brother Porter, Brethren, and friends. May I say to you in the very beginning that I am sincerely sorry that situations are such as to make necessary a discussion of this kind? But since the circumstances are what they are, I want you to know that I am truly grateful for the privilege of being here and having part in this discussion. I would like to suggest to you before going into other matters that I have tremendous respect for Brother Porter. I have known him for many, many years—more than he knows that I've known him and I have listened to him time and time again on the radio down in deep, East Texas. I appreciate his honesty and his sincerity and I am sincerely sorry that he is just as wrong as he can be in the matters that are before us tonight.

I am here to emphasize the truth; I have neither time nor inclination for personal reflections or anything along that line but at the same time I shall do my very best to constantly emphasize the inconsistencies that are involved in Brother Porter's position. And as Brother Porter has done in his affirmative, now, I shall throughout the course of this discussion, introduce a number of charts and Brother Porter will make a note of those charts and call for them as he cares to do so. And I apologize to him now for not having an extra copy of these charts ready for him tonight but will have by tomorrow night and will get them to you Brother Porter.

I want to emphasize also that it is my sincere desire and it's my determination to agree with Brother Porter on everything that I can possibly agree with him on. I would like to emphasize as we proceed in this study the points upon which we agree. Brother Porter's proposition is: *According to the scriptures, churches of Christ, each acting in its congregational capacity, are adequate to accomplish all the work of benevolent nature that God has given the church to do. And they should do this work without delegating it by the contribution of their funds to benevolent organizations.*

Now, Brother Porter had somewhat to say about that proposition and he said perhaps you never thought that you would live to see the day when a gospel preacher would sign his name to that proposition. I happen to know that just recently, Brother Porter signed his name to the negative of a proposition that baptism is in the name of Jesus Christ. I never thought that I would live to see the day when a gospel preacher would sign a proposition of that kind. He signed it because he knew what the man had in mind, and on the same ground I signed Brother Porter's proposition. Just exactly on the same ground that he has signed that and hundreds of other propositions—I know what Brother Porter has in mind and for that reason I signed the negative of his proposition.

So far as concerns the definition of terms, he says, "according to the scriptures" means in harmony with, especially the New Testament teaching and that is all right. By the word "scriptures" he says, the word of God—the Bible, and as far as concerns our matter now, the New Testament, and that is all right. By "churches of Christ," he means local congregations of the Lord's people and that is satisfactory. Each acting in its congregational capacity—he didn't give a definition on that or if he did, I failed to get it, Brother Porter. And I am wondering if you imply there that there is some capacity in which a congregation might act other than its congregational capacity. That's the reason why I was anxious to have a definition from you on that particular point, and Brother Porter, will take care of that in his next speech. Then "so far as adequate to accomplish all the work of benevolence, that God has given the church to do"—by the word "adequate," he says he means all-sufficient and that's right—it's able. Then to "accomplish," I didn't get a point on that. By the "work of benevolence," he said that means to relieve the distressed. Not one time in that definition did Brother Porter refer to orphans? He has in mind the benevolent work of the congregation. We are here as he knows, and as I know, to discuss benevolence as benevolence involves the work of orphans. Now benevolence is one thing and benevolence as it applies to the care of orphans is another thing entirely. And I'd like for him to give us some more information on benevolence as it pertains to this particular issue. Does this include, Brother Porter, an obligation to orphans? You tell the audience. I think that you certainly hold that position but you're duty-bound to tell us what you have in mind there. And then, has God given the church an obligation to orphans? And does this mean, now, does the fact that the church is adequate to meet its obligation to orphans, Brother Porter—do you mean by that, and I must know what you mean by that, and this audience must know what you mean by that, do you mean that the church as the church is sufficient, now, to meet all the needs of an orphan? Now you are dealing with the all-sufficiency of the church and I'm simply asking the question: is that what you mean by adequate or all-sufficient? You need to deal with that.

Then by "delegating" he says surrender. By a contribution of funds, Brother Porter, you say you mean donating funds and that's all right; that's a satisfactory definition of that so far as I'm concerned. Then by benevolent organizations, Brother Porter, I was a little bit disappointed here in that you didn't give all the information you should have given in defining your terms. What do you mean by "organization" in the first place? And may I mention that when Brother Chaffin read the proposition, he used the word benevolent societies. That isn't the proposition. I suppose from Brother Porter's viewpoint it wouldn't make any difference but the word is "benevolent organizations" in the proposition. Now what do you mean by that? Brother Porter says its association—it is a society—human in origin. But I need to know what exactly you have in mind by human in origin. I would like to know what it is that makes a thing human in origin, Brother Porter, and when you get me that information, I'll have some information for you that you're after. All right, does he mean an orphan home? That's the point that I need and that's the point that the audience needed and that's the point of this discussion. Did you mean, Brother Porter, by human organization, an orphan home? Brother Porter didn't tell you that, but let me tell you now; he does not mean an orphan home. When Brother Porter refers to benevolent organizations, in this position and proposition, Brother Porter doesn't mean an orphan home. And he'll not tell you that he does because he doesn't mean it. He means that there is something in between the church and the orphan home, and that's what he is calling a benevolent organization. And if you had in mind that when Brother Porter refers to benevolent organizations, he is talking about an orphan home, then you are disappointed. That's not his position at all. But by benevolent organizations, he pointedly refers to something in between. He does not refer to an orphan home. But he didn't tell us that as he came across the definition when he was supposed to have given us that information. And Brother Porter, you'll deal with that, won't you?

May I suggest to you that Brother Porter has the obligation to prove the points that are involved in his proposition? And he has the job of proving, number one, that God has given each congregation a work of benevolence.

Brother Porter, take them up one by one. You are in the affirmative and you prove to this audience that God has given the church—whether I deny it or not is beside the point—you have the job of proving that God has given to the church a work of benevolence. And then you have to prove—by the way, let me suggest to you here that we're here in this discussion to consider the matters pertaining to the orphan home issue, hence it's certainly clear that work of benevolence as involved in Brother Porter's proposition has to relate to the care of orphans—a church meeting its obligation to orphans. Now, Brother Porter must prove that God has placed upon each congregation, therefore, an obligation to orphans. Secondly, he must prove that each congregation, acting in its congregational capacity, is adequate to accomplish the work of benevolence which God has given the church to do. Keep in mind now that the work of benevolence here refers to a congregation's work in caring for orphan children. Now, Brother Porter, just what is a congregation's work in caring for orphans? It may be on that point you and I do not disagree one particle and I can't tell whether we do or not until I know what you mean by the work that God has given the church in connection with the care of orphans. Tell us what you mean by it; then we will know whether or not we agree on that point. It is certainly possible that there is disagreement between us as to what a congregation's work is in connection with orphans and Brother Porter must state plainly what a congregation's work is in caring for orphans and then we can discuss the matter. And whatever—Brother Porter you must prove now—whatever you say that is, you must prove that a church's work in caring for orphans, or that a church, now, is adequate to meet that, whatever it is. You tell us what the care is—what the obligation is—and then prove that the church is adequate to meet it. It may be that you are right and it may be that I'll agree with you. But I want you to prove it and you must prove it.

He must prove in the third place that each congregation must do the work which God has given it to do without delegating it to a benevolent organization. This simply means that each congregation must meet its obligation to orphans without delegating its work to a benevolent organization. Brother Porter, whether I agree with you on that or not, you prove it. You are in the affirmative and you have the job to prove it. And I believe you'll undertake to prove it.

In the fourth place, he must prove—and these are points in his proposition—we are here discussing the matter of the home—a church sending to a home. Now this is clear—this is certainly clear in view of the fact that

Brother Porter denies the affirmative which I shall discuss later. He believes that the Bible teaching concerning the church's obligation to orphans makes it impossible for a church to send a contribution to Boles home. Now then, he's got to prove that. He says Boles home is not in his proposition. You-bet-your-life it's in it. Your proposition means a church can't send to Boles home and Brother Porter—you've got to prove it. It's in your proposition and sure it's there.

All right, keep in mind now that benevolent organizations, as used by Brother Porter, does not refer to a home; it refers to that in-between organization and he must prove that there is such a thing as that in-between organization. And I'm here to try to get the benefit of that information. To save my life, I can't tell you how he's going to try to do it, but he says there is an in-between organization. Boles Home is not the organization, but there's one in-between. He is opposed to that. And if Brother Porter will show it—show where it is, it may be that we'll oppose it just like he does. In fact, if he can show that there is any such thing; I'll join him in his position of opposition to it. Brother Porter, that's all you've got to do.

All right, he must prove now, and here is the reason I signed this proposition in the first place, he must prove that any time there is a contribution of funds, there is an inherent delegation of work. Brother Porter couldn't prove that if his life depended on it. But it is in his proposition. A church can't delegate its work by sending funds—by contributing funds. He is affirming then that any time a church contributes funds; it's delegating its work. I deny that. I deny it with all the power that I have. And we'll deal with it. Brother Porter, you've got to prove it now—that when a church sends funds, it delegates its work. Then he's got to prove that the Bible teaching concerning a church's care for orphans makes it impossible for a church to send a contribution to Boles Home. I'd like to have my chart number 54 please, sir, right quick.

Here is a restatement briefly of what Brother Porter must prove; but because of time let's skip that. Let's go on to something else right here.

Brother Porter must prove these points. He must prove a church obligation. He must prove that each congregation is sufficient to meet its obligation to orphans, whatever that is. And he must prove that each congregation must meet its obligation without delegating its work to benevolent organizations. He must prove that when a church contributes to Boles Home, that there's an in-between organization, whether Boles Home or some other—doesn't matter. He must prove that contribution of funds means a delegation of work. And he must prove that the Bible teaching on this subject makes it impossible for a church to send to a home.

I'd like to suggest to you now my position. Lights please. My position with reference to Brother Porter's proposition. And Brother Porter, I'm in a better position to tell you my position than you are. Here's my position with reference to Brother Porter's proposition I believe that God has placed upon each congregation an obligation to orphans. I believe fervently that each congregation is adequate to meet its obligation to orphans. Now, whatever the obligation is, that God has placed upon each church with reference to orphans, that church is adequate to meet it. However, I'm not sure that Brother Porter and I agree as to what that obligation is, but whatever God gives the church to do, you can mark it down that the church is sufficient to do it. But let Brother Porter produce the passage that says that God gave the church the job of functioning as a home. That's his job. Now, whatever job that God gave the church to do, the church is adequate to do. All right, I do not believe that a church can delegate its work to benevolent organizations. Brother Porter, I stand with you on that. I do not believe that in the matter of churches contributing to Boles Home that there is an in-between organization. I deny that. All right, I do not believe that the Bible teaches regarding a church's obligation to orphans, such that it would be impossible for a church to send a contribution to Boles Home. Now, that's my position with reference to your proposition, Brother Porter.

Now, my chart 55, please. Here's what I am not denying. Brethren and friends and neighbors, regardless of all that Brother Porter has had to say, and he spent more than twenty precious minutes laboring on a misconception, I am not denying that each church has an obligation to orphans. I am not denying that each church is sufficient for doing all the work that God gave it to do. And as I said over at Borger, so say I now again: If there is any man on earth who believes more in the all-sufficiency of the church than I, it is simply because he's got more ability with which to believe it. I am not denying that each church must not delegate its work to benevolent organizations. Brother Porter, if you thought I was here to deny these things, you're wrong. I'm not denying these points.

My next chart, number 56. Here's what I am denying: All right, here's what I am denying now. I am denying that God has given the church the job of functioning as a home. I'm denying the existence of an in-between organization. I'm denying that contribution of funds means delegation of work. I'm denying that the Bible teaching regarding the church's obligation to orphans makes it impossible for a church to scripturally send a contribution to Boles Home. That's what I'm denying with reference to Brother Porter's proposition.

Now, give me Brother Porter's chart number "A" please. Brother Porter began his speech with this chart "A" which was designed to discuss his position and then mine. Here's the proposition: He says here's Brother Porter's position and here's Brother Deaver's position. On Porter's position, he says God has given a work of benevolence to churches and he says that Deaver says the same thing here. Well, he says the church is adequate to do that work and he says that Deaver says they are not adequate. Brother Porter, you're just as wrong as you can be. Deaver says no such thing. Deaver says the church is adequate to do any job that God gave it to do. God never gave it the job of functioning as a home. There's a difference in the church and the home. Brother Porter needs to understand. Then he says they should to the work and he says Deaver says they should not do the work. Deaver says no such thing. And church should do the work that God gave it to do. Then over here, should I surrender the work to benevolent organizations, Deaver says they should. Don't say any such thing. I say they should not surrender their work to any benevolent organization. Brother Porter, I'm in a better position to tell my position than you are. Your chart's no good.

All right. Now then, let's come to another matter please, Brother Porter's chart "B". I'd like to cover everything that he had if we possibly can—skipped number 1?

All right, let's get my chart number 60 before this. Just a moment here. Brother Porter's proposition is actually very verbose and technological. It has three propositions in one. And if I can get the time, I'd like to come back and suggest some things to you along that line. Look at this chart number 60. This is my chart number 60. Brother Porter's admissions on the written questions and answers the first night. I asked him some questions a while ago, and here they are. Brother Porter, if there is an orphan home now being provided by a church or by churches, which you indorse, please specify which home, and tell where it is located. He said, I'll endorse any congregation taking care of its needy when acting in its congregational capacity. Well, that's what you have at Boles Home. Each congregation acts in its congregational capacity and sends a contribution to Boles Home. That's all in the world that I want and that's all that I'm concerned about. Now let him deny it. He didn't answer this question actually. He complained about some of mine. I could come back and say, "Now Brother Porter is that taking place anywhere? Do you know of a home in connection with which now, being operated by churches relative to which brethren are sending to, or churches are sending to, acting in their congregational capacities? And which you will endorse? Why, you didn't answer that question?"

All right. Are there any circumstances conceivable to you—notice carefully—Brother Porter—are there any circumstances conceivable to you under which a church might scripturally sends funds to a private home so that the needs of orphan children might be adequately supplied? And Brother Porter said yes, a church can send to a private home. There's a home in Brother Porter's proposition as sure as the world and he knows it's there. And I hope that I can get the time to show you his position on that. There's a home in his proposition and there's a home in mine. And if you thought that Brother Porter's proposition was designed to preclude the possibility of a home, and then you're disappointed, just like you were over in Borger. Because both men believe in a home. I asked him the question then: If your answer to number 2 was yes, could this private home be incorporated? Brother Porter said it might be. All right. (But a corporation that provides a home is another matter. That's the figment of his imagination.) But he says that a private home might be incorporated. If your answers to numbers 2 and 3 are yes, would this be a church meeting its obligation to provide a home for orphans? And Brother Porter says yes, that's what it is. When a church sends a contribution to a private home incorporated, that's a church meeting its obligation to orphans and so I contend. That's all in the world you've got at Boles Home.

Number 5, since you believe that a church may provide a home for orphans, will you please list the component parts of a home which you will endorse. And here's his answer. Such as food, clothes, shelter, supervision, and simply the necessities, Brother Porter says that home meets the necessities for those children and I'll endorse it. All right, so here's what you have. Here's what Brother Porter admitted on those answers handed to me just a few minutes ago. That a church incorporated—he knows that's all right—an incorporated church can send funds to a private home incorporated that the necessities of orphan children might be supplied and he says that this is a case of a church meeting its obligation to provide a home for orphans and that's all under the sun that I'm concerned about.

Simply coming to understand the Bible teaching regarding the fact that the church can send a contribution to a home to provide the necessities of orphan children and that that home can meet the legal requirements and Brother Porter said that's all right. But in spite of all of that, he'll labor long and hard to try to establish an in-between organization. Let me tell you about that organization. If he can give me the name of it, and tell me its address, I will personally mail it a $25.00 check. You just tell me, Brother Porter, where to send it to. Now, I don't want it to go to Boles Home, mind you. I want it to go to that organization that stands between a church and Boles Home. I want you to fix it so they can get it. All right, those are Brother Porter's admissions there.

Let's cover then, Brother Porter's chart number "C" right quickly. Brother Porter's chart "C"—he spent a good deal of time on this now. That's the one I referred to a while ago when I said Brother Porter spent, I think, about twenty minutes on the all-sufficiency of the church. In evangelism: well, I believe that just as strongly as Brother Porter does. The all-sufficiency in edification I believe that just as strongly as Brother Porter does. The all-sufficiency in benevolence: I believe that just as strongly as Brother Porter does. Brother Porter, in this benevolent matter, you've got a home; you've got a private home; you've got an incorporated; tell me what it is. Now the church is all-sufficient; so you say and so I say. But the church is not a home; so I say and I don't know what you say. But both of us say that a church can send a contribution to a private home incorporated. Now where is it, in this all-sufficiency chart, on benevolence? Brother Porter, you've got to deal with that. You won't forget it. Wait just a minute. On his chart number "C", I want you to notice that this benevolent organization—is that chart "C"?—that's not the chart I want. "B"—his chart number "B".

All right, notice carefully his chart number "B" that he clearly distinguishes between these benevolent organizations. I told you that when Brother Porter referred to benevolent organizations, he doesn't have in mind a home. Here's what he's got over here. He doesn't have in mind this home. He distinguishes between this home and this benevolent organization and he says that this benevolent organization stands right here. It's kind of hard to get, his position's a way down here, but that is what he says is happening; that this stands between the church and the home so he's not opposed to this, he's opposed to this thing and so am I. It just doesn't exist. All right, notice carefully, he distinguishes between the benevolent organization and this. He refers to supervision and Brother Porter, you will tell this audience now, who is that supervision please, sir? Is it elders? Functioning as elders? Is it a board or what is it? You say there are supervision and this home's separated from that benevolent organization, mind you. The supervision's not over here, not by a long sight. It's over here in the home. Seven minutes? All right, sir.

Now, my 61 chart. All right, sir. Now here's what Brother Porter should have had on that chart "B". Brother Porter, here's exactly the situation: that a church incorporated can send to a home incorporated. That's all I say. And if you want to talk about this benevolent organization down here, let's just both mark it out. That thing doesn't exist. It exists only in his imagination. And when he tries to tell you or give the proof for his conclusion that it does exist, he's going to get into trouble; more so than he's already in. He admits that an incorporated church can send to an incorporated home. And that's all in the world I'm contending for and we'll just mark out this thing down here.

All right, let's proceed hurriedly then. Brother Porter then spent a long time in connection with his chart discussing the all-sufficiency of the church. Brother Porter, all I can say there is "amen" and me, too. I believe in the all sufficiency of the church just like you do and I appreciate your great work along that line and I believe it just as strongly as you do—unless you've got more ability with which to believe it. Then you discussed the all-sufficiency of the Lord's plan and of God's gospel and again, I say "amen" and me, too. Absolutely so. There is no disagreement there. He labored long on the misconception that Deaver denies the all-sufficiency of the church. I don't do any such thing. Deaver upholds the all-sufficiency of the home and the all-sufficiency of the church. Now it's just as wrong to vitiate against the all-sufficiency of the home as it is to vitiate against the all sufficiency of the church. God separated them. And what God separated, let no men join together.

All right, he referred to my answers to his questions; let me get that hurriedly. I asked him these questions. Lights please. Well, we referred to those. All right. We've covered his questions. He complained a little bit about them. But he admits that a home—that an incorporated church can send to a private home; that it can be incorporated and that's a church meeting its obligation to orphan children. All right, Brother Porter's proposition actually has the three points in one. All right, sir, as mentioned a while ago, so far as I can see—unless he's got an extra point, it has a great deal of tautology in it. Each congregation acting in its congregational capacity. Not much to that. I don't see any point in that unless he's got a point in it. I'd like to know what it is. I'm entitled to know what it is. If he has a point in that—if you simply mean a congregation acting, well—that's all we'll have to say about it.

All right, in the first place, it's actually three different propositions. Here is the first one: the first proposition is: A congregation is adequate to accomplish all the work of benevolence that God has given it to do. Brother Porter, that proposition I would not deny. Your second proposition in your proposition is: A congregation must do its work of benevolence without delegating it to benevolent organizations. And that proposition I would not deny. No sir. The third proposition is: By the contribution of funds, a church delegates its work to the recipient of those funds. This is the proposition which I emphatically deny. And I sincerely doubt if there's another brother in the house who will say that any time you send a contribution to something, you inherently delegate your work to them. You get in deep, deep trouble when you take that position, as will be shown as we proceed.

All right, and that's a very fundamental point in Brother Porter's proposition which I emphatically deny. And will you keep in mind please that a very basic matter in Brother Porter's proposition is that the Bible teaching concerning a church's obligation to orphan children makes it impossible for a church to scripturally contribute to Boles Home in Quinlan, Texas. There were lots of things in Brother Porter's proposition that couldn't be understood. Or at least were ambiguous. But there's one point that I knew from the beginning. That in that part that the Bible teaching on the subject was that a church couldn't send a contribution to Boles Home. I'd like to impress upon your minds the point that there is a home in Brother Porter's proposition. That he's got a home in it; his proposition doesn't eliminate a home. And if you thought that it did, then you're mistaken and disappointed. Brother Porter has a home in his proposition just like I have. Brother Porter's home can be incorporated just like mine can. And a church can send funds to his home just like a church can send to my home. The only difference between us is, he says, there's an in-between organization. And I deny any such thing. I want to prove to you that there's a home in Brother Porter's proposition. I have his statement—numbers of them—just trying to decide which—two minutes, all right, sir.

Keep in mind now that benevolent organizations as used in Brother

Porter's proposition do not refer to a home for orphans. What Brother Porter says when he says that a church can't contribute to a benevolent organization; he has in mind that in-between organization. In the *Gospel Guardian*, May 23, 1957, on page nine, Brother Porter makes this statement: "I do not know of anyone who has ever said that the benevolent society and the missionary society are identical but they are parallel in that they are both human organizations doing the work that God has designed the church to do." Note carefully then the following points: Here's a point I'd simply like for you to get there. Brother Porter says there's an in-between organization. This in-between organization is parallel to the missionary society. And it's parallel to the missionary society because it's doing the work now that God gave the church to do. He opposes the church sending a contribution to Boles Home, because there's an in-between organization that is doing a job that God gave the church to do. And the inevitable conclusion is, Brother Porter, God gave the church the job of providing Boles Home. There's no way around it. And if that conclusion doesn't grow out of that there is no such thing as a conclusion coming out of premises. It's wrong because it's doing the work that God gave the church—what's it doing? What's it doing? It's providing Boles Home. But that's a work of the church, according to Brother Porter, and there's lots of other statements. Keep in mind there's a home in Brother Porter's proposition. But I'm not denying—what I am denying, Brother Porter, is that God has given the church the job of functioning as a home. I deny that and if you want to stake this discussion on that, I'm prepared for it. If you want to affirm that God has given the church the job of functioning as a home, we'll get on that point, and we'll stay there. All right.

Porter's Second Affirmative

Brethren Moderators, Brother Deaver, Ladies and Gentlemen: I appreciate the privilege of returning to the stand to continue my part of this discussion concerning the question before us tonight as involved in the proposition which we have signed and which we are to discuss for the first two nights of the debate.

Brother Deaver said that he had known me for a long time and appreciated my sincerity and so on, but he is sorry that Brother Porter is so wrong about this thing. It seemed to me that before he got through, he had just about endorsed everything that I had affirmed. Yet he felt so sorry for me because I was so wrong about it. He says he wants to agree with me upon all points on which we can agree and I appreciate that; I want to agree with him on every point that we can but we do want to discuss our differences concerning these matters. And he made the statement regarding some other matters right in that connection concerning his position—that he was better able to tell you what his position was than I am. I wonder if the thing might work in reverse. Could it be that I am better able to tell you what my position is than Brother Deaver is able to tell you? It might work both ways, Brother Deaver.

And regarding the proposition which we are discussing that says, and *According to the scriptures, churches of Christ, each acting in its congregational capacity, are adequate to do all the work of benevolence that God has given the church to do. And they should do this work without delegating it by the contribution of their funds to benevolent organizations.* Now that's the proposition before us tonight. And Brother Deaver agrees with most all that's on the proposition he said. He said, "I signed that proposition because I knew what he meant." We are debating the proposition because you signed what it said, Brother Deaver. We are debating this proposition because you signed what the proposition said. Not what I meant—but what the proposition said. If I meant something else, then you simply signed what the proposition said. He said, "I happen to know that Brother Porter signed a proposition recently to deny that baptism should be administered in the name of Jesus Christ." I know that Brother Porter did no such thing. Your information is wrong, Brother Deaver. Oh, so you didn't put the word on the end did you? (Deaver I thought I did.) Well, you didn't. You didn't; you'd sign that too, wouldn't you? If the word "only" is in it, yes sir. But during that debate, I said if that word "only" had not been in there, I would affirm the proposition. But the word "only" was there—"only" in the name of Jesus Christ or in the name of Jesus Christ "only." Certainly I believe that men are baptized in the name of Jesus Christ, but I didn't believe that proposition—so I signed the negative of it. And the reason that Brother Deaver signed the negative of this one tonight is because he doesn't believe it.

Now, before we get to some other matters along that line, I want to call attention again to two of the questions at least, that I asked him a while ago. Question number two. Would you endorse in the field of evangelism, an organizational set-up for the church like that you accept and endorse in the field of benevolence? Of course, he said that legal requirements can be met in both benevolence and evangelism. But I told him that that was not what I was trying to find out. I want to know, would you endorse in the field of evangelism, an organizational set-up like that which you have in benevolence? And he said, now there's not any organization in-between; there's no in-between organization in benevolence. Well, whatever it is—let it be what it may—I'm just asking if you'll endorse one for evangelism just like it. Will you? Whether it's in-between or where it is. Will you endorse one in the field of evangelism just like the one you endorse in the field of benevolence? Wherever it is—whether in-between or where? Will you endorse it, Brother Deaver? Why didn't you tell us? Are you going to? If you don't, I'll not let you forget it. So I'm wanting to know and this audience needs to know whether or not you will endorse in the field of evangelism the same kind of organizational set-up, where ever the organization may be, that you have in the field of benevolence. Will you do it? I challenge you to answer. I'm just about ready to dare you to. We want to know, Brother Deaver. You haven't told us yet.

Number 4. Would you endorse as scriptural or oppose as unscriptural, the home for orphans or for the aged if placed under the supervision of the elders of a local congregation? He said we don't have anything like that. The men who are elders may oversee a home but in their oversight of the home, they do not function as elders. Then I said if we don't have anything like that, then I want to know if you would endorse one that would be like that. Would you? Would you endorse one like that if we did have it? Or would you endorse setting up one like it. By the way, if you would, will you tell me how to set it up? If what we have is not that, would you tell me how to set up one like it? You haven't done it yet. We want to know how to set up one like that. You said it isn't there and I'll deal with that later on in the speech because you came back to it, and dealt with it quite elaborately. And he says now I want to know what Porter means about this and what he means about that—what does he mean by congregational capacity? What does he mean by benevolence? And what does he mean by it being all-sufficient? And what does he mean by delegating and all of that? Why, I thought you knew what Porter meant. And I thought you signed the proposition because you knew all about what Porter meant in the proposition—not because of what the proposition said—but because of what Porter meant. But if you knew before you signed it, why are you asking me now what I meant? I meant what I said. And you ought to know what I meant. Just read the proposition again that's there, and that's what I meant—just what I said. And he said Brother Chaffin read the proposition "benevolent societies" instead of "benevolent organizations." He said, of course, as far as Brother Porter is concerned there wouldn't be any difference. Well, is there any difference with you? Brother Deaver, is there any difference with you whether it is an organization or a society? Will you tell me what is the difference between an organization and a society? If there's a difference with you, I want to know what the difference is between the two.

And he came to a number of things that Porter must prove. First, he must prove that God has given each congregation a benevolent work to do. Second, he must prove that it is adequate. And third, he must prove what its work is and fourth, he must prove that they must not delegate it—that they must not delegate the work to benevolent organizations. And fifth, he must prove that there is an organization. And sixth, he must prove that the contribution of its funds would be a delegation of it. And so all of that is what he says that Porter must prove. Well, I've proved enough now; he ought to begin to pay some attention to what I have proved. The fact is he is admitting already the things I've sustained and the things that sustain my proposition. I want to look at chart "A" again right in this connection. Let us have it, Brother Shaw. We want chart "A". This is the analysis of the proposition which I'm affirming tonight. Switch off the lights for us please; now, here's the proposition. *According to the scriptures, churches of Christ, each acting in its congregation capacity, are adequate to do or to accomplish all the work of benevolence that God has given the church to do and they should do this work without delegating it by the contribution of their funds to benevolent organizations.* I signed that in the affirmative. Brother Deaver, did you sign the negative of it? Did you? Does negative mean "deny" or what does it mean? Brother Deaver says I don't deny this and I don't deny this and I don't deny this and the only thing I deny is something I thought he meant. Is that your conception of a negative to a proposition? Would he say that it is denying what he thought the affirmant meant instead of what the proposition said? He says, I believe churches are adequate but the proposition says they're not, according to your signature. You denied it—you signed the negative of it. I always thought that in the negative, a man was denying. I have found out now that it means he is affirming the very thing that I thought he was denying. Brother Deaver says so. The way Brother Deaver denies is by affirming and he can't deny without affirming and I suppose he can't affirm without denying. Because to him it all means the same thing. He says, I'll affirm everything on there. I'll affirm that according to the scriptures, churches of Christ, acting in their congregational capacity, are adequate to do all the work that God gave it. He says, I'll affirm that—I believe that—I wouldn't deny that at all. And he said, I won't deny that they should not turn that work to benevolent organizations—I don't deny that at all—I don't believe they should—I won't deny that. He says, I won't say they should not do the work—I believe they should do the work. Well, what is he denying? He says, the thing I'm denying is that you are trying to prove that a church is delegating its work when it makes a contribution—that's all I'm denying. Can you now read a proposition like that with a man's name signed to the negative and think the only thing he is denying is what he *thought* his opponent meant about a certain expression in it—instead of denying what is said in the proposition? Here's the proposition; there's Deaver's position; here's what he must say or give up the proposition. Here's what I'm affirming. Here's what the proposition lays out for me to do: That God has given a work of benevolence to the churches. He says I must prove that. I've proved it already. Chart "C" proved that sufficiently, absolutely and definitely, and he agreed with me all along on the chart. And furthermore, I am affirming that churches are adequate to do the work. He says, I agree, but you must prove it. Well, I did. I proved that they did it in New Testament days; they can do it now. If not, why not? And furthermore, I should prove that they should do the work. Well, that's a very easy matter. If God gave it to them, certainly God expected them to do it and God thought they should or he wouldn't have given it to them in the first place. And he should prove that they should not surrender it to benevolent organizations. Well, that's the very thing I've done—they didn't do it in New Testament days. If so, what were the organizations? I gave you chart "C" and you made no effort to upset it or throw it aside. You just say, I agree that it's all-sufficient in benevolence; I agree that it's all-sufficient in edification; I agree that it's all-sufficient in evangelism. Then what are you denying? Why did you sign the negative of it? You can't get out of this thing by saying, I simply signed to deny what I thought you meant. You knew what the proposition said, and you signed the negative of it and you are going to stay with it. And until you surrender it; until you give it up and say I don't believe I'm occupying the right position toward that proposition, I don't want the negative of it any longer, I am going to hold you to it. So you had just as well get busy.

Another thing he said now. You thought there was a home in this proposition, didn't you? You said you were disappointed, Brother Porter is not talking about a home—this benevolent organization out here—he doesn't mean a home by that and then he turned right around and said there is a home in this proposition. But he says there is—there's not, but there is. Now then, I'm affirming that this should be true: The churches are adequate to do the work. They should do it and they should not surrender their work to benevolent organizations.

Brother Deaver in the negative, is saying by that negative signature that he placed there, that churches are not adequate to do the work and they should not do it if they were able. And furthermore, that they should surrender their work to benevolent organizations. That's what his position demands—that's what the negative of this proposition requires of him, and until he tackles that job, he hasn't even touched top, bottom, side, nor edge of his responsibility tonight.

Let us have the lights again just a moment. We'll see where we are here. He said, by that benevolent organization there, Porter didn't mean an orphan home, but an organization in-between the orphan home. All right then, if that's what Brother Porter meant. You knew that before you came didn't you, Brother Deaver? All right, Brother Deaver says that he knew that I meant an organization in-between before he came—you knew it when you signed the proposition didn't you? All right. He knew it when he signed the proposition, yet he denies that the church should not delegate its funds to that sort of thing. In other words, he has signed that the church should surrender its funds to benevolent organizations. He says I knew you meant an organization in-between the church and the home; therefore, he signed that the church should surrender its funds and its work to an organization in between the church and the home. Thank you all, let's shake hands and go home. What do you say? Just as well. Just as well shake hands and go home. That's what he says should be done, because he is denying that they should not do it and if he is denying that they should not do it, he is affirming that they should do it. And he says, I knew you meant by benevolent organizations, not a home—but an organization in-between the church and the home. And I knew it when I signed the proposition, Brother Deaver said. Then he says there is not any such thing but it should be done, that way. Well, you had better start one then. And since you say there isn't any such thing, I'm still demanding of you, Brother Deaver, to tell me how to set up one like it. Will you tell me? Will you tell this audience tonight how to set up one like that where there would be one in-between. What would we have to do to get an organization, a benevolent organization, in-between the church and home? Just what would we have to set up—what kind of an arrangement would we have to have to have a thing of that kind? Will he tell us? We'll wait and see.

Well, he brought chart 55 and I've already dealt with that. Let's just throw it back on the screen because he said, that's what I'm not denying. He said, I'm not denying the church is obligated; I'm not denying its sufficiency; I'm not denying the church should not send its funds to benevolent organizations. Yet, he is occupying the negative of this proposition. There's a debate on this proposition tonight and then he says, I don't deny anything on it. Now, isn't that something? I don't deny anything that's said—I'm just denying what Porter meant by this and what Porter meant by that.

And then chart number 56—I believe that was the number—I didn't quite see the number of it—fifty something the best I could see—was what I am denying, and so that was with respect to this matter of denying—put it on the screen and let us see it—I didn't get to see the number of it so I couldn't make a notation of what the number was. Can you slip it up or down one way or the other—I can't see the number yet. The other way. Number 56 or 36—56 I believe. Anyway, it has the 6 at the end. What I am denying. He says, I am denying, that God has given the church the job of functioning as a home. Does the proposition have anything about functioning as a home? You said home is not even in the proposition. He says, I'm denying the existence of an in-between organization. All right, but that's not what the proposition said. The proposition doesn't say there is an organization in-between. The proposition says they shouldn't contribute to an organization like that and you are denying that they should not do it. You are affirming therefore, that they should do it because you are denying that they should not do it. And that the contribution of funds means a delegation of work. And that by the teaching regarding the church's obligation to orphans makes it impossible for a church to scripturally contribute to Boles Home. Well, Boles Home comes up the third and fourth nights of this and we'll deal with that when the time comes and we'll have plenty of it for him when we get there. We have some other things tonight because we are on this proposition tonight.

Now, let us have the lights back on. Regarding the matter of my questions, he said, that Brother Porter admitted that a church could send funds to—that was his chart 60 regarding my admission to the questions—that the church could send funds or contribute funds to a private home; that the private home might be incorporated and the church would be meeting its obligation and the component parts of it were the necessities and so on. Well all right, now he says that's what Porter admits in his answer to the questions. That he can send to a private home and the private home might be incorporated. If it were, I don't know whether it would remain a private home or not. I don't know what effect the incorporation might have upon it. But let that be as it may. We are not discussing the matter of whether or not a home is incorporated. I want to show you what we have tonight; I want—let me see—chart "M." Let us have my chart number "M" in this particular connection. Then I have some others following that. And to show you what we have in this situation tonight, that's before the brotherhood that we're discussing with respect to these issues regarding benevolence. Now here is the question: What's wrong with incorporation? And sometimes, they present ideas like that—the church can send funds to a private home and a church incorporated can send funds to a private home or a church incorporated can send funds to a private home incorporated or a church incorporated can send funds to a church unincorporated or a church incorporated can send funds to a church incorporated or a church incorporated can send funds to Boles Home incorporated and so on. And so they put that in there that, if and when a private home can be incorporated, then they seem to think that justifies the arrangement for Boles Home. We are not discussing whether or not a home may or may not be incorporated—let that be as it may. The thing that we are discussing is this in-between organization, in between the church and the private home and I shall prove to you that we do have it. And so the question is not whether or not the church could send to a private home or whether the private home could be incorporated or anything of that kind. The question is this: Can the church send its money to a human organization or benevolent organization, either incorporated or unincorporated? And then let that organization spend the funds in a private home? Could a church incorporated send funds to that kind of organization and let it spend those funds in a private home or could it send to that organization and let them spend the funds in a private home incorporated or in a church unincorporated or a church incorporated or in Boles Home incorporated or unincorporated? The question is this: the existence of the institution between the two. The church has an obligation and over here is the home. And the church sends its funds to the corporation which in turn provides the home that we are concerned about in this discussion tonight. And it is this organization that is called a benevolent organization.

Brother Deaver, is the home a benevolent organization? Is it, Brother Deaver? Please put it down and tell me. Is the home a benevolent organization? Just what is the home? Is that the design of it? Is it designed to be a benevolent organization? Is that the purpose of the home? What is the purpose of the home anyway, benevolence? What is the benevolent organization? We have benevolent organizations. You don't deny that, do you? If you do, I'll prove it. We have benevolent organizations; now I want to know where they belong. Are those organizations the home or are they something that provides the home—something this side of the home? Which are they? It's not a matter of incorporation but it's the thing that's incorporated. And in this case, it is a human organization which they have set up and incorporated to provide these things which we call homes for the orphans and homes for the aged. There's the thing I'm opposing. Do we have it? If we don't, Brother Deaver, tell me how to arrange one. I'm still begging you to do it. Will you? I want to know how to arrange one, if we don't have it.

Now then, I want to use another chart or two here. Get my chart number "K", no K1, and also "L". I want those three charts in succession. First number "K" and then "K1" and then "L". All right, here is the question: Is the corporation the home? Now that's the position that has to be maintained by Brother Deaver—that the corporation is the home. It is not something in-between the church and the home, but it's the home. And they resort to such statements as these, taken from their charters, to prove it. First, the name of this corporation shall be the Tipton Orphan's Home, Article 1. Second, the name of this corporation shall be the Church of Christ Home, that's of Turley, Article 1. And third, the name of this corporation shall be the Sunny Glen Home and that's Article 1. And fourth, the name of this corporation shall be Boles Orphan Home, Article 1. And so they reason that since the name of the corporation is the home that therefore the home and the corporation is the same thing. All right, if that's true, then this follows: the name of this corporation shall be Shultz Lewis Children's Home and School, Article 1. Second, the name of said corporation shall be Christian Home and Bible School—that's the Mount Dora charter—Article 1. And third, that this corporation shall be named and known as the Potter Orphan Home and School Corporation, Article 1. Now then if because that here it says that the corporation shall be named the Tipton Home and the Church of Christ Home and the Sunny Glen Home means the corporation and the home is the same thing, then since the same charters say the name of the corporation is the school, the Bible School and so on, then that makes the corporation and the school the same thing. All right, if the corporation here means the home then the corporation here is the school. And so the corporation and the school is the same thing and yet the corporation and the home is the same thing. Give us the next chart now.

Is the home and the school the same thing? This is a chart that derived from that I've just had—the same title: "Is the Corporation the Home?" Now if the corporation equals this, the home, and also equals this, the school, then this, the home equals this, the school. Two things which equal the same thing equal each other, don't they? All right, if these two things equal the same thing, or the same thing equals the two things, then those things equal each other. So if the Corporation equals the home and the corporation equals the school, then the home must equal the school and therefore the home and the school would be the same thing. Now the fact is the corporation is not the home and the corporation is not the school. But the corporation provides the home and the corporation provides the school. Let us have the next chart. Chart number "L."

All right, the corporation provides the home. This was taken from the charters—photo static and certified copies of the charters of these homes. First, the purpose for which this corporation is formed is to maintain and operate a home, Sunny Glen, Article 2. Does it say it's the home? No. No the corporation is not the home. The corporation maintains and operates the home. The home is one thing and the corporation is something else. All right, the second, the purpose for which this corporation is formed is to establish and maintain a home. That's in the Turley charter, Article 2. All right, is the corporation the home? No. No, the corporation is the thing which establishes and maintains the home. The corporation is one thing; the home is that which the corporation establishes and maintains. They are two different things. All right, the third; the purposes of this corporation are to provide a home, Boles Article 2. Is the corporation the home? No, the corporation provides the home. The corporation is one thing, the home is something else. All right, and number four: This corporation is organized to provide a home, Maude Carpenter, Article 5. The corporation is not the home; the corporation provides the home. And so on the fifth: The purpose of said corporation is to establish, maintain and operate an orphan's home, Mount Dora, Article 4. The corporation is not the orphan's home; the corporation establishes, maintains, and operates the orphan's home. And that which the corporation operates is not the corporation itself. And when it operates something else, it is called an orphan's home. All right, number six: The purpose for which the corporation is formed is to establish and provide a home, Child Haven, Article 3. The same thing, the corporation is not the home but the corporation establishes and provides the home; and these are statements, taken my friends, not from somebody else, but from the charters of those homes and organizations themselves. And those very things are contained in them and I've copied them just as they are in the charters. Number seven: The purpose for which it is formed, referring to the corporation, is to build and operate this home and maintain an orphan's home, Shultz-Lewis, Article 2. Eight: The purpose for which this corporation is formed is to provide a home for aged men and women, The Gunter charter, Article 2. Now in every case, you see the corporation is one thing; the home which it provides is another thing. Therefore, we have an organization which is incorporated in between the church and the home. The church sends to the corporation that provides the home. Oh, he says, they send it direct to the home.

I want to know, Brother Deaver, do they spend it under the direction and oversight and according to the wishes of the corporation? Do they or not? And yet if the church would send its funds directly to the field of evangelism instead of sending to the definite corporation that forms the Missionary Society, would it be all right? And if the Missionary Society spent it under the direction of that board, would the corporation be working in that case? Just would you endorse it or what would you do about it? Let's have the lights now, please.

And there is the abundant proof that we do have an organization in between the church and the home. The organization is not the home. The corporation is not the home. The corporation provides, maintains, establishes the home and the home is one thing and the corporation is another. About two and a half minutes? That's all I need. I believe that about covers all my notes along that line. If I've overlooked anything, I've done it unintentionally, and if you will call my attention to it I will be glad to get back to it.

And another thing I want to find out just here in that connection with these questions, I asked him, number 3. Just what is the function or work in the field of benevolence that God has given the church to do? Whatever it is, Brother Deaver's position on the proposition says the church is not adequate to do it; I don't care what he says tonight. If he wants to back out on it and say I want to remove my name from it, let him say so. But until he says I've signed a proposition I don't believe, I occupy a position on that proposition which I don't believe, I'm going to hold him to what he has signed. Either give it up, Brother Deaver, or try to defend it, one or the other. It's up to you. You're not going to evade it by saying, I thought you meant this or I thought you meant that. You signed the proposition and you said you knew what I meant in those terms when you signed it and you are claiming that the church should contribute its funds to a benevolent organization—the church is not adequate to do it—that's what you are denying; anybody who reads the proposition can see that it is. There is no way that you can get around it. You had just as well face it.

So I want to know now, what is the function of the church to provide the needs or properly supply the needs? What do they do? Whatever it is; is it to send the money? Is that what you mean, the church sends the money? Well, if so then the church is not able to send it according to you, because you are denying that the church is adequate to do whatever God gave it to do in the field of benevolence. If that's providing the money, then the church is not adequate to provide the money according to your position with respect to this proposition tonight. So, whatever it is; I don't care where you put it, whatever it is; your position is on the negative of this proposition, the church is not adequate to do it. He wanted to know, is the church sufficient to do all the work God gave it? Yes. And, does the church function as a home?

The home is one thing; the church is another. We'll have some more on that but I haven't time in this speech. We'll have two more tomorrow night and I'll get you another chart along that line tomorrow night, showing you whose function it is and just what function the church performs and just how the thing operates on a scriptural basis. I don't have time to introduce that in the short time I have left and so I'll just save that for my first speech tomorrow night and deal with the function of the church and the function of the home. And we'll have some things that will be interesting I'm sure and some things that Brother Deaver will need to tell us about along that line. So don't forget, Brother Deaver, when you come to the stand, please Brother Deaver, please tell us: What is the function of the church? What does it do when it supplies the needs of orphans or those in need, whoever they may be? It's not orphans altogether. Benevolence covers more than orphans. We have the word benevolence but let it include them—the work of benevolence—whatever the work of the church is along that line. I want to know what does it do? When it provides for the needs of those who are in distress, what does it do? Just what is its work: What is its function? Don't forget to tell me how to set up a corporation or an organization that would be in between the church and the home. And be sure to tell me whether or not you would endorse a home placed under the supervision of the elders of a local congregation.

Deaver's Second Negative

Brother Porter, brethren Moderators, brethren, and friends: I'd like to remind you that Brother Porter referred several times in the course of his discussion to some things that I had not done and had not proved. And may I remind you as I remind him that he is in the affirmative tonight and he is in the proving business tonight and in spite of all the attempts he might make to put me in the affirmative, I refuse to go there until my time comes. He is in the affirmative tonight and I'm in the negative—he is in the proving business and we've called upon him to try to prove them and that's his job. And I maintain that he has not until this good day, told you just exactly what it is that brings that organization that he says stands between the church and the home into existence. Has he told you what it is? He complained for some few minutes about Brother Deaver's dealing with this proposition and he said, Brother Deaver knew my position and then he sought to leave the impression that perhaps I didn't know his position and yet the very point that he referred to in all that complaining was that I had said that he was talking about an in between organization and not a home. He has no objection right there to the home and by benevolent organization he does not mean a home, yet he came back and emphasized through the rest of his speech that that's exactly what he is talking about. That he is discussing that in between organization and I told you that's what he had in mind. He didn't mean by benevolent organization an orphan home; he means that in between organization. Now what brings it into existence? You know what Brother Porter said over and over again, "Brother Deaver, if we don't have it; tell me what to do so we can." Brother Porter, are you determined to have it? I'm purely opposed to that thing. There is no such thing. Brother Porter didn't tell you what brought it into existence; it's not incorporation because he says that's all right. You can incorporate a private home and that's not the issue, so it's not the incorporation that brings it into existence, but if it's there, then something brought it into existence. I say it's not there; he says,

Brother Deaver, if it's not, how can we get it there? As if he is determined to have it there, whether we have it now or not. Brother Porter, you say it's there and if you want to know how to get it there, just tell me what happened to put it there as it exists now in your mind. That's all in the world you've got to do. Tell us what happened to bring it into existence and I'll not have to tell you what put it there. I say it isn't there. Now if you want to know how to create a human organization, I can tell you. But you say you've got one there and I want you to tell me what brought it into existence and that's your job. I'm in the negative.

All right, Brother Porter complained again about the various parts in his proposition and he said that Brother Deaver denies all of these four points. He says there are four points in this proposition; Brother Deaver says he denies them therefore—or Brother Deaver signed the negative; therefore, Brother Deaver denies every point in that proposition. And I'm absolutely amazed to hear that kind of a statement from a man who has had the experience in polemics that Brother Porter has. He knows perfectly well that, if there is one single point in a man's proposition, even though it may state a dozen truths that he believes, that he can sign the negative to it; and here is a direct illustration of it. Brother Porter, the Bible teaches that there is one church and that there is one God and that there is one Lord and that salvation is by faith only. Would you deny that? Would you sign that proposition? There is one point in it, Brother Porter, that you will deny and I would exercise the same prerogative.

All right, I'd like to have my chart number 62 please. He complained somewhat at length about what I had had to say regarding his position, yet came back and said that I had represented him correctly—that he is opposed to that in-between organization. And that even—or when his proposition refers to a benevolent organization, that it does not refer to a home. It does refer to that organization in between the church and the home and which provides for a home. According to Brother Porter now, his proposition does not exclude—his proposition does not exclude a church sending funds to an incorporated home. We had the specific questions on that, asking him about it and he said, that's all right. A church can send to a private home and the private home can be incorporated. He thinks that there is the possibility the incorporation may make it not private any more but regardless, he still says that it can still send to a private home incorporated. All right, this home is not a church. Brother Porter, if this church can send to this home, then you admit that this home is not a church. And you admit that this home is not an integral part of the church and you say that this church can send to this home incorporated so that a church may meet its obligations to orphans and this admits everything that I'm contending for in this discussion. Brother Porter admits them every one. He wages a battle against the straw man. And if he didn't have that straw man, he couldn't do a thing on earth and couldn't make either of the distinctions to which you've listened. He ascribes the position to Brother Deaver and he assumes that the audience assumes that Brother Deaver is upholding this in between organization and he spends all of his time discussing that in between organization and if he could prove the establishment of it, I would oppose it just exactly like he does. I'm saying that a church incorporated even, just like he does, can send to a home incorporated and that that's one way that a church can meet its obligations to orphan children. All right, the lights please.

Brother Porter complained about what I had to say regarding his proposition here. I said that Brother Porter signed this proposition because he knew what Mr. Hicks meant by it. The scriptures teach that water baptism should be administered only in the name of Jesus Christ. All right, Brother Porter denies that. He denies that baptism is to be administered only in the name of Jesus Christ. And if only in the name of Jesus Christ means only by the authority of Christ, which is the only way that the Bible ever authorized baptism and he is denying it. That's not Brother Porter's position; he knows what he means by it. And so he signed it. Certainly, baptism cannot be administered in anybody's name excepting the name of Jesus Christ. That's the only way it's authorized. And if Brother Porter wants to quibble on it, in the name of Christ means by the authority of Christ and the only way that Christ ever authorized baptism was in the name of the Father and of the Son and of the Holy Spirit.

All right, he says, will I endorse the same arrangements in evangelism that we have in benevolence? Brother Porter, I've answered that question. I answered that in the written questions—you can read it. I said, we can meet legal requirements in evangelism just like we can meet legal requirements in benevolence. It just so happens that before this congregation here can have this property that the law says you've got to have some trustees to own it legally. I say you have a right to do it. You have a right to meet the legal requirements whether it is in evangelism or in benevolence. You couldn't own this property without meeting the demands of the law and the law says you've got to have legal trustees. Those trustees may be the elders but if they are, they are functioning in two capacities. They don't hold the property in trust as elders. They oversee the church as elders and this is not the church. But the same men, who are elders, may legally be the trustees of that property. And I maintain that the church has a right to meet those legal demands.

All, right, he wants me to tell him how to set up a human, benevolent organization. He begs me over and over, Brother Deaver, if we don't have it, tell me how to set it up. Brother Porter, I hope you don't want to set it up. And if we don't have it, you just forget that thing. And if we do have it, you tell me what happened to bring it into existence and we'll discuss that what happened. I wish he would tell us, but I predict he won't—he has already gone too far. Let him tell us what happened to bring that organization into existence. And if he says it's incorporation, then he is gone lock, stock and barrel. Because he has already said—(no head shaking, Brother Chaffin)—because he has already admitted that a church can send to a private home incorporated.

All right, he wants me to tell him now—referred to the definition of terms in the opening part of my speech, I have learned some things that he had not defined. Well, he said, Brother Deaver knew my position, and that's right, but I didn't know what he meant by some of these phrases and terms. I asked him, therefore, to give us the definition. He talked about my calling for those definitions and lo and behold never elaborated one particle more on what he meant by it. He says the church is adequate to meet its obligation to orphans, functioning in its congregational capacity. I said, Brother Porter, what do you mean by "is sufficient" or "is adequate"? Do you mean by that that the church must function as a home? Now if that's what you mean, I deny it. If you mean by that that the church simply provides the funds, to enable the care to be rendered by a home for orphan children, then I'll agree with you on it if that's what you mean by it. And then we will know whether or not we are agreed on that point. But did he do it? He still has left some very vital points undefined and that's the first job that he had in the affirmative.

I'd like to see Brother Porter's chart "A" please. In this connection, he said I denied all of these because I had signed the negative and we covered those points a while ago. He said, here's Deaver's position that God has given a work of benevolence to churches or that it is his position and that Deaver agrees to that. He says that churches are adequate to do that work and that Deaver says they are not adequate and I don't do any such thing.

He says they should do this work and Deaver says they shouldn't—I say they should. And he says, they should not surrender their work to benevolent organizations and Deaver says they can. Deaver doesn't say any such thing. I say they can't. But there's a number 5, Brother Porter. There is a number 5 that you don't have here—the very reason that I signed your proposition. Your proposition says number 5 over here that when a church sends funds it delegates its work. Brother Porter, why didn't you put that on there? Deaver denies that. You put that over here—Brother Porter says, when a church sends funds it delegates its work. Over here number 5, Deaver says, that isn't so and you'll have that right. You've got a number 5 that belongs on that chart but you didn't put it there.

All right, lights please. Well, let's see, he spent his time dealing with these matters. That was the straw man that I've already referred to and I'd like to beg him and plead with him to deal with the issue. He has somewhat localized the issue. He admits that we are discussing this in between organization. He wants me to tell him how to set it up but its already there according to him and it seems to me that it's his job to tell us what happened to bring it into existence and what we can do to get rid of it if it does exist. And then just allow a church incorporated can send to a home incorporated that the needs of orphan children might be supplied and get back to practicing just what we practiced back in 1951 by this good congregation.

All right, I'd like to see Brother Porter's chart Number "C" please. Brother Porter, your chart number "C". Let's notice the chart. Notice carefully, it's on the all-sufficiency of the church. And the church is all-sufficient, Brother Porter says, in the field of evangelism and I'd say that's exactly right. And it is sufficient in the field of edification and that's exactly right. He is opposed to the missionary society up here and he is opposed to a Sunday school society down here and that's exactly right. But he is not opposed to a Bible class remember. All right, in benevolence, he says, the church is all-sufficient and that's exactly right. He is opposed to a benevolent society down here and so am I. But he is not opposed to an orphan's home and neither am I. He is not opposed to that home being incorporated and neither am I. He is not opposed to that church being incorporated and neither am I. He is opposed to this in between organization which I say doesn't exist anywhere except in his imagination. And he has also the job of proving the existence of it. And Brother Porter, I asked you—and brethren, you know I asked him and you keep watching for the answer to it—I asked you, Brother Porter, where is your home on this proposition? On this benevolence here—the church is all-sufficient in benevolence but you say the church meets that obligation by providing a home for orphans, now you tell me where it is. And if you could put up a home here and a home that's incorporated and a home to which an incorporated church sends a contribution—if you can do that and not vitiate against the all-sufficiency of the church then why can't I do it. It comes down to the position: Brother Porter says, it's right if I do it and wrong if Deaver does it. Just a matter of who does it. Not a matter of what's done. Brother Porter, where is your home on this all-sufficiency in benevolence? You've got the job of putting it there. And I want you to put it there. You used the word "dare" a while ago, Brother Porter, didn't you? I dare you to put it there. Brother Porter, you need to do it. Where is your home on that proposition? On this phase here—the all-sufficiency in benevolence. Lights please.

He said, I said, Brother Porter didn't mean a home by benevolent organization. I'm amused Brother Porter at the way you handled that. He said, that I said, that he didn't mean a home when he used the word benevolent organization. And so then he talked all around in his proposition, referring to the word benevolent organization and said, Deaver said that when I used those terms I didn't mean a home. He never did come out and tell you he didn't mean it—right there—he did later. But when he was discussing that, and what Deaver said about it, he never did tell you that when I used the word benevolent organization, I didn't mean a home and Deaver was right when he told you what he told you when he told you what he told you. Brother Porter knew I was right on it. But he just wouldn't admit it on that particular point.

He complained about what Deaver didn't do. Remember again, he is in the affirmative and I'm in the negative. And it's my job to show you what he is not doing. Now he can have that job of showing you what I'm not doing on Thursday and Friday nights. Brother Porter, you let me do that now. It's my job to outline what he is not doing and yet what he is supposed to do. He said, tell me what to do to set up that organization in between. Two or three times he made that statement. And we've dealt with it each time we have come across it in the notes here. He said that I said I didn't deny his proposition. Give me my chart number 56. He made the statement that Brother Deaver said he didn't deny my proposition. Brother Deaver didn't say that but that's what he said that Deaver said. Deaver said he didn't deny my proposition and while discussing the idea that I didn't deny his proposition, he called for my chart number 56, which is a chart showing what

I deny, with reference to his proposition. What I am not denying—what I am denying now, that God has given the church the job of functioning as a home. Brother Porter, if that's what you mean, by the church being adequate to meet its obligation, then I deny it. Now if you don't mean that, just tell me and we'll get that off of there. And if you mean that the church can function as a home then I deny that. If that's what you mean in your proposition by being adequate, then I deny that or of the existence of an in between organization, I deny there is any such thing. I deny that a contribution of funds means delegation of work. And he has not one time attempted to prove that and he can't and he won't and this debate will close without his having made an attempt to prove that when you send a contribution you delegate your work. Let him face up to the task that he's got. Brother Porter, you signed the affirmative of this proposition, didn't you?

All right, I deny that the Bible teaching regarding to a church's obligation to orphans, makes it impossible for a church to scripturally contribute to Boles Home. Regardless of whatever else you meant that's one thing you did mean; that's one position you do hold. That is absolutely unquestioned that the Bible teaching regarding a church's obligation to orphans makes it impossible for a church to scripturally make a contribution to Boles Home. All right, the light please.

He said, the proposition does not refer to an in between organization. Brother Porter, it does refer to an in between organization. I might have misunderstood you there but I have in the note here that you made the statement that the proposition didn't refer to an in between organization. But you know perfectly well that the word "benevolent organizations" there refers to an in between organization. You were making this statement with reference to what I had to say about a home. I said there is a home in your organization. But you said that Deaver said benevolent organization doesn't refer to a home; therefore, you said Deaver said there's not a home in it. That's an erroneous conclusion. And it kind of suggested to me how you had drawn some of the conclusions you had. Just because benevolent organizations doesn't refer to a home doesn't mean there's no home there. Not one particle. That word benevolent organizations in Brother Porter's proposition doesn't mean a home. But there's a home in his proposition. Let him tell you that his proposition eliminates a home for orphans. Why, it doesn't. It's there.

All right. Then again, let me have Brother Porter's chart "M". Chart number "M". Chart number "M", what's wrong with incorporation? Brother Porter has the details outlined here of a church sending to an organization in between—it's a human organization—it's unincorporated—a human organization unincorporated—a human organization unincorporated. Brother Porter that reminds me of a statement I've read from you, that you're opposed to this organization in between incorporated or unincorporated, chartered or not chartered. And brethren, that means this: that there is the possibility of the existence of this in between organization without its being chartered and without its being incorporated. Now you keep that in mind when he comes back to tell you what it is that brings it into existence. Now, if it's not the charter and if it's not the incorporation that brings it into existence, pray tell me what it is. And yet he says it can exist, chartered or not chartered or incorporated or not incorporated. All right, he's got the in between organization, the church sending to that which they say is to the private home. Brother Porter, I'm opposed to that just like you are. There just isn't any such thing in the world—so far as concerns our brethren. What I'm concerned about is this: Can an incorporated church, a church can incorporate, can't they Brother Porter? Can incorporated churches send to a private home incorporated? That's all in the world I'm concerned about. And he says that's all right. I don't want this thing down here and I'll oppose it just like he does. But I know that an incorporated church can send funds to an incorporated home in order that the needs of orphan children might be supplied. And he said, it is not incorporated but the thing incorporated—a human organization. And if you can find it, Brother Porter, I'll join the fight with you. I made the statement one time to Brother Leroy Garrett: If you can find that kind of a preacher, I'll oppose him just like you are. If you can find that kind of a system, I'll oppose it just like you do. And if Brother Porter can find that kind of an organization, in between, then I'll join him in the fight against it. I'm concerned about an incorporated church sending to an incorporated private home. You may wonder why all the talk about incorporation. But Brother Porter ought to explain that to you; he is in the affirmative and if he doesn't, I will when I get into the affirmative. It's a very fine legal matter. And the church has the right to meet the demands of the law and also exercise some good business sense. All right, now let's have the lights, please.

Brother Porter's chart N. The thing we are discussing now. Brother Porter says here is the thing we are discussing; here's the issue. It's like I told you it was in my first speech. Here is the issue: the in between organization.

Brother Porter, I'll ask you again to tell this audience again what is it that creates that in between organization? Now, it's not incorporation according to your chart M. It's not a charter according to your Chart M. Now, what is it? All that we're concerned about when all of that's said and done is that a church can send to a home, that the needs of children might be supplied. All right, is the home a benevolent organization? Brother Porter asked me if the home a benevolent organization? Well, Brother Porter, I can't answer that until you tell me that—or what you mean by benevolent organization. If you mean by benevolent organization what you mean in your proposition, no. But if you mean, is it a benevolent organization in that it involves itself in benevolence, yes. Now, I just don't know what you mean and that's the only way I know to answer it. And if you can rephrase your question, I'll try to do a better job of answering it. That's all I know. If you mean by benevolent organization what you mean in your proposition by it, then the answer is no. If you mean that a church can involve itself in benevolent activities, then yes. You just tell me what you mean and we'll see which way we go.

All right, if you don't have to tell me. Or he said, if we don't have it, then tell me how to arrange it. How many times, I wish I had counted, did he make that statement? If we don't have it, tell me how to arrange it. Brother Porter, are you determined to have it regardless? Brother Porter's chart K, please. Brother Porter's chart number K. And it's on the matter of incorporation. Is corporation the home? And Brother Porter gave all of these statements to prove that the corporation is one thing and that the home is something else; that the corporation provides the home. Brother Porter, I wish in my last speech I had asked you the question: Is Boles Home, in your opinion, incorporated? Would you make a note of that and answer it for me? Is Boles Home incorporated? I'd just like to know the answer to that. Does Brother Porter believe—does he think that Boles Home is incorporated? I want to know the answer to that question. All right, he says, in these cases it's the corporation that provides the home. And that is actually the mistake in Brother Porter's reasoning. May I suggest to you that the corporation provides the home in exactly the same sense that a parent provides for his family. The father's an integral part of that home and so is the corporation. And that's the way the charters read—some of them. That the corporation stands *en loco parentis*. They occupy the same position—with reference to those children that the parents do with reference to their own children. They're legal parents—they're legal guardians. Let him get up and tell you that a man's no part of his family simply because he provides for them. That's the ridiculous position that he is holding tonight. It's the corporation that provides it. Well, it's the husband that provides for his family. But the corporation, if it provides it, is no part of the home. And therefore, it takes the husband out just as sure as the world. If not, why not? Let Brother Porter explain it. By following the same reasoning which he exercised here, I use the word reasoning lightly there—but by following the same kind of reasoning that he followed here, I can prove to you that every incorporated church is provided by a corporation and that therefore, the corporation is no part of the church. It has no integral connection with the church. It has no integral connection with the church and has nothing integral—or has no integral connection with meeting the legal demands of the law. I can read from charter after charter just like he has on the chart here, where the corporation formed, in Wichita Falls for example, is done so to provide for worship and for benevolence. Now the corporation provides it. But it's simply meeting for the demands of the law. I'd like to read to you some of those if we had the time but to be sure to cover everything that Brother Porter had to show you that regardless of what he did say, do you have his answers to my questions here? Regardless of what he had to say on this incorporation, he spent a great deal of time on it yet he is not opposed to it. He's not opposed to an incorporation *per se*. All of which means you could have an incorporated church and an incorporated home without having that in-between organization, and that's all that I am concerned about.

I asked him the question: Are there any circumstances conceivable to you under which a church might send funds to a private home so that the needs of orphan children might be adequately supplied? And he said yes. A church can send to a home. I said, could a private home be incorporated? And he says yes to that. But he says a corporation that provides a home is something else. But he says the private home can be incorporated. And a church could send to it—an incorporated church, could send money to an incorporated home that the needs of orphan children might be supplied and he says that's all right. And that's all in the world I'm concerned about.

All right, notice then—let's get his chart K-1 right quickly please. I need his chart K-1. Brother Porter says that because things that equal the same thing are equal to each other, that here you have a corporation and he says this sends to a home and equals this and the corporation equals the home there and that this sends to the school and the corporation equals the school and if the corporation equals the home and if the corporation equals the school and then of course, the home would equal the school. And the whole thing is, the corporation is an integral part of the home and the corporation is an integral part of the school whatever set-up he had in mind and that doesn't prove that a home and a school are the same thing. It simply proves that the corporation is an integral part of two different things. And that's all there is on that chart.

All right, let's turn please, to my chart number 60. Notice carefully, let me emphasize to you while we are getting this ready, there is not an orphan home among us which Brother Porter will endorse that's being supported by a church or by churches. Furthermore, he is not about to start one and furthermore, he can't start one because if and when he does, he is going to have to meet the same requirements as these that are characteristic of Boles Home and have to oppose it just like he does this.

All right, my chart number 60—Brother Porter's admissions now, on the written questions and answers in this first night session. An incorporation—rather, an incorporated church, he says, can send to a home incorporated in order to supply the needs for orphan children and he admits that in this above situation a church would be meeting its obligations to provide for orphan children. I want my chart number 61 and get number 62 ready. Here's how Brother Porter should have gone on his chart number B. His B chart had a church sending to a benevolent organization standing between here—and here's the way it actually is Brother Porter, when a church sends to an orphan home—when a church sends to a private home incorporated; you don't have this in between organization. You simply have a church incorporated sending to a home incorporated that the needs of orphan children might be supplied and you said, yes Brother Deaver, that's all right. According to Brother Porter his proposition does not exclude—his proposition does not exclude a church sending funds to an incorporated home. And this home is not a church, keep that in mind, this home is not a church and this home is not in any way an integral part of the church. Any time he says a church can send to a home, he recognizes the difference between that church and that home. And if he knows the difference, then he knows the home is not the church. And the church is not the home. And if so, that a church may meet its obligations to orphans. And this admits everything in the world that I need him to admit in order that my proposition might be sustained.

My chart number 55 and 56 please and have I that much time? Don't have time. Thank you for listening.

Porter's Third Affirmative

Brethren Moderators, Brother Deaver, Ladies and Gentlemen: Through the goodness of God we are permitted to gather once more upon this occasion to make a further investigation of those things that concern the church of the living God in the field of benevolence. The proposition which we are discussing tonight as you understand is the same proposition we had for consideration last evening in which I am affirming that *according to the scriptures, churches of Christ, each acting in its congregational capacity are adequate to accomplish all the work that God has given the church to do. And they should do the work without delegating it by the contribution of their funds to benevolent organizations.* Brother Deaver says he signed the proposition not because of what the proposition said but rather because of what he thought Porter meant by the proposition. He indicated during the progress of the discussion last evening that he endorsed about everything in the proposition. He says he believes the church is given an obligation in the field of benevolence. He believes furthermore, that the church is adequate to do that work. And he believes the church should do that work and the church should not surrender that work to benevolent organizations. Frankly, everything involved in the proposition, he agrees with according to his procedure last night. And he signed it because he thought something else was in it and not because of what the proposition actually said. He indicated he might sign just about any kind of a proposition as long as there might be one little thing in it that he didn't agree with. In fact, he said if someone would present the proposition that the Bible teaches that there is one church, and one God and one Lord and salvation is by faith only, he should sign the negative of that proposition. Well, I wouldn't my friends. I wouldn't deny that the scriptures teach that there is one God; I wouldn't deny that the scriptures teach that there is one church; I wouldn't deny that the scriptures teach there is one Lord in order to deny that salvation is by faith only. I could not sign that proposition without denying all of them for the simple fact that each of them is an independent clause. When you say the scriptures teach that there is one God, that's an independent clause—a sentence complete within itself. It has no relationship to the rest of the proposition. When you say the scriptures teach there is one church, the same thing is true. And when you say the scriptures teach there is one Lord, the same thing is true. It's an independent clause, and does not depend in any way for its significance upon any other part of the proposition. And I would not deny those things in order to deny that salvation is by faith only, Brother Deaver to the contrary notwithstanding. He would deny all of that in order to deny that salvation is by faith only.

Well, he said in the beginning of the closing speech last night that Brother Porter is complaining—continues to complain about the proposition. And I suppose that Brother Deaver continues to complain because Brother Porter complains about the proposition. Well, we will let that go for what it may be worth and proceed to an investigation of some things along the line. He said, another thing in that connection, that Porter is in the proving business. I had called upon him to prove something. He said Porter is in the proving business in this proposition and he would be in the proving business the last two nights of the discussion. Well, I realize that full well, but at the same time, he is in the disproving proposition and therefore, I have been calling upon him to disprove some things which he has not undertaken to do. And I am still insisting that he deny because he is in the position of the negative of this proposition tonight.

Now, we have been exchanging questions a little different from the arrangements usually made in discussions of this kind. Instead of asking the questions during the speeches we make, we are presenting our questions, five in number, each night in advance of the session. The answers are being written in, and then returned to the one who gave the questions and then the speaker introduces the questions and the answers as he sees fit. And here are my questions tonight that I handed to Brother Deaver with his answers: First, if a congregation contributes its funds for the work of evangelism, to a missionary society, does it delegate its work to a human organization? Brother Deaver answers, the mere transfer of funds does not necessarily constitute a delegation of work. Well, that isn't what I asked. I didn't refer to a mere transfer of funds. I said, when a congregation contributes its funds for the work of evangelism to a missionary society, does it delegate its work to a human organization. Brother Deaver did not beg the question; as he did not last night; he evaded the question. The question referred not to a mere transfer of funds but to a contribution, Brother Deaver. If a congregation contributes its funds for a work of evangelism to a missionary society, does it delegate its work to a human organization? I'm still demanding that you answer.

And number two: Is the Buckner Corporation that provides the Buckner Home in Dallas, Texas, an organization between Baptist Churches and the Home? You know, last night he had a great deal to say about the in between organization and denied that there is any such thing, that the idea of an in between organization existed only in my imagination and that there wasn't any such thing. And hence I asked him this question: Is the Buckner Corporation that provides the Buckner Home in Dallas, Texas, an organization between Baptist Churches and the Home? And Brother Deaver answers, so far as I know, Buckner Home is an incorporated orphan home and an integral part of the Southern Baptist Convention. Now, I'm wondering Brother Deaver, if in Boles Corporation, the corporation is an integral part of the home, why wouldn't the Buckner Corporation be an integral part of the home? You make one reach one way and the other reach back the other direction. With Boles Home, you say the corporation reaches to the home. It is an integral part of the home. It reaches back the other way and becomes an integral part of the Southern Baptist Convention. Now, I wonder why. Did he see the handwriting on the wall? I wonder why he made one reach one way and the other reach the other direction. Now, according to that, if he means it becomes an integral part of the Southern Baptist Convention, because the members of the Baptist Churches who provide the corporation or provide the home are members or are allied or associated with the Southern Baptist Convention, would make it become an integral part of that Convention, then upon the same basis, since members of the church form the corporation, that provides Boles Home, why wouldn't that corporation reach back the other way and become an integral part of the church? If one reaches one way, why doesn't the other reach the same way? Why does the corporation in Buckner Home reach one direction while the corporation in Boles Home reaches the other direction? We will be interested to find out.

Number three: Is the missionary society that provides the work of evangelism an organization between churches and that work? He says the missionary society stands between the churches and the work, but not because of the fact of incorporation. Nobody ever claimed that it did. Nobody ever claimed that it stood between the churches and the work because of incorporation. Nobody claims this other organization stands between the church and benevolence or the home by the mere fact of incorporation. Just why—why does the missionary society stand as an organization between the church and the work? It is an in between organization. Now, why? We want to know why, Brother Deaver?

Number four: Is Boles Corporation a divine organization because it stands *en loco parentis* to the children? He made a statement last night about it standing *en loco parentis* to the children and was therefore an integral part of the home. His answer is, Boles Home is a divine institution which is incorporated like the home in your proposition. Well, in the first place, you said there wasn't any home in my proposition. Now you say it's like the one in my proposition therefore it's like nothing, you see, according to his reasoning, because he says there's not any home in my proposition. Now, he says, it is like the home in your proposition. But again, notice he did not answer my question. I said, "Is Boles Home a divine organization because it stands *en loco parentis* to the children?" I asked for the reason for its being divine institution. He says, it's a divine institution which is incorporated. Why? That's what I'm trying to find out, Brother Deaver. Why is Boles Home or Boles Corporation, whichever you put it a divine organization? Why is it a divine institution? That's what I'm trying to find out. You haven't told me.

Number five: What are the legal demands for a congregation to meet in order to minister relief to orphans and other needy people? And if the same legal demands were made for evangelism, would you endorse that? His answer is, the legal requirements in each case would be different. The church is not a home, hence must provide a home for the orphans and this home must meet legal demands. The legal demands relating to evangelism can be met. Well, do you understand what he said in answer to the question? I said, what are the legal demands for a congregation to meet in order to minister relief to orphans and other needy people? Did he answer? No. No, he didn't answer. He didn't tell me any of the legal demands. I want to know, Brother Deaver, what the legal demands are. You say we have to meet legal demands. Now, I want to know what they are and that's what you haven't told me. And then when you tell me, if the same demands were made in the field of evangelism, would you also accept that? That's what I'm trying to find out. And that's what you are evading.

Now we proceed to an investigation of some things said last night and other arguments and charts as we introduced them in this speech as we go along. And people have said sometimes that debates of this kind accomplish nothing—that they will do no good but I'm certain that we have accomplished a great deal already in the debates we have had during the past two years. Because now it is being admitted and has been definitely admitted and elaborated upon that Brother Deaver, in this discussion, that the thing which we oppose, if it exists, is wrong. That our opposition to benevolent organizations to do the work of the church is a valid objection. That we are proceeding in a scriptural course upon that and the only thing left is: Does the organization actually exist? Now, in former debates, men have affirmed that the church has a scriptural right to build and maintain benevolent organizations. But now Brother Deaver says there is no such thing. The benevolent organizations do not exist. It exists only in your imagination, he says. It isn't there. And so they have come to the place now where they say the only issue is if there is such an organization. If there is, he says he will oppose it just like I do and he will make the same arguments I'm making if there is such an organization. So it resolves itself into that one thing: Is there an organization in between the church and the work of benevolence? That's the only thing we have to prove now in this and future discussions that may develop because it has been agreed that our opposition is valid—that our opposition is scriptural if there is any such thing. And so the whole thing hinges upon the idea: Is there such an organization? And that's what we shall endeavor to prove and sustain before you tonight and as we go along during the discussion. A number of things were introduced last night. And we want some more of them now.

I want to use just at this time my chart V. The one a way over toward the last—chart V. We want to get that at this particular point in order to get before you some ideas along this line. Instead of chart V, he said, its chart F that I wanted. We will get to these others presently but chart F is the one I want now. This deals with some definitions concerning the matters before us tonight. We have first, "organization" and it is defined: A body of persons organized for some specific purpose as a club, union or a society. That definition is taken from *Webster's New World Dictionary*, page 1033. Second, "association" is defined: An organization of persons having common interests, purposes and so on as society or a league, from the same dictionary, page 89. And third, "society" is defined: Any organized group of people joined together because of some interest in common, as a medical society, the same authority, page 1384. And fourth, a "corporation" is defined: A group of people who get a charter, granting them as a body certain legal powers, rights and privileges, page 330 of the same authority. Now, here we have definitions of what an organization, an association, a society and a corporation is. And we find that an organization is a body or group of persons set up to perform some specific purpose—that endeavor to accomplish some mutual interest of some kind. And association and society are but terms that may be used interchangeably referring to the same sort of group of people. And when a group of people obtain a charter, then that kind of organization becomes a corporation. It's still the same kind of organization, but it becomes a corporation when it gets a charter. And so keep those things in mind.

Now then, down beneath there: A divine organization is one that exists by divine authority and a human organization is one that exists by human authority. Now keep in mind the difference between a divine organization and a human organization; it's because of the authority back of it. A divine organization exists by the divine authority; a human organization exists by human authority. And so that will suffice for definitions concerning organizations.

All right, we proceed now to some other matters on that particular point. And remember that Brother Deaver is admitting that organizations in between the church and the work are wrong if there are any such thing. And I asked him how to set up one if we don't have it—how to set up one. If what we have is not an organization of that kind, how would we go about building one? He said, Brother Porter, I hope you are not determined to have one. Why no, I'm not wanting one. I'm not determined to have one. But I'm determined to find out whether we already have them or not according to you. And I'm wanting you to tell me what you would do to set up an organization of that kind and when you tell me what you must do, I think I can show you that that's what we already have and therefore we do have them and that's why you haven't told me how to set up one. I'm still insisting that you tell me how.

Also, he wanted to know how to determine its existence—how did the corporation come into existence. That's the idea he presented in that connection. Well, a human organization may exist before it's incorporated or it may come into existence at the time the charter is obtained. It may exist one way or the other but which ever way it comes into existence, if by human authority, it's a human organization, regardless of when it began in that particular matter.

And then now, we want to use chart T in this connection in order to get before you this idea of the organizations in between the church and the work. And here we have chart T that concerns two associations. On the left hand column, I have Christian Restoration Association. On the right hand, I have Southern Christian Association. Christian Restoration Association is a Missionary Society, chartered by a conservative group of Christian Churches at Cincinnati, Ohio. Southern Christian Association is a corporation chartered by some of our brethren over at Morrilton, Ark. Now then, these statements are taken from their charters—they're not my statements—they're what their charters say. And here, regarding the Christian Restoration Association it said, First, The name of said corporation shall be the Christian Restoration Association—Article 1. Concerning Southern Christian Association, First, The name of the Association is the Southern Christian Home—Article 1. Under Christian Restoration Association, Second, Said corporation is to be located at Cincinnati in Hamilton County, Ohio, Article 2. Second, under the Southern Christian Association, the location of this association shall be in or near Morrilton, Conley County, Ark., Article 2. And third, of the Christian Restoration Association, Said corporation is formed for the purpose of promoting the cause of the Christian religion and of receiving, soliciting and holding in trust and dispersing bequests, gifts, funds and monies for the preaching of the gospel of Jesus Christ—for the organization of churches of Christ according to the New Testament pattern, Article 3. Third, under the other, The purpose of this association shall be to care for, adopt, keep, train and educate orphan children and to find homes for and place in Christian homes children committed to this association and to act for and on behalf of orphan children and dependent and neglected children, Article 3. Now there we have two associations; one of them is a missionary society—the other is a benevolent society. I want to know, Brother Deaver, on this hand over here, is this Christian Restoration Association an organization between the churches and evangelism? I want to know. And if it is, I want to know why. And then tell me why this one over here wouldn't qualify in the same way. Here, we have one in between the churches and the work they are doing and I want to know, when did this one come into existence, Brother Deaver? When did this corporation here come into existence—this organization on the left hand side of the chart—the Christian Restoration Association—this missionary society—the group of men set up to promote the cause of the Christian religion and to disperse funds and gifts and so on for the preaching of the gospel and the organization of churches of Christ? I want to know, is that a human organization? And why is it? Would you endorse one of that kind? In the field of evangelism? Why will you endorse this one in the field of benevolence but will not endorse that in the field of evangelism? Well, we shall await his response to that.

Now then, I want chart V following that. Here we have another chart dealing with in between organizations. Now, we have drawn here on the chart some in between organizations. At the top we have over there, some figures drawn to represent churches—you see the word spelled up and down there by the side of those blocks. In the center we have the missionary society corporation just as that to which your attention was called a while ago. Over here we have evangelism or the work of preaching the gospel of Jesus Christ. All right, then down here we have the same arrangement with churches over there and in between a benevolent organization or corporation. Then over here, benevolence—the work of relief to those who are in distress. Now I want to know, Brother Deaver, if this is up here an in between organization? When the churches send their funds or contribute their funds to a missionary corporation, which takes charge of their funds and does the work in the field of evangelism—I want to know if that missionary corporation is an organization between the churches and the work? And if so, I want to know what makes it so? Then I want to know again, if down here when the churches contribute their funds to a benevolent organization—corporation and it takes charge of those funds and spends them in the field of benevolence, if that is not also a corporation or an organization in between the churches and the work of benevolence? And if not, why not? Why is one of those a human organization down here but a human organization up there? He says this is divine. He has made the statement already, here is the divine organization. I want to know why this is divine and that's human? And why that one is between the churches and evangelism and this one is not? I want to know.

He says the church is not a home and it cannot function as a home and he gave me chart 56 along that line which we have had on this screen before in which he says he is denying that the church can function as a home. So he said, the church is not a home and therefore it cannot function as a home. I don't know whether the audience generally understands just what Brother Deaver is driving at but the idea is this. It's the work of the church to raise the money and it's the work of the home to give the care. In other words, the church can't feed a baby; the church can't clothe a little child; the church can't bathe a child; the home has to do that and the church simply furnishes the money. And when the church furnishes the money, its work ends, and then when the home takes over, the home's work begins. And therefore, he has the function of the church one thing and the function of the home the other and says the one cannot overlap the other—that the church cannot function as a home. Well, certainly the church is not a home, Brother Deaver. Did it ever occur to you that the church is not an automobile? And the church is not a train. And the church is not a gospel meeting or a church building. But, while the church is not an automobile, I believe the church can provide a automobile in which to transport its preacher to train to provide the means by which he can ride the train to a place where a gospel meeting is to be held and have the meeting conducted. Do you believe they can do it? Or do you think that when the church buys the automobile, that its work ends there and then the automobile takes over and performs its function? And then the train takes over and performs its function? Certainly the church is not an automobile; the church is not a train and actually, Brother Deaver, the church is not a bus. But I've known of churches operating buses, haven't you—to send out a bus to bring in people to the services and then take them home? Is the church doing its work or does the church end its work when it buy the bus and then the bus takes over and performs its work and therefore the church cannot bring anybody to services or send them home because the church cannot function as a bus? Don't you see the absurdity of his argument?

All right, I want now chart D. To get that a little plainer before you. How much time do I have? We want to get chart D there to further illustrate that point. And here we have the question—Whose work is it? And first, if an individual, by his own arrangement and the use of his own funds, does a work, the action and work is that of the individual, as for example: Dorcas in relieving the needy, Acts 9:36 to which we might compare Ephesians 4:28. And second, each one may edify (Rom. 14:19; 15:2). All right, third, there is Philip preaching in Samaria (Acts 8:4, 5). We have there individual action—individual work. And second, if a congregation arranges the work and provides the personnel and funds, the action or work is that of the church. Such as 1. In gospel preaching (Acts 13:1-3; 15:22, 23; Phil. 4:15, 16; 1 Thess. 1:8) and 2. self edification (Eph. 4:16). And 3. in benevolence (Acts 6:1-6; 11:27-30; Rom. 15:25, 26). And 4, the same would be true of the home as in Acts 18:24, 26 in which Aquila and Priscilla took Apollos unto them and expounded unto him the way of God more perfectly. Now then, 5. if furnishing the money is the function of the church and furnishing the care is the function of the individual or the home, then, Brother

Deaver says that, the church cannot do the home's work; and the church cannot administer the care. All right; then that being true, if it is true, then on the same basis the individual or the home could not furnish the money. If the church gives the care; has any part in the care, then it's functioning as a home. All right, then if the home furnishes the money, then the home is functioning as a church, Brother Deaver, and you have the thing going each way, or both ways, thank you.

On the trustees of the church property, he said, you have the same thing. Well, the property can be deeded to trustees but does that authorize or does that set up an organization such as he has in the field of benevolent work or benevolence? I have a chart on that but I haven't time to use it just now. But we shall get to it a little later.

And then getting to the matter of chart C, he dared me to put the home on that chart. Where is your home on chart C, he said, I dare you to put it on. Well, the word "home" in the sense of providing food, shelter, clothing and things of that nature; when they made provision for the needy, they certainly provided those things but they did not set up a human organization either incorporated or unincorporated to do it. And that's the thing we are after in this debate.

And he wanted to know, "Is Boles Home incorporated?" And I have a chart on that. I believe I might have time to use that chart; chart W now. We want to get that one if we have time for it, "Is Boles Home incorporated?" All right, which is the corporation? Here we have on one hand the square over there to represent the missionary society; over here another square to represent evangelism or a gospel meeting. And over here in the missionary society, we have set up, a group of men that corresponds with the definition of an organization which I have on the chart a while ago, from Webster's dictionary. All right, here is a group of men that form a missionary society and that group of men provides evangelism or a gospel meeting. Here is the preacher, the song director and the audience. Now I want to know which is the corporation. Is the corporation the preacher, the song director and the audience over here in the field of evangelism or is the corporation that group of men over there that provides these things? Which is the corporation? All right, then the same thing down here. We have the benevolent society which is also a group of men set up between the church and its work. And over here the benevolence or the home, and we have the matron, the cook, the janitor, and the children and so on. I want to know, Brother

Deaver, which is the corporation? Is it the matron, the cook, the janitor and the children or is it that group of men over there that provide this work in the field of benevolence? Which is the corporation? Now then, if this is merely an incorporated home down here and that's not a corporation over there that provides the home or an organization that provides it, then this up here is merely incorporated evangelism and that's not a separate group or organization over there. Brother Deaver, do you accept evangelism, either incorporated or unincorporated? Is this incorporated evangelism; is that what you mean? Or is the group of men over there the corporation that provides the evangelism? We have another group of men down there that's a benevolent society or organization that provides the work in the field of benevolence. And so there is your answer to the matter of whether or not Boles Home is incorporated.

He said that he did not endorse, or rather indicated he would not endorse a home under elders. And I haven't time for my chart on that. I'll get that in the beginning of my next speech I believe. And one other point, he said, Porter did not define certain terms in his proposition. Time.

Deaver's Third Negative

Brother Porter, Gentlemen Moderators, Brethren and Friends: The proposition which Brother Porter is affirming tonight reads as follows: *According to the scriptures, churches of Christ, each acting in its congregational capacity, are adequate to accomplish all the work of benevolence that God has given the church to do and they should do this work without delegating it by the contribution of their funds to benevolent organizations.* Now last evening, Brother Porter spent just a few moments in an attempt to define the terms of his proposition. In my two speeches, I called attention repeatedly to the fact that there are some very important terms in that proposition which he has not as yet defined. And I'd like to mention briefly now just one or two of those. I want him to state specifically what he means by the term "adequate" in his proposition. He's gotten fairly close to it tonight; in fact, close enough that I think we can know definitely just exactly what his position is with reference to the adequacy of a congregation in meeting its work to orphan children. And we shall discuss that then in the light of what he has had to say. But if he'll take just a moment—give me another statement regarding what he has in mind by adequacy there, I'd certainly like to have it.

On the word "benevolent organization" in his proposition, may I keep before you the definite fact that Brother Porter does not mean orphan home. When you have the word "benevolent organization" in his proposition, he does not refer to orphan homes. But rather, he does refer to an in between organization. He refers to an organization that stands between the contributing church and the home. Now that's the entire center of this discussion so far. He maintains that there is such a thing as that organization in between. I deny very emphatically the existence of any such organization. But you keep in mind, now, because the terms is in his proposition and it's an important term, or a term so important that when he refers to benevolent organizations in this proposition, that he does not refer to an orphan home. He has reference to an in between organization which exists only in his imagination and also the imagination of those who stand with him. I'd like to keep before this audience just exactly what Brother Porter is obligated to do.

Now we called attention last night to some of these points and I shall review them very hurriedly here. But I think the audience needs to know, and I know that all of us need to recognize that Brother Porter has a tremendous obligation here in attempting to prove his proposition. And according to that proposition, he is under the responsibility of proving that what is—rather that God has given each congregation a work of benevolence. Keep in mind, that whether I deny that or not doesn't have anything to do with his responsibility to prove the point. Let him give a scripture on it, and so far he hasn't—let him just give the passage now—I'd like to see the mode by which, or the method by which he arrives at that conclusion and I shall have use for it. Let him give the scripture that proves that point. Keep in mind also that benevolence as is involved in his proposition refers to the care of orphans and so he has the job proving that a church has the responsibility in connection with the care of orphans. He must prove secondly that each congregation, acting in its congregational capacity, as he has it, is adequate to accomplish the work of benevolence which God has given it to do. Now benevolence here means providing for orphan children. And the church is adequate to do the work that God has given it in connection with providing for those orphan children. And we raised the question last night then, Brother Porter, do you mean by that that the church has everything that it needs to meet that need or to supply the needs of orphans? He has gotten fairly close to answering that question tonight and we shall press him on it at the proper time.

But by being adequate now, does he have in mind that the church has everything that it needs to meet the needs of an orphan child? He must prove in the third place that each congregation must do the work which God has given it to do without delegating that work to a benevolent organization. That simply means that each congregation must meet its obligation to orphans without delegating its work to benevolent organizations.

He must prove, in the fourth place that in the matter of the churches contributing to Boles Home or a similar home, that there is such a thing as that in between organization. And he must prove, in the fifth place, that when a church contributes funds, that it automatically or inherently delegates its work. Now that's in his proposition. He must prove that when a church contributes funds, that it is inherently delegating its work to the recipient of those funds. He must prove, in the sixth place (here's a very fundamental point in connection with his proposition), that the Bible teaching regarding a church's care of orphan children makes it forever impossible for a church to make a contribution to Boles Home or to a similar home.

I'd like to have my chart number 54 right quickly now and this chart no. 54 is simply a brief statement of what Brother Porter is obligated to do. I'd like for you to keep in mind the chart as we proceed and see just exactly has he proceeds in his attempt to establish these points. Let him prove that a church has an obligation to orphans. Let him prove that each church is sufficient now to meet its obligation to orphans without calling upon anything else under the sun. And let him prove that a church must not delegate its work to a benevolent organization. Let him prove the existence of an in between organization now—and that's what he means by benevolent organization I believe—he doesn't mean a home. Let him prove that a contribution of funds inherently means a delegation of work. And let him prove that the Bible teaching on this subject makes it impossible for a church to send a contribution to Boles Home. Now then, I want to suggest to you my position with reference to that. Keep the chart on the screen just a moment. Here's my position with reference to Brother Porter's proposition. I do not deny that God has given the church an obligation. I believe that just as firmly as does he. And I believe that each church is sufficient to do the work that God gave it to do but I emphatically deny that God gave the church the job of functioning as a home. And that's the position now that Brother Porter has found himself in tonight. The church is adequate. All right, if the church is adequate now, I asked him last night, what do you mean by that? Does the church have to call on something else—may it provide a home, or can the church function as a home? And now tonight his position is that the church has everything that it needs in meeting the needs of orphan children. And we shall deal with it. I deny that the church of the living God has the right or even could legally or scripturally function as a home.

Number 3: A church must not delegate its work and I do not deny that. Certainly a church must not delegate its work to a benevolent organization. I deny the existence of any such thing as that in between organization. I deny the position very emphatically that contribution of funds means inherently a delegation of work. Brother Porter's position is, when you send a dime, you delegate your work. And I'm here to deny it. And that's in his proposition. I deny emphatically and regardless of what other things else are involved in his proposition, here's one thing that shall forever stand out, his proposition means that the Bible teaching regarding a church's obligation to orphans means that the church cannot scripturally make a contribution to Boles Home.

Now that's my position with reference to Brother Porter's proposition.

I'd like to have my chart number 55 please now. And this chart has to do with: What I am not denying. And you keep in mind as we proceed, what I am not denying. I'm not denying that each church has an obligation to orphans. I'm not denying that each church is sufficient for doing the work that God gave it to do. I'm not denying that each church must not delegate its work to a benevolent organization. And the next chart please, no. 56. Here is what I am denying. And Brother Porter needs to keep it in mind and the audience needs to keep it in mind. I am denying that God has given the church the job of functioning as a home. I do deny the existence of an in between organization. I do deny that contribution of funds means a delegation of work. I do deny that the Bible teaching regarding a church's obligation to orphans makes it impossible for a church to scripturally contribute to Boles Home in Quinlan, Texas. There are the four points related to his proposition which I deny. There are several points in his proposition which I do not deny. Now Brother Porter said a while ago, and he has made the statement two or three times so far, that Brother Deaver virtually endorses my proposition. That just isn't so. Here are four points with reference to his proposition which I deny. Now there are some things in his proposition which I admit, and with which I agree. And Brother Porter, I'm here to agree with you on everything that it is possible for me to agree with you on, but here are four points related to your proposition which I emphatically deny. And don't you tell this audience again that Brother Deaver virtually agrees with me in my proposition. It just isn't so.

All right, there are some points then with which I do agree but here are four points on which we don't agree. And let's discuss those points. You're in the affirmative now.

All right, I'd like to have my chart number 60 please. And let me read to you—review very briefly here Brother Porter's answers to my questions on the first night because this is exceedingly important. Over in the Borger debate, we had the privilege of going into the first speech with everything under the sun having been admitted in the first speech. But we had an unusual experience last night in being privileged even to go into the debate before a word was ever said with everything that we needed having already been admitted in the written questions answered by Brother Porter. Now here's his questions: I asked him last night, Are there any circumstances conceivable to you under which a church might scripturally send funds to a private home so that the needs of orphan children might adequately be supplied? Are there any such circumstances under which, and Brother Porter won't disagree, he will not object to that incorporated church there? Can this church send a private home? Brother Porter said, that's all right. I have the yes here in the notes now, and it's in his handwriting. All right, number 3. If you answer number 2 yes, could this private home be incorporated? And Brother Porter said yes, that's all right. Now then, if your answers to 2 and 3 are yes, would this be a case of a church meeting its obligation to supply a home for orphans? And Brother Porter said, that's all right. He said yes to that question number 4. This is a case of a church meeting its obligation to orphan children. How? A church sending funds to a home incorporated. Brother Porter, by the way, here's your admission now, and when this church sends these funds to this private home incorporated, Brother Porter, what's the relationship of that church to that home? That's the home that you admit. Now what's the relationship of that church and those elders to this home to which they send the funds? Does that mean that the elders of this church take oversight and manage this home? Now you answer it. That's what you say here tonight. And his position is, based upon what he said tonight, when the elders send funds to this home that they become the managers of that fund. They become the directors of, or the managers of that home. They become the directors of that home.

And our question number 5 was this: Since you believe that a church may provide a home for orphans, would you please list the component parts of the home which you would endorse. Here's his answer: Such as food, shelter, clothing, supervision, and similar necessities. And that's the reason for this statement. If a church wants to send funds to a private home incorporated, in order that the necessities of orphan children might be supplied, and this be a case of a church meeting its obligation to orphan children, Brother Porter said, I'll not object to it. And neither do I. And that my friends and brethren is the only thing under the sun for which I'm contending in this debate whether I'm in the affirmative or on the negative side. And Brother Porter has admitted everything in the world that we want regardless of all things else. He says a church can send funds to a home incorporated which meets the needs of orphan children—that this is a method by which a church can meet its obligations to orphan children.

All right, I'd like to have my chart number 63 now in connection with what Brother Porter has admitted and some things that he has had to say. Notice carefully, according to the session late last night, Brother Porter recognizes now—this is number 63, Brother Porter—Brother Porter recognizes that an incorporated church can send funds to an incorporated private home so that the needs of orphans might be supplied. He recognizes that this home is not a church. Brother Porter, when you said a church could send to a home, you admitted that the home is not the church. Otherwise, you have the church sending to itself and that's ridiculous. He admits that this home is not a church. He admits that this home is not an integral part of the church. And admits that a church may thus meet its obligation to orphans. And he has admitted everything under the sun that's involved in this proposition. Now this entire battle has been waged against that in between organization. But it doesn't exist. Brother Porter, if a church—if a church like we had on the other chart—if a church can send to a private home incorporated that the needs of orphans might be supplied, and there would be no in between organization, that's all in the world I'm concerned about.

All right, now we come to the things that he's had to say in the speech to which you have listened. He said that I had endorsed his proposition. Well, we've covered that sufficiently. I just don't endorse his proposition. There are four points in it specifically that I deny emphatically in spite of the fact that there are some points with which I can agree. I want my chart number 65 right here. And Brother Porter had somewhat to say along this line. He complained last night because I had signed the negative of this proposition and he says that means that Brother Deaver denies everything in that proposition. It just doesn't mean any such thing. And I said then and I say now, I'm absolutely amazed that a man who has had the polemic experience that Brother Porter has had would make a statement of that kind. He knows perfectly well that when a man signs the affirmative of a proposition, that he has obligated himself to prove every point here in his proposition. That's on the affirmative side. But if there is a single point with which he disagrees, he can sign the negative of it. And I have signed plenty of them that way and so has my good brother, Brother Porter. Just because there's one single point in it which he denies. Brother Porter, look at this proposition, chart no. 65: Will Brother Porter affirm or deny the following proposition? The Bible teaches. He tried to make you think that these were all separate sentences—they are simply component parts of the same sentences—he needs to know the very significance of a comma and the word "and." All right, the Bible teaches. that there is one church and that there is one God and that there is one Lord and that salvation is by faith only. I said, Brother Porter, will you sign the negative of that? I'll sign it. Now you said tonight you wouldn't sign it, because it would mean that you would be denying that the Bible teaches that there is one church. That doesn't mean any such thing. There's one point here that I deny. And if there is a single point in that proposition which I can deny, then I can sign the negative of that proposition. And in the discussion on this, we've emphasized over and over our agreement on these points where there is agreement but here's where we differ. And because of that one point on which we differ, I'll sign the negative. Brother Porter, that one statement is either wrong or right. Now, if you won't sign the negative, will you sign the affirmative? I'll sign the negative. Now then, lights please.

He referred to my answer to his questions and let me get those now. Here are the questions which Brother Porter handed me. (How much time, Tom?) If a congregation contributes funds for a work of evangelism to a missionary society, does it delegate its work to a human organization. Now that society is a human organization, but the church doesn't delegate simply because it sends funds. Brother Porter, that's your position and I deny it. And when I signed your proposition, there on that particular point, that's one of the very points I had in mind. Is the Buckner Corporation that provides the Buckner Home in Dallas (get ready my chart number 57), is that Buckner Home—the Buckner corporation that provides the Buckner Home at Dallas an organization between the Baptist churches and the home? Here's my answer: So far as I know, Buckner Home is an incorporated orphan home. Brother Porter said, Deaver said, the corporation here works the other way. Didn't you see my word incorporated home? It's in the home, Brother Porter. That's where I said it was. You said, Deaver said it wasn't here. Well, it's in your answer there if you'll just read it. I said Buckner Home is an incorporated orphan home. All right. What he had in mind that Deaver had the corporation going one way this time and another way another time. Here you have a situation, the Baptist Church and the Southern Baptist Convention of which the Baptist Churches are an integral part, and then the Southern Baptist Convention provides the Buckner Home and the Buckner Home is an integral part of these and it's all connected together. But so far as concerns Buckner Home, it is an incorporated home and the corporation belongs to the home here. This particular corporation. Now if you've got the Southern Baptist Convention incorporated and you have because I've got it in my brief case—I've got the incorporated papers or the charter of the Southern Baptist Convention right here. All right, it's incorporated. So is this Baptist Church over here and each one of them have formed a corporation, and I told you that Buckner Home is an incorporated home. And that incorporation or that corporation is a part of that home over here. You've got three corporations there.

All right, the lights please. Is the missionary society a corporation? I want you to notice the shifting of gears there. Is the missionary society a corporation that provides the work of evangelism of the church—an organization between churches and the work? My answer is: The missionary society stands between the churches and the work but it's not because of incorporation. It's not the fact that incorporating put it there. Brother Porter knows that—admits it. It's not the fact of incorporation that makes it in between. It's in between anyhow. That's the very design of it, to stand between and it's not the fact of the corporation. And he's already said that's so.

All right, is Boles Home—is Boles Corporation a divine organization because it stands *en loco parentis* to the children? Here's my answer. Boles Home is a divine institution which is incorporated like the home in your proposition. There's a home in Brother Porter's position. Brother Porter said this home could be incorporated and the home in his proposition or his position which is incorporated is a divine institution just like the home in my proposition. And Boles Home as in the question here.

Question number 5. What are the legal demands for a congregation to meet in order to administer relief to orphans and other needy people and if the same legal demands were made for evangelism, would you endorse such? Brother Porter can't get it into his mind evidently that legal requirements in each case would differ. The fact of the matter is, if you have different types of homes, and there are a number of them, the legal requirements in each case will be different. Brother Porter said, Brother Deaver tell me what they are. You tell me what kind of a home you are talking about and I'll tell you. Are you talking about a child care agency; are you talking about an adoption agency; or are you talking about a child placing agency? The requirements are all different. But we emphasized last night whether in evangelism—evangelism or benevolence, that a church had a right to meet the demands of the law. If the law says you've got to have a board of trustees to hold church property, I maintain that the church at this place can meet that demand. All right, that's on the questions which he had asked me.

Now then, Brother Porter, the mere fact of incorporation doesn't mean the existence of an in between organization. Brother Porter, you made that statement and I have it in quotation marks and you are just exactly right. The mere fact of incorporation doesn't mean an in between organization. Certainly that's so. But if that's not what brings it into existence, pray tell me what does. Now it's not the incorporation and we are forever settled on that. Incorporation doesn't bring in the in-between organization. He said that I said there was no home in his proposition. Brother Porter, I did not. You said that last night. I said over and over that when you said benevolent organization, you didn't mean orphan home but I emphasized over and over that there is a home in your proposition. And I took several minutes in my first speech to emphasize that just as much as I knew how. Benevolent organization doesn't mean a home. But there's a home in your proposition.

All right, he said, I believe debates do good and so do I. It's somewhat encouraging to me to know that this thing is constantly shifting. We have one issue down in Houston; we had another issue over at Borger; and we've got a different issue now. Over in Borger the home was parallel to the missionary society, remember? Not so over here. It's parallel to something else but not the missionary society. And don't let all that Brother Porter had to say on that lead you to think that that's what he believes. Buckner Home is an incorporated home. And that incorporation or that corporation is a part of that home over here. You've got three corporations there

All right, the lights please. Is the missionary society a corporation? I want you to notice the shifting of gears there. Is the missionary society a corporation that provides the work of evangelism of the church—an organization between churches and the work? My answer is: The missionary society stands between the churches and the work but it's not because of incorporation. It's not the fact that incorporating put it there. Brother Porter knows that—admits it. It's not the fact of incorporation that makes it in between. It's in between anyhow. That's the very design of it, to stand between and it's not the fact of the corporation. And he's already said that's so.

All right, is Boles Home—is Boles Corporation a divine organization because it stands *en loco parentis* to the children? Here's my answer. Boles Home is a divine institution which is incorporated like the home in your proposition. There's a home in Brother Porter's position. Brother Porter said this home could be incorporated and the home in his proposition or his position which is incorporated is a divine institution just like the home in my proposition. And Boles Home as in the question here.

Question number 5. What are the legal demands for a congregation to meet in order to administer relief to orphans and other needy people and if the same legal demands were made for evangelism, would you endorse such? Brother Porter can't get it into his mind evidently that legal requirements in each case would differ. The fact of the matter is if you have different types of homes, and there are a number of them, the legal requirements in each case will be different. Brother Porter said, Brother Deaver tell me what they are. You tell me what kind of a home you are talking about and I'll tell you. Are you talking about a child care agency; you talking about an adoption agency; or you talking about a child placing agency? The requirements are all different. But we emphasized last night whether in evangelism—evangelism or benevolence, that a church had a right to meet the demands of the law. If the law says you've got to have a board of trustees to hold church property, I maintain that the church at this place can meet that demand. All right, that's on the questions which he had asked me.

Now then, Brother Porter, the mere fact of incorporation doesn't mean the existence of an in between organization. Brother Porter, you made that statement and I have it in quotation marks and you are just exactly right. The mere fact of incorporation doesn't mean an in between organization. Certainly that's so. But if that's not what brings it into existence, pray tell me what does. Now it's not the incorporation and we are forever settled on that. Incorporation doesn't bring in the in-between organization. He said that I said there was no home in his proposition. Brother Porter, I did not. You said that last night. I said over and over that when you said benevolent organization, you didn't mean orphan home but I emphasized over and over that there is a home in your proposition. And I took several minutes in my first speech to emphasize that just as much as I knew how. Benevolent organization doesn't mean a home. But there's a home in your proposition.

All right, Brother Porter's chart F, please. Brother Porter's chart number F right quickly. He, in this chart, I believe it's the one where he discussed organizations, gave you several definitions of organizations and in spite of all these organizations, he knows perfectly well that the word organizations can mean and it's a very legitimate definition of it; a systematic arrangement. I'm not denying that Boles Home is an organization. I never have denied that. I'm denying there's an organization in between—between a church and Boles Home. And I told you last night, if you'd just tell me where it is, what its name is and what its mailing address is, I'll send it a personal $25.00 check. You just tell me where that organization is, and so that I could send this check to it, in such a way that Boles Home will never get it. I want to mail it to that organization right now, then, lights please. That's all he has on that, the matter of organization. It becomes a corporation when the homes gets a charter. That's Brother Porter's statement. It becomes a corporation when it gets a charter. Therefore, Brother Porter, no corporation, no charter. Remember that, no corporation—no charter. And the law of the state of Texas says if you have a home, you've got a charter. You can't have it without it. And Brother Porter says, no charter, no incorporation, or you can't have incorporation without a charter. And when you get the charter, you've got to have incorporation. And he's right. That's what they told me down at the office just a few days ago. You can't have the charter without it.

All right, now then, he says, tell me what to do to set it up. You just tell us what has already happened to set it up, Brother Porter. I'll tell you how to set it up when I get in the affirmative. You tell us what's already happened to set it up. You say it's not incorporation. That doesn't set it up. All right, Brother Porter's chart number T and that's regarding missionary societies now and notice carefully what he has here. The two different associations. He talked about the two different missionary societies. Why certainly I recognize there are two different missionary societies in that arrangement. And I told you that not one particle and if he could prove that there is any such thing under the sun, in connection with our brethren, and Boles Home, then I'll love to oppose it just like he does. Give me chart number 58. Everything that he had to say on the missionary society and to it, I'll say amen. Except when he gets down to the point of trying to make Boles Home parallel to the evangelism that that society provides. And now here's Brother Porter's position on Boles Home. Brother Porter does not say—bless his heart for this—he does not say that Boles Home is parallel to the missionary society. He doesn't help the situation much. But what he says is that Boles Home is parallel to the evangelism which the society provides. Here's a church for example, and here's a benevolent society which exists in his mind and the benevolent society provides Boles Home. Here's a church down here with a missionary society here to which the church sends and the missionary society provides evangelism here. He does not say that the missionary society is parallel to Boles Home. Now that was Brother Finley's position. He said that Boles Home was parallel to this. Brother Porter doesn't say that. Brother Porter says the missionary society is parallel to the benevolent society up here and that Boles Home is parallel to the evangelism which the society provides. Now give me chart number 59 and I want Brother Porter to deal with it. And that's his position. That is his position on chart number 58.

Now then, Brother Porter, when you come back up here, you answer these questions; you'll tell this audience that that's your position and that you believe that Boles Home is parallel to the evangelism provided by the missionary society. All you have to do is just answer these—you have a copy of this and you can just check it. All right, here's the item, Does Boles Home have a right to exist? Brother Porter, yes or no? Does the evangelism of the missionary society have a right to exist? Now they are parallel. Does Boles Home have a right to exist? Does the evangelism provided by the missionary society have a right to exist? Will you fellowship those people who support Boles Home? Will you fellowship those people who support the evangelism provided by the missionary society? Can an individual support Boles Home? Can an individual support the evangelism of that missionary society? Can a church buy service from Boles Home? Can a church buy the evangelism of that missionary society? Now the parallel, Brother Porter. You say they are parallel, now you answer these questions. And I want to see you answer them. That's your position—lock, stock, and barrel.

All right, I'm not upholding any such thing as that in between organization, as a missionary society. I am simply saying that a church can send funds to a home incorporated in order that the needs of orphan children might be supplied, and Brother Porter said that's all right. Now give me my chart number 68, in connection with the care of orphans. Three minutes? All right, let's skip those and come down just a moment now to my chart no. 14 please.

Brother Porter has taken the position on some of these charts—I've forgotten whether I or whether D or T. But Brother Porter has on this chart now, some things regarding a church and the church providing. I'd like to have my chart number 14—number 14—let's get this one right here while you're getting 14. Brother Porter says that Boles Home is parallel to the evangelism of the missionary society. And so he has the society injected into this thing. I want you to notice here exactly what the missionary society is. These churches send funds—or they send delegates rather to the missionary society and the missionary society makes decisions and the delegates carry these decisions back and these decisions are bound and that's the meaning of that fact. These decisions of the society are binding upon the churches and the missionary society—or the same thing on this side—either way—you've got the decision of that society binding upon the churches. Now, I'm opposed to that just like Brother Porter is.

Here's what Boles Home is not, parallel to this. There is no such thing as churches sending to Boles Home or Boles Home invading in any sense the autonomy of the congregation. It's simply a home. It is not parallel to that but here is what it is parallel to. Churches send to a private home or a foster home just like Brother Porter says can be done and if the law says incorporate, Brother Porter says that's all right, and so the churches send to the home in order that the needs of children might be supplied. And that's what you have here and Boles Home is parallel to the private home or the foster home and it's not parallel to a thing like you have up there.

All right, my chart number 14. Brother Porter has tonight now, taken the position that the church is sufficient to do all the work that God has given it respecting its obligation to orphans and by sufficient, he means that the church can function as a home. Notice his statement a while ago, Brother Porter used the word direct—the church can supply the funds and direct the care. Brother Porter, if that's not what you mean by direct care then you correct me when you come back up. But you said the church can supply the funds and the church can direct the care. I want to raise the question—who is authorized to have the oversight of or to manage or to direct the church? What's God's law on that point anyhow? And if somebody had told me, even last year, that we'd ever have the obligation and the need of having to emphasize to brethren where God put elders, it would have surprised me beyond measure. But that's what we're doing now. Where is the passage that says that elders can be over anything except the church? God put elders over the church. Brother Porter, where did God put elders? God put elders over the church and God put parents over a home. Or when you come up, take it like it is the other way here. Over a church, who has oversight or who directs? Is it parents or is it elders?

Porter's Fourth Affirmative

Brethren Moderators, Brother Deaver, Ladies, and Gentlemen: I am grateful for the opportunity of appearing before you again and to continue my part of this discussion concerning the proposition we have for our consideration tonight. One very interesting and amusing statement made by Brother Deaver during the speech that just proceeded was: Brother Porter has admitted everything concerned in the proposition. Well, actually that's what I'm affirming. I'm affirming everything that's contained in the proposition, Brother Deaver. I don't have to admit it. And when I signed the affirmative to it, I signed the affirmative to affirm everything that's contained in it. Not just one or two things but everything that's contained in it. And so that was a rather interesting and amusing statement.

I want to get back to the beginning of his speech and to some things in that connection. And I want to use one or two charts I didn't get time to use a while ago; I want to use them just at this juncture and then I shall proceed with the notes concerning the speech which he has just made. I want to use chart number 17, Brother Shaw. In this chart number 17, I started to present it a while ago and didn't have the time—regarding the church property deeded to trustees. And Brother Deaver is claiming that, if I accept this over here, then I will have to accept this over here; that these two are parallel. Now then, I'm asking the question: If this, the church property deeded to trustees justifies this, churches' contribution to a benevolent organization or society, whatever you want, and let them operate a home, a school, a clinic and a farm, then why wouldn't that same thing justify this? Since he endorses that, would not that also justify this church sending to a missionary organization or society that they might provide a home, a school, a hospital, and meeting? Now what's the difference between this and this? And if that justifies one, why doesn't it justify the other?

All right then, let us have chart number 19. Now he is claiming that the home—Boles Home—and so on is parallel to the private home. And he says these are parallel and therefore, if you can contribute to a private home, you can contribute to Boles Home—they are parallel. All right now, to the top here, churches are parallel to churches, that is on the one hand, and on the other as I have them represented—the rectangles over there representing churches and also over here. And down here we have a benevolent society providing benevolent homes. He is denying that that society exists but there's something that exists there that's providing the orphan homes and homes for the aged and these are benevolent homes. Down here we have private homes. He says these are parallel to these and therefore, if you can contribute to private homes, you can contribute to benevolent homes. Well, the difference between them is that, if you set up a similar organization here to provide the private home that he has over there to provide the benevolent home, then he might have a parallel, but he doesn't have it. Over here he has the church sending directly to private homes and there is no organization, incorporated or unincorporated, between the churches and the private homes to whom they surrender their funds or turn their funds that that corporation may provide the home. But he does have it over here and therefore, they are not parallel. And so his argument on that has gone with the wind.

Now then, I want chart U. I want to get these because these are necessary to come in just here and then I shall take up his speech. Remember we are on the same proposition for two more nights though he takes the lead of course, in the discussion the following two nights. Now I asked him last night if he would endorse the home under elders of a congregation. He never would tell me exactly whether he would endorse it or not but then he indicated that there was no such thing existing. All right, you can't see this in all parts of the audience I'm sure, but these are little clippings taken from the masthead of the official publications of some of these homes. Over there we have the Old Folks' Home which is the home for the aged, operated by the Chapel Ave. Church of Christ in Nashville, Tennessee. And it says that it's under the supervision of the elders of the Chapel Ave. Church of Christ. That's what the masthead in their paper says. Here we have the home journal of the Maud Carpenter Home at Wichita, Kansas, and it says that this home is supervised and directed by the elders of the Riverside Church. And they use the name elders and so does that over there. Here we have the Children's Home at Lubbock, Texas, which is also said to be under the supervision of the elders of the Lubbock Church. And over here we have—you can't quite see this one—advertising put out by the Central Church of Christ in Houston,

Texas on which they are establishing a Christian home for the aged, and it says that it's under the elders of the Central Church of Christ in Houston. And a number of others that we had their mastheads but we will have just these for the present time. And so these homes are saying that they are under the elders of a church. Brother Deaver says they are not—that there is no such home operated under the elders of a church. He says the same men are elders of the church and they are the board over the home. That isn't what these papers say—that isn't what the homes say. The homes say in the masthead of their official publications that they are directed and are under the supervision of the elders of the church, and actually names the elders. Now either they are telling the truth about it or they are not.

If Brother Deaver's position is so, these homes haven't been telling the truth about it. Therefore, they have been misrepresenting before the brotherhood a situation and obtaining money under false pretense. And if what he is saying about it tonight is true, then elders doing this should apologize to the brotherhood; these homes should apologize to the brotherhood because they've been claiming and making the brotherhood believe that they are under the direction of the elders, when they are not according to Brother Deaver. Therefore, they should send all the money back to the elders that came under that impression made upon them, by such an advertising procedure. All right, let us have the lights now and we will go on to the speech to which you have just listened.

Brother Deaver said that there were certain terms in the proposition that had never been defined and one was "adequate." I defined that in the very first two sentences I uttered in my first speech last night. That the word "adequate" meant sufficient or that was able to do so. And he didn't know about benevolent organizations—and then he says Porter does not mean that refers to orphan homes, but he says organizations in between. Certainly, that's what I mean—that it's the organization in between. I thought he understood that to begin with. And I'm insisting that a congregation should not contribute its funds to any such organization that God gave the church to do. Now he said, he is obligated to prove that it's adequate. And third, he is obligated to prove that it must meet its obligation. And fourth, he must prove that there is an organization in between and that contribution of its funds is a delegation of the work and that such would be wrong if sent to Boles Home. Now he says here are three things he must prove. First, each congregation is obligated to care for the needy. He says, I agree that it is but he has got to prove it. And second, it's adequate to do its work. He said, I agree to this but let him prove it. And third, a church must meet its obligation. He says, I agree that it must but let Porter prove it. And so if he were denying that proposition he put on the board a while ago—what chart was that?—he will look at that right in this connection—that chart on the proposition he signed and wanted to know if I would sign. Do you remember the number of it? Number 65. We want to look at this right in that connection. He says he would sign this. Here is a proposition: The Bible teaches that there is one church, and that there is one God and that there is one Lord and that salvation is by faith only. He says, I'll sign the negative—will Porter sign the affirmative? No, Porter will sign neither the affirmative nor the negative.

But actually, Brother Deaver ought to sign the affirmative because he believes more of it than he denies. He believes more of it than he denies; therefore, he ought to sign the affirmative instead of the negative. He only denies one fourth of it; he believes the three fourths of it. And so it's up to him; he should sign the affirmative instead of the negative because he believes more of the affirmative than he does of the negative. Thank you, Brother Deaver. But here's what he would have to say if he signed the negative. He said, now you must prove that there is one church and you must prove that there's one God and you must prove that there's one Lord. A man getting up in a debate and crying before an audience that his opponent must prove that there's one God would certainly indicate that he doesn't believe it. Why demand a man to prove something that he already accepts? That kind of course would be something that would tend to produce infidelity on the part of the people who sit and listen to any such defense made of a thing of that kind.

All right, let us have the lights again and we will go right on. On this, regarding my position in chart 54 which is along the same line as this; in fact, chart 54 was the one that involved that that I just read. He said, in my position, I agree on number one, number two, and number three, but I deny number four, number five, and number six, one of which was of course, that there is a benevolent organization in between. Well, I've given some proof along that that he hasn't even referred to yet. And then he gave chart 55, what I am not denying—and we have dealt with that already because it's involved in the other and we had it last night. And then chart 56, what I am denying. And he said he did not endorse my proposition; he just denied that portion of it that he didn't believe and he denied a part of it and he'd be willing to affirm a part of it and of course, he should have signed this proposition both in the affirmative and in the negative because he believes part of it and he denies part of it.

Now his chart number 60, on the questions which he gave me concerning the admissions that I had made. He said, Porter has admitted everything we need. Now first could he send funds to a private home and he said yes—and can the private home be incorporated and he said yes—and the church can meet its obligation, yes; the component parts of the home such as the shelter, food and raiment and so on, and he said yes, and he wants to know if the church can oversee the private home in that connection. Does the church oversee the private home? And he has another chart along that line that we will get to a little later on in the speech, as I get to it in my notes. And so here we have the matter in which he says that he presents as proof that Boles Home can be supported because the private home is the same as Boles Home—that's his reasoning. And since the private home is a divine organization, he reasons that Boles Home is also a divine organization. Well, we want to look at a chart in that connection here.

I want chart E. I want chart E just there concerning the matter of divine organization. All right, we have here two divine organizations, on the one hand the church and on the other, the home. Over here the church is a divine organization because it has a divinely ordained relationship. First, the Lord said, "I will build my church" (Matt. 16:18). Second, "all baptized into one body" (1 Cor. 12:13). Third, "we, being many, are one body in Christ" (Rom. 12:5). Fourth, Christ is the head of the church (Eph. 5:23). And therefore, the church we recognize as a divine organization because of a divinely ordained relationship. And without that divinely ordained relationship, there is no divine organization called a church. That divinely ordained relationship must exist or there is no such thing as a divine organization called the church. We have them presented there. When we refer to that church as a divine organization, we mean more than a place. Although a church building may be sometimes defined as a church, in fact, you can turn to authorities—dictionaries on it and they will give you as definitions of the church as a building set apart for public worship. But we mean more than that when we refer to a divine organization. We don't mean a place where the church meets. Paul referred to the church in one place (1 Cor. 14:23) and second, "come together in the church" (1 Cor. 11:18) and third, "church in their house" (Rom. 16:5). We do not believe however, the place or the house where the church assembled is a divine organization. But the divine organization assembled there is more than a place. It's an institution that sustains its relationship to the Lord and without that relationship, there is no divine organization called the church. All right then, we believe the home is a divine organization because it sustains a divinely ordained relationship. First, "he which made them at the beginning" (Matt. 19:4)—we are told he made them male and female. Second, "He said they shall be one flesh" (Gen. 2:24). And third, he declared that "what God had joined together, let no man put assunder" (Matt. 19:6). And fourth, "the husband is the head of the wife" (Eph. 5:23)—just as Christ is the head of the church. And without this divinely ordained relationship, there is no home that is a divine organization, any more than there is a church that can be called a divine organization without that relationship. Therefore, when we talk about a home being a divine organization, we mean more than a place. Certainly the word "home" sometimes means a place—a place where a person lives, just like the word "church" is sometimes defined as a building set apart for public worship. As, for example, "they returned home" (Acts 21:6). Second, "let him eat at home" (1 Cor. 11:34). Third, "servant lieth at home sick" (Matt. 8:6). In those places, the word "home" refers to a place. But when we talk about a home being a divine organization, we do not mean a place. We mean a home that sustains this divinely ordained relationship which is brought about and brought into existence by means of a marriage relationship and without that relationship, there is no divinely ordained home that we may call a divine organization. If this relationship does not exist, then there is no divine organization called a home just as there is no divine organization called a church if this one does not exist. And the private home is like this and Boles Home is not like this; the relationship is not sustained and it is not a divine organization. Now, we will let him grapple with that.

On chart number 63, Porter recognized that funds can be sent to an incorporated home; that the home is not the church; and not an integral part of the church, and that the church may meet its obligation this way. And this, of course, will take care of that chart too, because he is paralleling Boles Home with a private home which it does not parallel from the standpoint of being a divine organization at all. Well, back to chart 65 that he wanted to know whether I would affirm or endorse and I've already dealt with that—I would neither affirm nor deny that proposition because of the things stated in it. Now let us have the lights back, and we will see some more here.

He came to his answers to my questions: I asked, Is a missionary society a human organization? Or rather, Whenever a church contributes its funds to a missionary society to do the work of benevolence, is it delegating its work to a human organization? He says, now the missionary society is a human organization but the church is not delegating its work when it gives its funds to the organization. Well then, when the church gives its funds to the organization, I suppose the church is performing its work and when the missionary society takes over and spends the funds for the work, then it's doing its work. And so the missionary society does not rival the church. The missionary society is doing its work which is not the work of the church and the church does its work when it gives the money. And so the church performs its work and the missionary society performs its work and there is no rivalry between them at all, according to Brother Deaver's position, now.

On the Buckner corporation, I said he made it point two directions. He denied it. He says—no, that isn't so, that I spoke of it as an incorporated home. Said it didn't point the other way. But you said the corporation is an integral part of the Southern Baptist Convention. That pointed the other way, didn't it? The Southern Baptist Convention is the organization you said back of the corporation that provides the home—whatever it is. And yet you say that that corporation is an integral part of the Southern Baptist Convention. All right, it points back the other way. And yet you say the corporation in Boles Home is an integral part of the home. I want to know, Brother Deaver, and you haven't told me, is that corporation that provides Buckner Home an integral part of the home? Is it? And if so, is it divine? Is Buckner Corporation divine? Was the Baptist home that was destroyed a divine organization or are private homes only divine if they are Christian? Now you tell us about that. Is this matter of the private home limited to a Christian's home? Is it only a divine organization when Christians marry? Or if Baptists marry, is the home provided—or the home brought into existence a divine organization? And if that home is destroyed, and those corporations provide a home, is that provision made by them also a divine organization? Yet you claim Boles Home is; if not, why not? You have the same situation exactly. I want to know now. He is going to have to endorse Buckner Home and recommend that brethren send contributions to Buckner Home because it's a divine organization provided by an incorporation that's an integral part of the home just as the Boles Corporation, he says, is an integral part of Boles Home. But he said there are three incorporations here. He said the Southern Baptist Convention is incorporated then you have this other corporation here and then the home is incorporated. Well, you would have three on the other then, if you have an incorporated church. Sending funds to a corporation there and then that home is also incorporated; you have three there and so you'd still have your parallel. Thank you Brother Deaver, very accommodating.

And I then asked him about this other—number three—as to whether or not a missionary society is an organization in between the church and the work. And he said, yes, it's an organization in between but not because it is incorporated. Well, that's exactly what I said all the time. You have tried to leave the impression that I have been opposing the idea of incorporation—that the incorporation makes it unscriptural. Well, the fact is, according to your position, it takes the incorporation to make it scriptural. If it's not, it can't exist, he says, without the incorporation. You can't provide one in Texas without the incorporation and therefore, he would oppose it until it's incorporated. When it's incorporated, it becomes scriptural. I suppose he would do that because he would on evangelism. He would oppose it for evangelism but if the state requires it—it becomes a law—then he would accept it upon the same basis of meeting legal demands and so an incorporated—or incorporation for this would become scriptural in evangelism because he got a charter for it. And so the incorporation makes it scriptural. It was unscriptural before, according to his position. Then he said, Boles Home is a divine institution just like yours and I have dealt with that already.

Now, I asked about the legal demands. I wanted to know what the legal demands were and he hasn't yet told me. He said, now the legal demands are different, what kind of home are you referring to? What are the legal demands? He said the legal demands were different even for different homes; what reference are you making? Why, I thought you knew what we were talking about. We were discussing Boles Home and similar organizations. We will just say that I'm referring to Boles Home and Buckner Home then—we'll just take those two—I'm referring to those. Now you understand, don't you, Brother Deaver? Now then, what are the legal demands? What are the legal demands? What legally is necessary to operate homes like Buckner Home and Boles Home? What are the legal demands? We may have a little more on that presently.

He said now, on my chart number T—was that it?—number T, that C.R.A. chart—I believe that's right. That's it. All right, now then, he said I agree that both of these are missionary societies. Well, bless your life, Brother Deaver, I will deny it. I deny that they are both missionary societies. One of them is a missionary society—that's the Christian Restoration Association with headquarters at Cincinnati, Ohio. This other is the Southern Christian Association, pertaining to the Southern Christian Home at Morrilton, Arkansas. And he says they are both missionary societies. Well, they are not. This over here is a missionary society and this is a benevolent society. Now I want to know what makes a human organization out of this and a divine organization out of that one? Has he told you? He hasn't even started to tell you yet, and he doesn't intend to. What makes one a human organization and the other divine? And why is this one all right, and this one wrong? Why? And when this one came into existence by reason of charter it was all right, then if this one came into existence the same way—would it be all right? Since incorporation is not wrong, if this one came in by incorporation, he says it's all right. Well, this one came in by incorporation also, and so therefore, it's all right and you have a missionary society, the Christian Restoration Association that Brother Deaver will endorse in the field of evangelism. I challenge him to get out of it.

Now, the lights please. He says these debates have proved one thing that positions are being shifted. I am sure you are aware of that very readily. Positions are being shifted because heretofore brethren have maintained that churches can build and maintain benevolent organizations for the work of the church in the field of benevolence. And now, Brother Deaver says there is no such organization in existence. Somebody is shifting positions. Make your own choice as to who it is. Now he said regarding Porter's chart T that "organization" can sometimes mean a systematic arrangement. Nobody denies that. Is that all you have? Is that all you have in Boles Home—just a systematic arrangement? Is it? If so, then that's all you have in Buckner Home because you have the same kind of arrangement, Brother Deaver. And so you have only a systematic arrangement and therefore you must support both Buckner and Boles. He wants to know, "Tell me where it is and I'll send a check to it." Well, can you tell me where the Christian Restoration Association is? You can find out where it is—where people can send a check to it. Maybe you can find out where the Boles corporation is.

All right, now he said, Porter has said that some of them become a corporation when it gets a charter or that it becomes a corporation when it gets a charter. And he said, that's right. And then he said, no corporation, no charter. And I say, Brother Deaver that's right. I might even shake hands with you on those two points. That it becomes a corporation when it gets a charter and no corporation, no charter. We agree upon that. And then Brother

Deaver said, the law of Texas says, that you must have a charter. And I deny emphatically that the law of Texas says any such thing. I demand him to prove it; but first, I have no chance to reply to what he says about it tonight in giving his proof. But I want him to give it and then tomorrow night I'll have a chance to reply to his proof that he presents tonight. I deny that the law of Texas requires any such thing, and challenge him to prove it. Now then, we will proceed. In chart 58—Porter's position on Boles Home—he says here that Porter does not make the church parallel to the home but parallel to the missionary society, and the home parallel to the evangelism. And the home is not parallel to the missionary society and then he gave chart 59 in that connection and wanted to know if I believed that Boles Home was parallel to the missionary society after having said in the other chart that I didn't believe it and that I thought evangelism was parallel to benevolence and that the benevolent society was parallel to the missionary society and the church to the church. And turned right around with a chart fixing it the other way and wanted to know if I believed that when he knew that I didn't believe it in one chart, why put it in another chart and ask me if I believe it on that when he has it pictured both ways and says I believe one and don't believe the other.

And then his chart number 14. If I have time, I want to get to that. This will cover the notes that I have on his speech if we have that. Here we have—it was another one I had in mind. Maybe it was number 40. But we'll get this one out. Who is authorized to have the oversight of managing? First, the church: parents or elders? Why, elders oversee the church. And a home—and I suppose he refers to a private home and parents oversee and look after the private home, of course. They are the ones who established the home by reason of marriage relationship, and therefore, he is claiming that elders cannot provide a home, and when I say the elders can provide the care—the funds and the care—or direct the care of the home, I mentioned the home which they provide. Why didn't you read the answer, Brother Deaver? You left out a part of it and made it apply to a private home and the answer didn't apply to a private home at all. Now then, chart 40. He wanted to know—that still isn't it but let's get the other here. The parallel to this orphan is parallel to this private or foster home and the Boles Home. The church sending money to Boles—I deny that the church sends money directly to Boles Home and is spent except under the supervision and direction of the corporation. Now then that chart in which he wants to know if it has a right to exist. I have forgotten what the number is. Maybe I failed to get the number of it down. Here we are. Does Porter believe they are parallel? And so here he gives some ideas. First, the right to exist. Does Boles Home have a right to exist and does the missionary society have a right to exist. Yes or no. Neither of them, Brother Deaver, has a right to exist for the purpose of doing the work of the church. All right, fellowship. Will you fellowship Boles Home and will you also fellowship the missionary society? Well, I suppose I would occupy the position on that just about like you do, Brother Deaver. You say that the church is parallel to the missionary society—you are on record as having made that statement the church is parallel to the missionary society. Will you fellowship the missionary society because you fellowship the church? You will fellowship the church won't you and the brethren in the church? Will you fellowship the missionary society? You say they are parallel. And if not, then your argument breaks down here. So therefore, I occupy the same position on that as you do on the other. Can the individual support Boles Home and the missionary society? And as operated right now, I would say no to both of them. And could a church buy service from both of them? I would say no to both of them as they are now operated and arranged, no.

All right, now then, do I have any extra time? About two minutes? Fine. Now then, friends, I want to have you keep in mind—let us have the lights back please—keep in mind the issue before us tonight. And Brother Deaver has not noticed a number of the charts which I gave. I gave him numbers of charts there to deal with that he paid no attention to whatsoever. The in between organizations, he paid no attention to the things I said there. He did come to a chart regarding benevolent organizations and the missionary organization, the C.R.A. and the Southern Christian Association, but he said they were both missionary societies. And paid no attention to some of the others that I gave. Now I want to know about the legal demands and I aim for him to tell us that please when he comes. And I'm still demanding him to tell us why Boles Corporation and Boles Home provided by Boles Corporation is a divine organization and yet the same arrangement for Buckner operation does not hold true. If Buckner corporation provides Buckner Home and is an integral part of the home, that home is a restored home just like Boles Home is a restored home for our brethren. Then I want to know why it is also not a divine organization. Why is one human and the other divine? You wait and see if Brother Deaver tells you. Why is one human and the other divine? If he doesn't tell you, I may put it on the chart and let him do some checking. And see something about it. We'll find out just where he stands on it—what his position actually is. And I'm still wanting to know why the missionary society is a human organization. Brother Deaver, you haven't told me. You said it's not because of incorporation. We'll agree on that. Why is it a human organization? It is not because it serves *en loco parentis* for the children. Last night he said it was an integral part of it because of that and I suppose he meant it was a divine organization because of that. But now, seemingly that isn't so. But it's for some other reason, that Boles home is a divine organization. I want to know about Buckner Home—why that is not a divine organization too. If one of them is, the other is. And so there is a group of men set up—a group or body of people set up out there that is incorporated, to provide the home and I brought that chart there and asked which is incorporated? And I gave you the missionary society and over there the work which they did in the field of evangelism—the preacher, the song director, and the audience. I asked him, which is the corporation, the preacher, the song director and the audience, or the group of men over there—the organization that provides it? What did he say about it? Absolutely nothing. I asked also about the next one and in the same way there—a benevolent organization or society and they provide in the field of benevolence, a home with matron and cook and janitor and children and so on. Which is the corporation: the matron, the cook, the janitor and the children—are they the incorporation or is the incorporation the group of men over there set up to provide that work in the field of benevolence? Which is the corporation, Brother Deaver? Did you tell us? Thank you very kindly.

Deaver's Fourth Negative

Brother Porter, Gentlemen Moderators, Brethren and Friends: I'd like for you to notice now carefully my chart number 60 right quickly and then we shall proceed to give attention to the remarks that have been made by Brother Porter and the preceding speech. I'd like for you to keep in mind that, regardless of what Brother Porter says or may say, regardless of the objections that he may file, he has admitted every basic and fundamental characteristic of Boles Home and similar homes. Would you keep in mind please in connection with this that Brother Porter admits that a church can be incorporated. He does not think that there is an inherent sin in incorporation. A church incorporated may send to a private home.

Furthermore, he has no objection if that private home is incorporated. An incorporated church may send to a private home for the specific purpose of enabling the private home to provide the needs or necessities or to administer the care for these orphan children. And he says that is a way by which a church might meet its obligation to orphans. Now then, brethren and friends and neighbors, in a situation where a church sends a contribution to Boles Home, that's all under the sun that you have. His entire speech has been designed to emphasize that there is a benevolent society in between. Now then he says the benevolent society does not come into existence simply because it's incorporated and yet when he takes the time to deal with the matter of incorporation, you would somehow draw the conclusion that that's the very point which Brother Porter is objecting and yet it's not.

In spite of all he has to say about the matter of incorporation, he recognized that the very fact that incorporation is not inherently sinful; that it's not the thing that brings into existence a separate organization—an in between affair here—and you don't have that in between affair in connection with the church sending to Boles Home. You don't have a Southern Baptist Convention in here or anything parallel to it. You don't have a missionary society like you have in the Christian church or anything similar or parallel to it. Mark out the Southern Baptist Convention, mark out the missionary society. Just allow the church to send to a home incorporated. And that's all in the world that I need. Now you can think about all that has been said or done in the thirty minutes that are already gone and in the entire speeches made by Brother Porter for that matter, he admits that a church incorporated can send to a home incorporated, that the needs of orphans might be supplied and that this is a way by which a church might meet its obligation, God given, to orphan children. And that's all you have in the situation which I shall be affirming tomorrow night and this is all you have in the situation which he has been opposing for two nights. His speech has been a discussion of that in between organization. Where is it? What brought it into existence? It's not incorporation. But he has discussed about and fussed about and argued about incorporation and yet he knows its all right. It does not inherently bring an in between organization into existence. He has admitted here everything in the world that we need and all that is involved in connection with Boles Home and a church sending to it.

Now then, my chart number 63 please. And these are basic matters as we shall proceed to give attention to the things that have been said by Brother Porter. Brother Porter now, in connection with his proposition, recognizes perfectly well and has already admitted as much; that an incorporated church can send funds to an incorporated private home so that the needs of orphans might be supplied. Now then, brethren and friends and neighbors, you just keep in mind that there's a home in Brother Porter's proposition; there's a home in what he believes; it's an incorporated home; whether human or divine doesn't make me any difference as far as concerns this part. Boles Home is just like the home which he upholds. If the home which he upholds is a divine home, then so is Boles Home. If the home of his proposition is a human home, then so is Boles Home; either way, you take it doesn't make me any difference. Just like the one you are defending, Brother Porter, and that's all we are concerned about. Whether human or divine is all beside the point. It's just like the one that he's upholding. I think it's human. If he wants to call me, but I believe it's divine. If he wants to call it human, let him call it that. It's just like the home that he says can exist. I believe he is right; that that home can exist. He recognizes that this home is not a church. He sought to leave the impression tonight, in fact that's the point to which he is coming now, that the church is sufficient to function as a home. But when he says a church can send to a home, he recognizes that this home is not a church. And he recognizes that a church may thus meet its obligation to orphans. And so I maintain, as we have already said, he has admitted everything that's vital in my proposition. He has admitted everything that is in my position. Already, he has sought to oppose the very thing that we shall be affirming tomorrow night. And his proposition is designed to eliminate the possibility of a church making a contribution to Boles Home. Yet as he has discussed that—he has admitted everything that is involved in that totality.

Now my chart 40 please right quickly. Notice carefully. Here is what you have in a missionary society arrangement. It is a thing that exists in the field of the church; it's a human arrangement operating in the field of the church and which assumes unto itself authority and prerogatives that God has restricted to a local congregation and in particular to an eldership. But the churches send delegates down here; the missionary society makes decisions which are binding on the churches that are members of it. Now that's certainly true—these churches don't have to be members of it, but if they are, they have to be bound by those decisions and if you are not bound by those decisions, then out you go. There is no such thing as that in connection with Boles Home. Churches do not provide in any way and manner arrangements by means of which Boles Home makes decisions that are binding upon churches. A church simply sends to Boles Home, a home incorporated, because the law says you've got to incorporate—Brother Porter denied it—but he had already said, you can't have a charter without incorporating. How can he come back and say the Texas law don't demand it? He has already said it in the other speech, and spent some time discussing it. And I'll read it to him—the Texas law. We regret to have to. You simply have the situation that a church is sending to a home. Boles Home is not parallel to that thing up there and is not parallel to the evangelism provided by that thing up there. Boles Home is parallel to the private home or the foster home or the home to which Brother Porter said a church can send funds and which home can be incorporated and in which he says a church thus meets its obligation to orphans. Now that's Boles Home. That's that to which its parallel. He mentioned chart number 40 a while ago, but if he came back to deal with it, I failed to catch it and I'm sorry if I did, Brother Porter.

All right, my chart number 17, please. I want you to keep in mind please, that the church is not a home. Brother Porter's position is that the church can function as a home. He has made the statement that the church can send funds and direct the care. Now if they direct the care, Brother Porter, you are meaning that elders as elders are overseeing that home. Is that right? And if it's not right, then you tell us it's not right, because that's what you said and I think that's what you mean by it. And if that's not what you mean by direct the care, then I want to know about it. All right, a church can send funds and he says that in connection with the sending of the funds now, that the elders direct the care. That puts the elders in the oversight of that home. And it's my firm position that God put elders over the church and that God put parents over the home and that you and I must respect the fact that there are two institutions and we cannot combine them. In these passages I've called this chart ???. In these you simply have an oversight, subjection or relationship in each case now. The elders are over the church and over here you have parents or guardians or parents over the home. And down here, if you can change the situation around so as to put elders over the home or an oversight of children, why in the world can't you put parents over the church? On the same ground and based upon the same reasoning by which he concludes you can put elders over a home, I will arrive at the conclusion that you can also put parents over the church. God separated them. God put elders over the church and parents over the home. And in connection with this matter of a church meeting its obligation to a home, a church can't function as a home—**God** didn't put elders over a home. But a church can send funds to a home that that home might administer to the needs of orphan children. And so Brother Porter believes and so I believe. But he has taken the position tonight that the church can function as a home and that's the very point that I deny. The church is sufficient to do the job that God gave it to do, but God never gave it the job of functioning as a home. He gave it the job of providing for orphans. It can send the funds; it cannot function as a home. What God has separated, we must not join together.

Now then, my chart number 19—or Brother Porter's chart number 19. And get my chart number 7 ready. Brother Porter's chart number 19—notice it now. Here you have the private home. Churches over here parallel to churches. Churches sending to benevolent societies—the benevolent society providing the home and home for aged here. Over here the same thing—the benevolent society and the home, private home, orphan home and home for the aged. Now Brother Porter, this is not my position and I'm not upholding anything like this and I've told you time and time again that if you can prove that this thing exists I'm going to oppose it just like you do. And I've told you that if you would give me the name and address of it, I'd mail a check to it. What I am saying is that a church can send a fund right down here and you don't have any such thing as that. You can send funds to a home. And that home can incorporate. And you said it's all right. We don't have any such thing as that—not a thing in the world in that chart.

Give me chart number 7 please now. Brother Porter had a great deal to say about these in between organizations and discussed incorporation somewhat in detail. Now you keep in mind, and I know that because of the length of the speech that was made by Brother Porter, and the same thing would be true with reference to any speech, that because of the length of it, and the great ?????, that it's easy to become confused on the matter: but you keep in mind, that regardless of what Brother Porter had to say about incorporation, he does not believe that the fact of incorporation brings into existence an in between organization. If it did, look what you've got. Brother Porter, a church incorporated can send to a private home. Brethren and friends and neighbors, mark it down. If the mere fact of incorporation means you've got a separate organization in between, then when you have an incorporated church sending to a private home, you've got an in between organization because the church is incorporated. Brethren, the incorporation is over here and over here. You've got an in between organization if that's what produces it. Brother Porter says it's not but yet he spends his time on that. All right, can an incorporated church send to a church? If so, and if the incorporation means an in between organization, then you've got an in between organization in this situation where an incorporated church sends to a church unincorporated. Now if a church incorporated sends to a church incorporated, Brother Porter says it's all right, you don't have one organization in between; you've got two, if the fact of incorporation brings something else into existence. You have two organizations here and Brother Porter said, that's all right. He won't deny that an incorporated church can send to an incorporated church; why certainly not. But if the fact of incorporation should bring a separate organization into existence, then you've got two of them.

Give me chart number 7, I believe there's another part to that. How many organizations in between here brethren? And what brought it into existence? Here you have the case of a church incorporated sending to a private home incorporated. Brother Porter, if the fact of incorporation brings into existence a separate organization, in this situation, you don't have one separate organization, you've got two. Because the church is incorporated and the home is incorporated. And he wouldn't oppose that at all. But if there is anything that even looks like a distant relative of a corporation, in connection with Boles Home, he is opposed to it. Here you have a church incorporated sending to Boles Home which is simply a home incorporated—Brother Porter says you can send to a home—a home so that the needs of orphans might be supplied and that home can meet legal requirements, that home can be incorporated, but you can't send to Boles Home. That's Brother Porter's position. How many organizations between there?

I want Brother Porter's chart number W please. This one has to do with the home and the position of elders in connection with that home. And Brother Porter refers to the oversight now in connection with this chart W—Missionary Society—group of men which provide preacher, song director and such like now. And down here, benevolent society which provides matron, cook, janitor and such like. Brother Porter, I've said time and time again and I say again that in connection with the church sending to Boles Home, we don't have a missionary society and we don't have a benevolent society. Up here, if you had evangelism and a church on the other side, we would mark this thing out and let the church provide the evangelism here and down here we would mark this thing out and let the church send to Boles Home—and that's all that we are concerned about—mark these things out. I oppose them just like you do.

All right, Brother Porter said in connection with the home under the elders now, I want to give you some information on that. I emphasized a while ago that certainly a church cannot, or elders, cannot oversee a home and they cannot legally or scripturally function as elders over a home. Now it's certainly a definite fact that the men who are trustees of this property, this very church property, is legally held in trust and it could be legally held in trust whether you had elders or not, and likely was held in trust before you had elders and was held in trust by legal trustees—that's the way the law regards it—now the same men who are elders might also be those legal trustees to hold this property for you, but if that be the situation, they do not function as elders when they serve as trustees in control of this property. This property is not the church. And God put elders over the church. And just so in connection with Boles Home, the same men who are elders may also serve as the trustees for a home. But in the latter position, they are serving as trustees; they are serving as legal guardians *en loco parentis* to those children and they are not functioning as elders. I have a statement signed by one of the very men, representing the other elders, and he refers to the elders of a certain church shall function as the trustees with so and so home, and that's right. And that's the way the law says it is. Not long ago, may I suggest to you kindly and it would do some brethren a whole lot of good—if they would simply take the time to see what the law has to say on these matters. I asked the very question a while back; Do you regard men who are elders of a church, as being trustees or guardians in connection with a home on the ground that they are elders? They said, no sir. Not on the ground that they are elders. And the person to whom I was talking said, when we speak of those particular men with reference to their relationship to the church, we call them elders. When we speak of their work with reference to their relationship to that home, we call them trustees. And they said, Brother Deaver, we have faced that same problem. That's the information that comes straight from the department of public welfare.

All right, notice this. I carried this statement down, which I copied, and the statement was, when I asked the question now: Would there have to be a recognized governing body, in connection with so and so home and the answer was yes, there would have to be a recognized governing body. I raised the next question: Would elders of a local church constitute such recognized governing body simply on the ground that they are elders? Here is the following answer to that statement now. No, there must be a legal organization; this is not a legal body until chartered. That's the information directly from the State Department of Public Welfare, with headquarters in Fort Worth, Texas. If anybody wants to question that and argue with them about it, that's their business, but that's the law on it. All right, and these men, simply because they are elders, do not function as elders over a home. They are elders with reference to the church. Now, they can also be the legal trustees in connection with a home. That don't mean that they have the oversight of running that farm as elders. Where did God ever put elders in the business of spanking children, and running a farm and operating a school, and providing discipline. These are home affairs.

All right, now then, Brother Porter, you referred to a home under elders. In fact, you had a chart here that had several homes under elders as you regarded it.

I'd like to raise the question: Did you mean to imply that you endorse those homes? You gave a list of homes; homes for orphans and homes for aged which were under elders you said. The law says they are not. But now, if they are, did you mean to imply that you endorse them?

All right, my chart number 67 right quickly. How much time do I have? All right, 67 then—get my chart number 65 ready. Number 67, here you have a Baptist Church and Southern Baptist Convention providing Buckner Home up here: this is incorporated; this is incorporated; this in incorporated; those different corporations there and are related here Brother Porter, and you know that that's so; this is a part of the Southern Baptist Convention and this is a part of the Southern Baptist Convention, but down here in connection with the part we are discussing, you have a congregation of God's people sending over here to Boles Home and you have nothing like that Southern Baptist Convention in between. You introduced the matter here to discuss the incorporation a while ago. Each of these is incorporated; you have a corporation here which is an integral part of Buckner Home. You've got one here which is an integral part of the Southern Baptist Convention. You've got one over there which is an integral part of the Baptist Church. But we don't have any such thing as a benevolent society, missionary society, or Southern Baptist Convention or anything else. And this is the very point that Brother Porter had in mind. This—to his mind—would occupy the position of the benevolent society but in connection with the church sending to Boles Home, it is conspicuous for its absence. It just isn't there.

And my chart number 65. Brother Porter needs to get more information about legal demands now. And we shall give him more information as we have the time. Notice here. Regarding this proposition; the Bible teaches that there is one church and that there is one God and that there is one Lord and that salvation is by faith only, Brother Porter, in his quibbling in connection with this simply needs to go back and restudy something about the law. Brother Porter, did you ever read that? Why certainly you have. And you know perfectly well that you can sign either the affirmative or the negative of that proposition and if there is one single point in which there is disagreement, you can sign the negative of it. And whether you sign it or not doesn't make me any difference, I'll sign it. There's one point in it that I deny and I'll sign the proposition. But that does not mean that I'll deny everything that's in it. The scriptures teach thus and so. Brother Porter, signed the negative. Does that mean that he denies the scriptures teach? Why certainly not, you know he doesn't.

All right, now then, if Brother Deaver believes—he says, if Brother Deaver believes it, I don't have to prove it. I've pressed him throughout the discussion thus far to prove some of these points Brother Porter. But now he has shown tonight why he hasn't attempted to prove a church obligation.

He says, Bother Deaver agrees with it—Brother Deaver believes it and I don't have to prove it.

And may I tell you that's not my conception of debating. I think I have an obligation to prove what's in my proposition whether the other man believes it or not. I'm not down here for the benefit of Brother Porter primarily. He is not down here for my benefit or Brother Porter primarily. He is not down here for my benefit—we are here for the benefit of the audience. And the audience wants to know how he will go about establishing the fact that a church has an obligation to orphans. And if he will just show me the line of reasoning that he follows in arriving at that conclusion, I'll have use for it. But do you think he is going to do it? He knows I'll have use for it.

Now then, with reference to his answers to my questions, notice carefully, I asked him: In your opinion—lights please—in your opinion, is Boles Home incorporated? He says, not as you use the term. Brother Porter, it is as I use the term. The people down there say it's incorporated. Brother Porter says it's not incorporated. Let me tell you here's the reason why he had to say that Boles Home is not incorporated. The charter says it is. Brother Porter says it's not, as I use the term. Because, if Boles Home is incorporated, there's not the corporating that produced the in between organization. And if it isn't incorporated, then there is no in between organization if it's true that the incorporation is what creates the in between organization. And so, he says it's not as I use the term. Well, as I use the term, just like the charter, they say it's incorporated. You need to instruct those people down there, Brother Porter. They think that they are protected by the law. They think they are incorporated. Brother Porter says they are not. In your opinion, does the fact of incorporation automatically create a separate organization? Not necessarily. And away goes about eighty percent of his speeches. Does the fact of incorporation automatically create a separate organization? And he says, not necessarily. There are some other things there I'd like to get to but some more things more important.

Let me have Brother Porter's chart number E please, sir. And I have how much time? All right, Brother Porter's chart E. This is on divine organizations. Now then, he said, Is Boles Home divine? Or is it a Human organization? And I've already said, whether human or divine. He said over here's what you've got to have in connection with a divine situation. And in connection with the home that this would be divine. And he came down, brethren and friends and neighbors, he came to take the ridiculous position, that in order to have a divine home, you've got to have a husband and wife. And I'm sorry to see him take that position. Mary and Martha and Lazarus didn't have a home. And a widow doesn't have a home. Brother Porter, I'm ashamed of that. I'll tell you the truth, I'm ashamed of it. Two old maids and a bachelor brother can't have a home. That is, it's not divine. You've got to have a husband and wife.

All right, Is Boles Home a divine institution? Brother Porter, it doesn't make me any difference a great deal, how you regard that. It's just like the home that you endorse. Now, if you say that the home that you endorse is divine, I'll say Boles Home is divine. If you say the home which you endorse is human, I'll say it's just like the one that you endorse. It doesn't make me any difference which way you go. I maintain it's divine. I maintain it's God's will that every child have a home. And many, many times, because of tragic circumstances, children can be left in an orphan situation. They are entitled to a home and the church of the living God may make possible the existence of that home and I believe that then if the home that was lost is divine, the home that is restored—and if Brother Porter wants to quibble on that word, I'm ready for him and his whole bunch—the home that's restored is divine. You can have a divine home without a husband al wife relationship. If there are any widows in the audience, regardless of how many children you may have with you and may be caring for, if there is no husband and wife relationship, you don't have a divine home; you just thought you did. Brother Porter. Keep in mind if you will that there's a home in Brother Porter's proposition. There's a home in his thinking. A church can send to a home, an incorporated home that the needs of orphan children might be supplied.

All right, I want to have my charts number 60 I believe—60 and 63 and then come back to some further matters. All right, let's get number 66 ready after 63. 60, 63 and 66 I believe is what I need. Brother Porter has agreed this is the very point to which we just referred, and you keep it in mind, regardless of everything else that has been said, a church can send to a home and that home can be incorporated and the church is doing the sending for the purpose of enabling this home to meet the necessities of orphan children and this is a way—it's not the only way—but it is a way and it's a scriptural way by which a church might meet its obligation to orphan children and Brother Porter said, I endorse that. And that's all you have in the world in the church—Boles Home matter, when a church sends a contribution to it. Number 63 now. Along this same line. Brother Porter admits now, in this connection, that an incorporated church can send funds to an incorporated private home, so that the needs of orphans might be supplied. That this home is not a church. And that this home is not an integral part of the church. He spent some time discussing the fact that the elders direct that care, but when he says that a church can send to a home, he is saying that this home is not a part of the church or an integral part of the church and that a church may thus meet its obligation to orphans.

Number 66 now. And notice carefully Brother Porter's answers to the questions. Question number 4. If they might—a church—and here is his very statement—can send these funds to the home but he says the elders direct the care. Brother Porter says the church sends the funds to the home here, and that the church directs the care. Question, Brother Porter: In the situation, do the elders of the sending church direct the care and when they do what are they functioning as—elders? That's the only point left that I want you to deal with. You say that they are directing the care. Now in that direction, of the care, are they functioning as elders or are they functioning as trustees in connection with that home? Now if they function as elders, then it's certainly obvious that he has taken the position that the home is an integral part of the church. Because it's something over which the elders serve as overseers.

Now then, let's come back now to the matter of legal demands. Brother Porter said that he denied—he said what are the legal demands to operate Boles Home? He had asked about legal requirements—I said, give me the kind of home you are talking about, and so he says Boles Home. But Brother Porter, in the first place they've got to have a recognized governing body. In the second place, they've got to have a charter. In the third place, they can't have a charter until they are incorporated. And in the fourth place, they've got to have a license. And that's what they have and that's all they do have and a church sends funds to them. That's what you have down there. And he says, what about requirements in connection with Buckner Home. I'm not too well acquainted with Buckner, but I suppose the requirements are the same. But so what? Does that mean a church could send to it? You know there are lots of good Baptist homes in the land. Does that mean the church can send funds to them? There are some homes that involve members of the church to which a church can't send. If you've got a father in it that won't work, neither let him eat. There are some homes that involve members of the church to which you can't send. We are not talking about that kind of home. We are talking about the kind of home that properly supplies the needs of orphan children. And if you want to take the position that Buckner Homes does, we are ready for you on it. You just take the position that Buckner Home properly supplies the needs of orphan children, since it's an integral part of the Southern Baptist Convention.

Deaver's First Affirmative

Brother Porter, Brethren Moderators, Brethren and Friends: I would like in the very beginning of the study tonight to introduce to you my chart no. 69. And this chart is briefly a summation of what we have established thus far in this discussion. Brother Porter has admitted that a church may send funds to a private home. That both the church that is sending and the home that is receiving may be incorporated. In which case there is no in between organization. He has admitted this incorporated home is not a church. This incorporated home is not an integral part of a church. This incorporated home is not managed by the elders functioning as elders. And he has admitted when a church sends funds to this incorporated home, that the needs of orphans may be adequately supplied, and that this is a way that a church may meet its obligation to orphans. It is certainly clear, therefore, that Brother Porter says a church may meet its obligation to orphan children by sending funds to an incorporated home which is not a church, which is not an integral part of the church which is not managed by elders functioning as elders. Now regardless of what else he may have to say, and regardless of what else he has had to say, these are points that have been admitted by him.

Now then, I would like to have my chart number 72 which is also along the same line—some very vital admissions that have been made by Brother Porter. Now then, he has made these admissions, not in connection with Boles Home but to the home to which we have just referred now. He denies the same points when you come down to Boles Home but he has admitted that a home can receive funds from a church. Brother Porter admits that now. He has admitted that that home which receives these funds from a church can be incorporated—he admits that. He admits that the sending church or sending churches can be incorporated. And he admits that this home which is receiving is not a church. He admits that the home does not have to be an integral part of the church there. And he admits that the home does not have to be managed by elders functioning as elders—he has admitted that.

And he has admitted that the needs of orphans can adequately be supplied now by the church sending to this home. And he admits that the church may meet its obligation to orphans by sending funds to the home. And he admits that in the case of this church sending to this incorporated home, that there is no in between organization. Now these are points that Brother Porter has admitted in connection with a church incorporated sending to a home incorporated. These are points which he has admitted. But when you apply the points which he has admitted to Boles Home, he said, no, you just can't do that. These points have been admitted in connection with a home. But he won't admit them now in connection with Boles Home and that is the unenviable position in which he finds himself tonight.

Now then, with that brief reference to what has taken place and what has been established, I shall proceed now to my affirmation. We'd like to have the lights please. It is my pleasure to stand before you at this time in the affirmative of the following proposition: *The scriptures teach that a church may contribute to Boles Home, Quinlan, Texas.* If there has ever been a simpler proposition written than is plainer than that, I haven't seen it. The scriptures teach that a church may contribute to Boles Home, Quinlan, Texas. It is my duty and my obligation, as the affirmative speaker now to define the terms in that proposition. Brother Porter will listen carefully as I shall do that. By the word "scriptures," we simply mean the word of God, the Bible, consisting of course, of old and new testaments. By the word "teach," we mean impart information; give instruction. By the word "church," we simply mean a local congregation of God's people. By the word "may," we mean has the right to; liberty of action. By "contribute to," that simply means send funds to for the particular purpose of making possible care for orphan children. It is, in other words, a stipulated donation. By "Boles Home," I mean this: It is an arrangement existing as a home for needy children, which has a legal board of trustees standing in the position of parents to the children in the home, which board is selected by the elders of the church at Terrel, Texas, which home is chartered under the laws of the State of Texas, and which home is incorporated according to legal demands and good business principles. That is all there is in the proposition so far as I'm able to see, that needs definition. If there is anything further, Brother Porter can call my attention to it and I will give my attention to it.

I'd like for you to keep in mind now, what I am not affirming. I am not affirming that the church of the Lord is insufficient to do the work that God gave it to do. I am not affirming that brethren have a right to establish and maintain a missionary society as of the Christian Church, or anything parallel to it. I am not affirming that a church can delegate its work to a benevolent organization which then provides a home for orphans. I am not affirming that the only way that orphans can be cared for is to place them in Boles Home or similar homes. I am not affirming that a church can shift its responsibility. I am not affirming that a church can forfeit its autonomy. These are points which I am specifically not affirming. I am affirming however, that Boles Home has a scriptural right to exist which you saw Brother Porter deny last evening. I am affirming that Boles Home has a scriptural right to exist and secondly, that a church has a scriptural right to contribute to Boles Home for the particular purpose of making possible care for orphan children. And so I shall turn now to my obligation of proving that proposition.

I'd like to have my chart number 70 here as I introduce to you the syllogism upon which my entire affirmative shall be based. I'm simply referring now, brethren and friends, and neighbors, to the simple fact that when you prove—any time you prove the parts of a thing—a totality, you prove the entire thing. That is, when you prove the scripturalness of the parts, you prove the scripturalness of the entire thing. If you were to state that formally, here's what you would have. All total situations—the constituent elements of which are scriptural, are total situations which are scriptural. My friends, the total situation described in my proposition is a total situation the constituent elements of which are scriptural. Conclusion: the total situation described in my proposition is a total situation which is scriptural. Now, if you were called upon to write out formally, the syllogism upon which my affirmative is based, that is it. When it has all been said and done, it simply means that any time you prove the scripturalness of the parts of a thing, you automatically prove the scripturalness of the whole thing.

Now then,—lights please—in dealing with this syllogism, there are two questions that can be asked. In fact, in dealing with any syllogism, there are only two questions that can be raised. Number 1. Is the syllogism valid? And number 2. Are the premises true? A syllogism is valid according to Mr. Ruby, page 151—a syllogism is valid when the premises necessitate the conclusion. When the premises guarantee the conclusion, then the syllogism is valid. All right, that my syllogism is valid cannot be denied. I have a letter here—Brother Warren and I took the time to write, he in particular, to write to a number of universities and especially to their logical philosophy departments to ascertain the validity of this very proposition. I have a letter from Mr. Alan Ross Anderson, Department of Philosophy,

Yale University, regarding this syllogism. And he says—Mr. Anderson says, "In reply to your letter of Sept. 11, the syllogism is unquestionably valid." Now I think Brother Porter won't even attempt to question the validity of that syllogism. It cannot be denied.

All right, I want to prove to you then, some things in connection with my major premise. The syllogism is valid. Now are the premises true? It is my job to prove to you both the major premise and the minor premise. So far as concerns the major premise now, may I suggest to you brethren and friends, that it's an axiom and by the way, an axiom simply means a self evident truth and every high school student knows that—a self evident truth; that's an axiom. And it's a simple and fundamental axiom that the whole of a thing is the sum of its parts. Whether you and I like it or not and whether we are inclined to quibble about it or not, that's a definite fact that cannot be refuted. The whole of a thing is the sum of its parts. If you will simply pick up any good dictionary and check the word "whole," you will find that statement. The whole is—and here's the quotation from the dictionary—"The word whole simply means containing all its constituent parts or elements representing the sum or aggregate of its parts." That's the meaning of the word whole.

So far as concerns the scriptures on the point, in Psalms 139:17 the record says, "How precious also are thy thoughts to me oh God; how great is the sum of them." The sum of God's thoughts is made up of the individual thoughts, Psalms 139:17. In 1 Corinthians 13:10, Paul argued, "But when that which is perfect is come; that which is in part shall be done away." Back in 1951, I was preparing for a debate with Lester Hathaway, and was giving some attention to 1 Corinthians 13:10 when it occurred to me that Paul was working upon the very basis that the whole of a thing is the sum of its parts. I devised an argument on that particular passage which I called constituent elements, and by the way, all that I did to it was in effect give it a name. Brethren have used it ever since the days of the apostles, on every subject under the sun. And I have letters in my files from some of the brethren who are opposing it now, who complimented the argument then and said, if I ever debate an anti-Sunday-School preacher, I'll use it. But now, when you come down to some other matters, it's just no good. But that's the very argument in 1 Corinthians 13:10. In James 1:25, James refers to the perfect law of liberty or the word of God as being the perfect law of liberty. And where is the man who will deny that the perfect law of liberty is the sum of its parts? All right, the sure consequence of that action is simply this: Any time you prove the scripturalness of the parts of a total situation, you prove the scripturalness of that total situation.

Let me illustrate that to you. Suppose you tell an individual, here's what God would have you do to be saved. God wants you to hear the gospel, believe the gospel, repent of your sins, confess your faith in Christ, and be baptized. But someone objects and he says, Brother Deaver, how do you prove that? Well, there's not a passage in the word of God to which you can turn and get all five points. Not one. But you prove that a man must hear by citing Romans 10:17. You prove that a man must believe by referring to Hebrews 11:6. You prove that men must repent by referring to Acts 2:38. You prove that a man must confess his faith by referring to Romans 10:10. You prove that a man must be baptized by reading Mark 16:16. You prove the scripturalness of that totality by proving the scripturalness of its parts and there's no other way under the sun to do it brethren.

All right, suppose you want to prove to a man the scripturalness of what you do in a worship service, your regular service on Sunday. You prove that you can sing by this passage. You prove that you can pray by this scripture. You prove that you can observe the Lord's supper by this one. You prove that you can teach by this passage. You prove that you can contribute by another. How else would you do it?

Anytime you prove the scripturalness of the parts of a thing, you prove the scripturalness of the whole thing. For example, you are dealing with the anti-Sunday-School issue, and someone calls upon you to prove your work—prove what you are doing. All right, here is the way you do it. You prove that elders have authority. This work simply recognizes the authority of elders. You prove the scripturalness of the principle of dealing with individuals as they are able to receive. You prove that there can be teachers. You prove that it's right to study. You prove that there can be simultaneous teaching. You prove that it's right to take a small group out of a large group and teach that small group. And you prove that there can be religious gatherings larger than the home and smaller than the whole church. And that's the way you prove the Bible class subject or issue and that's the only way under the sun you can do it, and that's by the scripturalness of its parts. Or if Brother Garrett gets hold you, and says to you, "Preacher, prove your work," how are you going to prove it? You'd prove that it's right for a preacher to preach to a church—he says you can't do it—but you prove it to him. You prove it to him. And you prove it's right for a preacher to work where there are elders. An you prove to him that it's right for a preacher to stay for a period of time. And you prove to him that it's right for a preacher to receive a stipulated salary. And when you prove the parts of the whole thing, you prove the scripturalness of the whole thing and that's the only way you can defend your work.

All right, here's what I'm saying. When you prove the scripturalness of the parts of a thing, you prove the scripturalness of that whole thing. I want to read to you a statement; here it is: the wrong creed, the wrong doctrine, the wrong worship, the wrong organization and the wrong name could not possibly result in the right church. But the right creed, the right doctrine, the right work, the right worship, the right organization and the right name for a like reason cannot be the wrong church. The man who made that statement said that when you prove the constituent elements of a thing, you prove the whole thing to be right. You couldn't have said it better yourself than that. That's Foy E. Wallace, Jr., *Bulwarks of the Faith*, Vol. 1, page 38. That's the way you've got to do it brethren. In fact, that's the only way you can deal with any Bible subject. Get all it has to say on that particular point. It's certainly clear therefore, that when you prove the scripturalness of the parts of a thing, you prove the scripturalness of the whole thing. That's my major premise. It cannot be denied.

Now then, the minor premise. All I've got to do is prove the scripturalness of the various component parts that make up my minor premise. Here they are: the total situation described in my proposition. A church contributing to Boles Home involves these following points: No. 1. In Paul's recognition of the fact that God has given the church an obligation to orphans, I'm going to prove it to you—Brother Porter hasn't undertaken that job. The fact of the existence of thousands of orphan children cannot be denied. To these children somebody sustains a responsibility. And that's certainly proved in Acts 20:35; it's proved in Galatians 6:10 and James 1:27. God's people are to be concerned about the weak and support the weak. To these children, the church sustains a responsibility (James 1:27) and the man who says that that passage is restricted to individuals' action only, gets into deep difficulty in the light of 1 Timothy 5:16 and he takes the position that the church cannot practice pure and undefiled religion. Brother Porter won't quibble on that. He is way ahead on that point. He knows that James 1:27 shows a church responsibility to orphans. This point Brother Porter won't deny, because I have his statements along that line. In *Gospel Guardian* July 25, page 1, Brother Porter says, God has authorized the church to relieve the needy, both widows and orphans, as is indicated in the statements of 1 Timothy 5:16 and James 1:27. Church responsibilities to orphans, point number one, James 1:27.

Second point, my proposition involves recognition of the fact that God has given the obligation, but has not specified the details as to how to meet that obligation. It's a vital principle brethren that when God gives an obligation, and specifies the manner by which the obligation is to be met, that then the manner becomes just as binding as the obligation. But when God specifies the obligation but does not specify the details, as to how that obligation is to be met, then the details involved in meeting that obligation are left to the realm of human judgment and expediency. This is the ground upon which we've all defended the use of black boards, song books, church buildings, invitation songs, song leaders, prayer leaders, baptisteries, individual cups, contribution baskets and on and on. Brother Porter will not deny that principle. That is the very principle upon which he has labored in numbers of debates with the anti-Sunday-School people. God has given the church an obligation to orphans and he hasn't told them how—hasn't given the church the details as to how to carry out that obligation. Notice me carefully Brother Porter. God gave the church the job now, but God didn't give the detail as to how the church is to meet that obligation. If he did, all you've got to do is read the passage including those details and we will go home.

All right, point No. 3. This is the third point in my proposition now. It involves recognition of the true meaning of the word orphan. Some people object to the homes because it is said there are some there who are not orphans. And it is certainly true that there are some there who have a living parent—some who have both living parents but the whole matter comes to the point: Who is an orphan? The word occurs twice in the New Testament, James 1:27—translated "fatherless," and John 14:18, translated "comfortless" in the King James, "desolate" in the Revised, "orphans" in the Greek Testament. The Lord said, "I'll not leave you orphans." The word "orphan" there simply means one bereft of parental guidance and care. And those children who are bereft of parental guidance and care because the parents are dead are in much better condition than those who are bereft of that guidance and care and such even though the parents are still living. They are orphans none the less.

My proposition involves, No. 4. recognition of the fact that God's love extends to all men. Some have taken the ridiculous position that the benevolent responsibility of the church in this matter extends to Christians only.

You saw that over at Borger. And some have taken the position, and even the ones who occupy that position generally say yes, but you can also take care of an orphan such as whose parents were Christians. They can either be Christians themselves or their parents might have been. In any case, you can take care of them. The fundamental point is, you can take care of Christians only. So it's that situation, you've got to be wrong in order to be right. All right, God's law of love is discussed in Matthew 5:43-48. It extends to all men, to the evil and the good, and the just and the unjust and we are commanded to be like the father. Galatians 6:10, "Let us therefore, as we have opportunity do good unto all men, and especially unto those that are of the household of faith."

My proposition involves, No. 5, the fact that a church cannot function as a home. And that's one of Brother Porter's fundamental errors. The home and the church are two separate and distinct institutions. God put elders over the church and parents over the home. The church is all sufficient to do the work that God gave it to do and the home is all sufficient to do the work that God gave it to do. And it's just as wrong to violate the all sufficiency of the home as it is to violate the all sufficiency of the church. Some maintain that a home for orphans would be right if placed under an eldership. And those who make this statement simply fail to recognize that God nowhere authorizes elders to function as elders over anything except the church. And they fail to recognize further that it is legally and scripturally impossible to put a home under an eldership; men who are functioning as elders in the oversight of that home.

All right, No. 6. in my proposition I have this point: Recognition of the fact that the need of orphan children cannot be adequately met without its being a part of a home. By divine right every child is entitled to a home. What are the needs of a dependent child? Food, clothing and shelter; education, both secular and religious, recreation, medical care, discipline and custody. To supply these needs, is to supply a home for that child regardless of what you might call it. And the needs of an orphan child cannot be adequately met without its having or being a part of a home.

No. 7, my proposition involves recognition of the fact that there is no inherent sin in having a board. The legal board of trustees stands in the position of parents to the home and the children. The law demands a recognition of a governing body. The law demands this recognized governing body, a license and in many states the law demands incorporation. Now, is having a board inherently sinful? This congregation and every other congregation has to make provisions to hold its property in trust legally. And so you have a legal board of trustees. And if you have a legal board of trustees, every time you meet in this building, in connection with worship, we are using that which is held in trust by a board. Every time you meet in the Bible classes, you are availing yourself of facilities that are legally held in trust by a board. And when you establish a new congregation, you go out and buy a lot, that lot is held in trust legally by a board. And when the preacher lives in the home that is legally held in trust by that board, there's a point involved in connection with the place in which he lives. And why is it right to have it there but wrong to have it in connection with a place for orphan children.

All right, my proposition involves recognition of the fact that there is no inherent sin in incorporation. Now Brother Porter has already said, if my opponent agrees with me, I don't have to prove anything. And so I don't have to prove that but I am. What is incorporation? A corporation is an artificial being, invisible, intangible, existing only in contemplation of law, and that's the very legal definition of it. Incorporation insures perpetual existence and protection. If a person were to fall outside here and break his leg, and if this church is not incorporated, that person could sue every member of this congregation and likely collect if he wanted to. And so—to avoid that possibility, many states demand incorporation. That simply means they can't touch you individually. They can only touch the corporation. And as an individual, you are protected. And that's the reason why the laws of many states even demand that in order to hold property; all right, incorporation is involved in good business sense, even if the law didn't demand it, it is just good sense. And some states demand that a church must incorporate to hold property. And if you have an incorporated church, and Brother Porter doesn't object to that, then when you meet in your auditorium for the purpose of worship, you are availing yourselves in that that is involved in connection with incorporation. The same thing is true with your Bible classes, the same thing is true with a preacher's home. Now why is it wrong to have a corporation in connection with a home for orphans, but right to have it in connection with a preacher's home or the place in which the preacher lives.

No. 9, my proposition recognizes the fact that there is nothing inherently wrong in having a charter. This is simply another legal requirement. The law demands a clear statement of purposes and policies. Brother Porter, here it is. You said it didn't exist. Here it is. Before it is licensed, the institution must submit to the State Department of Public Welfare, a plan of operation including a statement as to its plans for financial support, proposed receipts and disbursements, policies of admissions and fees, previous experience of operator and staff. Section 1 A, minimum standards for child care institutions, State of Texas. That plan of operation is what they elsewhere call a charter. Now if you want to quibble on that term, I wouldn't fuss about it. I had just as soon call it one as the other, but that's what is.

All right, No. 10, my proposition involves recognition of that fact that we must meet legal requirements. In fact, the board and the charter and the corporation all come under this one heading here. The fact that we must meet legal requirements, Romans 13. Brother Porter, James 1:27 and Romans 13 is all under the sun I need to establish this proposition. The law demands a license, a recognized governing body and in many states, incorporation. No vital principle is violated when we meet the demands of the law. A thing that is right, brethren doesn't become wrong because you make it legal. Even a private home has to be legal. You've got to have a marriage license sure as the world.

My proposition involves, No. 11, recognition of the fact that the arrangement at Quinlan, Texas is simply a home and that's all there is to it. If brethren could simply get this point in their minds, much of the confusion and static would be forever gone. If Brother Porter—Brother Porter, do you deny that it's a home? It is God's will that every child have a home. Many times through tragic circumstances a child's original home is lost. Boles Home is simply an effort on the part of Christian People to restore or reproduce a home for the child. The churches—my chart No. 4 please—the churches' responsibility then is to make possible that home. All right, let me refer briefly then to the point—we have only three minutes left—I want Brother Porter to have all of these. Hold that just a minute and get my chart No. 71 ready, Brother Clements. My proposition involves recognition of the fact that this is simply a home down at Quinlan.

Now then, No. 12, it involves the recognition of the fact that a church can contribute to a home to make possible care for orphans. I want my chart No. 71 first. Recognition of the fact that a church can contribute to a home to make possible care for orphan children. This point Brother Porter cannot deny. Remember that there's a home in his proposition. There's a home in what he believes. If the church has an obligation to orphans and if the need of an orphan child is a home, and if God has not designed the church to function as a home, then it's clear that the churches' obligation to orphans is to provide a home or make it possible:

Brother Porter, here are the twelve points of my proposition. All you've got to do is come up here and say, this one is right and this one is right but this one is wrong and we will know where we differ. And we can spend our time on that and do a lot of good so far as concerns this discussion. Do you admit or do you not that the church has an obligation to orphans? That the details are not specified?

The meaning of the word "orphans"? God's love extends to all men? The church cannot function as a home? The needs of orphans cannot be met without a home adequately? No inherent sin in having a board of trustees or an incorporation or a trust? We must meet legal requirements? That the arrangement at Quinlan is just a home? And a church can contribute to a home that's incorporated? And meeting legal demands? Now, is there something wrong on that chart? If so, you just tell me what it is. And we will spend the time on that.

All in the world Brother Porter can do—either come up here and say that here's a part that's wrong and here's a part that's wrong right here or else admit that all of these are right and say that there's at least one more element that Brother Deaver doesn't have on that and which element is wrong. One or the other is the only way under the sun he can refer to it. Now Brother Porter, if I don't have it all in there, you just tell me. And I anticipate that's just exactly what he will say, that Brother Deaver doesn't have that in between organization. And he's right because it's not there. There is no in between organization.

Now my chart No. 4 please. I want to ask Brother Porter simply this: all right, Brother Porter, is this a home? We got down last night to the vital point of what is a home. I maintain that a home is that situation which attains when there is either the actual existence of or the partial existence of a guardian child relationship. Now, that's what a home is. Brother Porter, you tell us when you come up here. This is my chart No. 4. Here you have a husband and wife and three natural children. Is that a home? You have a husband and wife and three natural children and they become foster parents to three more. They don't adopt them; they simply take care of them now as foster parents. And is that a home? Then you have a husband and wife and they take in four more children here; three natural children, seven legal children. Is that a home? But when they cross this number six line, the law steps in. You then become a child care agency. All right, and so you then have a husband and wife, three natural children and seven legal children and the law says get a license and incorporate. And you can't get a charter without it. The state of Texas. All right, and you've got to have that charter.

Porter's First Negative

Brethren Moderators, Brother Deaver, Ladies and Gentlemen: It affords me a great deal of pleasure to be with you again upon this occasion to engage in this discussion regarding the benevolent work of the church. There were a number of things said in the closing speech last night that I need to pay a little attention to before I go into the speech to which you have just listened. Some of these things have been repeated in the speech which has just been made and they have been mentioned a number of times already during the discussion. But we want to deal with them a little more elaborately as we go along and so to these I call your attention first.

When I brought up some statements relative to some other situations that were total I suppose and that were parallel to the situation which he has in his proposition tonight in which I introduced the evidence regarding another home that's called Buckner Home down at Dallas, Texas. And also a missionary society that was incorporated as the Christian Restoration Association, that does not control churches; that puts no high pressure upon anybody for funds and every church is left to act in its own way; and that no high pressure methods of any kind are used; no domination of churches; just the same sort of arrangement as he has. Tonight, he says, well just mark off Buckner Home and mark off the missionary society. Just mark it off your chart. Well, that reminds me of the fellow that smashed the barometer, thinking it was going to stop the storm. You can mark it off your chart, Brother Deaver, but that doesn't mark it off the records of the states in which these operate. The thing is still there regardless of how much you may mark it off your chart.

That doesn't get rid of the fact that it exists and there will be further proof along that line as we go.

Now he said, there is no organization in between and wanted to know to whom he could send a check; he wanted to send a check for twenty-five dollars; there was no organization to which he could send it. Now, I asked my questions to him tonight—we've been passing our questions out in advance—and getting the answers back—and one question which I asked him was this: If a church should contribute its money directly to a person on the field of evangelism, who is hired and controlled by a missionary society, instead of sending it to the board or corporation, and then the money is spent by this person under the direction and according to the approval of the board of directors, would the church be doing its work through a missionary society? And Brother Deaver says, A church would be contributing to evangelism being provided by a missionary society and such would be wrong. He says, A missionary society involves an ecclesiasticism or is an ecclesiasticism. All right, now then, in that connection I want to use chart No. 25. I want first to look down at the bottom of the chart. We have represented here churches and a missionary corporation or a board. And this board hires definitely somebody that we will call a superintendent there. And the churches do not send their money to the board; they couldn't send it to all the members of the board because they live in different places. The only thing they can do is to send it to some place or some person which the board directs. To the place directed by the board and then that person, whoever he may be, takes charge and spends the money according to the direction and with the approval of the board. Now that's done. I asked him: Is the church or the churches operating through or working through a missionary society? And he said, yes and that's wrong. They would be doing their work in the field of evangelism that was provided by a missionary society and so that would be wrong. And then in that case we see that they could not send it to all members of the board since they live at various places, therefore they send it to some designated place or person. And when that person spends it under their control and according to their directions, it is just the same as if they had sent it to the board in the first place because it is being spent according to their direction. And therefore, it is operating through the board just as much as any other way.

Now then, at the top we have the benevolent corporation which we will let represent Boles Home. And we have the same board set up. And he wanted to know where to send his twenty-five dollars; he couldn't send it to the board. Well, the board of Boles Home, like the board down here to the missionary corporation, live in different places; one member here and another yonder. And so, of course, you couldn't send it to any one place and get it to all the board. Therefore, you must send it to a place directed by them for it to be sent. And that's sent over to the home where the superintendent takes charge and spends it. And when he does so, he spends it according to the direction and with the approval of the board. And therefore, up there they are operating through the board in exactly the same way they are here when they operate in the field of evangelism through the board of the missionary society. Now Brother Deaver can see that there is an organization here in between. But here he says the organization is not between because they don't send it to them, but they send it over here. But down here, if they send it over here instead of sending it to the board, he can see the board is still there and since it is spent according to their direction, they are still operating through the board. And the board is still in between and so it is up here. Now that board is a group of men, set up for the purpose of providing and promoting this thing. They have charge of it. They hire and control and all of that. And consequently you have there the group of men, the organization in between.

And I want that that there has the rubber band around it please. I forgot to bring it up with me. Let us have the lights now just for a moment. And keep in mind that chart and we will get back to it in just a minute, as soon as I get my place located here. I have in my hand the charter of Boles Home. Now then, turn it back on please—turn the lights back off so we can have the chart. Now, looking up there at the board of the benevolent corporation, I want to read to you from Boles Charter, Article A. And the charter says that the directors of this corporation shall employ a superintendent of said home for such salary and upon such terms as such directors may deem fair, just and proper and give to such superintendent the power to employ all necessary, proper and suitable aid and assistance with the approval of the board of directors. Therefore, what the superintendent does in the spending of that money has to be done under the direction of and with the approval of the board of directors. And there is your organization in between and as he said a while ago, I anticipate that Brother Porter will say that that's the element that he left out. And that is the element that he left out of all of his arguments throughout the whole thing. And his constituent elements break down because he leaves out the very vital part of it. All right, thank you and let us have the lights again.

Then he introduced his chart No. 17 again last night along the "rule over these"—The elders over the church and the parents over the home and wanted to know if they could be changed around. The elders do not oversee parents and so on and parents cannot oversee the church. And he declared that the function of the church is one thing and the home is another and the church cannot spank a baby and so on; the church can't spank a baby—the church can't do that because the function of the church is one thing and the function of the home is another. And I'm wanting to know if, since the church cannot spank a baby, then it can't provide a home and oversee a home of any kind as you say, then in the field of evangelism, I want to know if a church as such can sweep a floor; or erect a tent; or clean off the church grounds; or operate a bus; or anything of that kind. Can the church do it? And if so, is the church functioning as an automobile; does the church become an automobile or a bus or what about it? You didn't tell us anything about that though I gave it to you last night.

Now then, I want chart X, Brother Shaw, in this connection to get before you the function of the church and the home and the inconsistency of it according to Brother Deaver's position. Now, notice in this please, that we have here the functions of the home and the church. Brother Deaver says that the church provides certain things and the home provides certain things. That they have different functions and the church provides the money. Now that's his position; that's the thing he is saying tonight. The church provides the money; that is, it furnishes the pennies, the nickels, the dimes and the dollars and so on and then the home provides the care. That is, the home feeds, clothes, bathes and spanks the children and all of this goes into the care of the home. And the church cannot do this because this is the function of the home. And he says if the church does any of this down here, then the home loses its all sufficiency and the church becomes a home. And therefore the church cannot only minister the care—it cannot feed, it cannot clothe, it cannot bathe, it cannot spank and so on—because that's the thing that the home does; that's the care the home provides; the church cannot do that; that's the work of the home; not the work of the church. But up here he says is the work of the church. The work of the church provides the means. The work of the church provides the pennies, the nickels, the dimes and the dollars. And that's the work of the church and this is the work of the home. Now then, he says here the church cannot do this. If the church does this, it invaded the home and does the work of the home and therefore then becomes a home. All right then, Brother Deaver, I'm asking you, since this is the work of the church up here, according to you, then can the home do this? Can a private home furnish pennies and nickels and dimes and dollars for the care of the needy? If so, then the home invades the church and the home becomes a church, according to his argument. Now then, I challenge him; I dare him, every inch of him from the top of his head to the bottom of his feet, to deal with that and tell us about it. Let us know Brother Deaver, whether or not the home can do this up here that you say is the work of the church. You say the church cannot do this down here because this is the work of the home. The church cannot render the care. The home must do that. The church provides the money. Therefore, the home cannot provide any money. If it does, it becomes a church. And it's out of its field and it's out of its function and it has taken up the function of the church and so the home becomes a church according to his argument. Now, I want him to tell us something about that when he comes to deal with it.

All right, let us have the lights again. He said last night that Boles Home is divine because it's the will of God for every child to have a home. I said that the private home is divine because God ordained the marriage relationship. And I showed by the use of a chart last night that there is no divine organization called a home unless that relationship exists. Just as there is no divine organization called a church unless there is a certain relationship existing as I pictured on the chart last night. And therefore, in order to have a divine organization called a church, we must have that relationship. God ordained marriage and when he ordained marriage, he set up a home that is divine in its nature. Therefore, it is a divine organization. But you don't have that in Boles Home. You don't have that relationship there at all and therefore it is not a divine organization as the church is a divine organization. And so he said, Well, it's a divine organization because it's the will of God for every child to have a home. And I asked him the question in this list I gave him tonight, No. 3—Is it the will of God for children of Baptist parents to have a home? And he said, Yes, it's the will of God for every child to have a home, to have and be a part of a home. And then I asked—Do the Baptist people have a right to restore the home the child has lost? He says, No people have a right to set up an arrangement, one purpose of which is to propagate false doctrine. Now the thing resolves itself into this: he talked a while ago about the universal law of love of God—you know, that he sends rain on the just and the unjust and makes the sun to shine on the good and evil—and therefore he said, there are thousands of orphans everywhere and we have the responsibility to them; somebody must take care of them; God expects every child to have a home. But he said last night that there are many Baptist homes that you can't send to and we can't send to Buckner Home because they are advancing or they are advocating false doctrine. Remember Brother Deaver, it's just a home. Brother Deaver, it's just a home; it's simply a home; that's all; it's just a home. Remember that. And now you say that God's law of love must be restricted. That you can't send to Baptist homes and you can't send to Buckner Home because they are teaching false doctrine. And yet God wants every child to have a home and the Baptists can't set up one for their children that have lost their home. They can't do it; the Methodist can't do it; none of the denominations can; even the anti-Sunday-School brethren can't because they are teaching false doctrine too, he would say; and even brethren who stand with me in this can't do it because we are teaching false doctrine too according to him. And therefore, nobody could do it except those who stand with him. Therefore, he puts himself in the place that nobody can take care of orphans to provide a home for them except the brethren in the church that stand identified with the position he occupies tonight. Is that restricting benevolence? Is that as broad as the universal law of love that God had? As that you mentioned while ago Brother Deaver? We just wonder about that.

Now then, another thing I want to get to just here is about the legal demands. And he had more to say about it a while ago. He said now, the legal demands are these, and he gave a number of them last night, one of which was a charter and corporation. And he declared that you cannot have such a home as we have at Boles without having a charter and incorporation. And Brother Deaver, I'm willing to let you take this back if you want to, I hate to expose you. Do you want to take it back? Do you want to take it back? Are you willing to take the consequences? All right, we will just let you have it. Now then, he read from the minimum standards for a child care institution put out by the State of Texas, Department of Public Welfare. Under the topic of licensing, and he read "A" and it said this: "Before it is licensed, the institution must submit to the State Department of Public Welfare, a plan of operation including a statement as to its plans for financial support, proposed receipts and disbursements, policy of admission and fees, previous experience and training of operator and staff." Is there anything there said about a charter or a corporation? Not a word. It is dealing simply with licensing and not one word said about a charter or a corporation. And yet he says that's what this thing proves here. He deals with the rules and regulations of the minimum standards of Texas for child care institutions, like denominational preachers deal with the Bible. He takes something that applies to one thing and takes it out of its setting and makes it mean something else. And I am saying that there are no legal demands in Texas for any such charter or incorporation to be put up in order that such care might be rendered or ministered to children or those in need. He told us last night about an interview he had with somebody down at the State Public Welfare Department at Fort Worth, who told him there had to be a charter and there had to be a corporation. He didn't give us their words, that is, he had no written statement to the effect so far as I discovered. He simply told what was spoken to him orally and therefore, he said, there must be a charter and there must be a corporation; that it must be incorporated; it's not legal to exist—it can't exist without it. The law demands it.

I wrote the Attorney General's Office in Austin—the Attorney General of the State of Texas, and asked him some questions about it. And I have here a letter from the Attorney General's office, State of Texas which says he knows of no such statute in the laws of Texas. Why don't you inform him Brother Deaver, or let him know you have found out about it. The attorney General of the State of Texas doesn't even know that such a statute exists on the law books of Texas. And that isn't all, I'm not through yet. I also wrote a letter to the State Department of Public Welfare, not at Forth Worth, but at Austin, where headquarters are. And I have a letter from the headquarters of the State Public Welfare. And here is what they say about it : "It is not mandatory"—(get it now) "It is not mandatory that a separate corporation be formed and that a charter be granted in order for a person or an association to maintain or operate a child caring institution in the State of Texas."

And yet that's exactly what Brother Deaver said had to be done. That was the legal demand; he said, you can't operate one if you have more than seven or more than six. When you get to seven, he said, right then you have to obtain a charter. Well, Brother Deaver, it's not called a child caring institution until you get to seven, is it? Is it? You didn't mean to say it was, did you? You meant to agree with me, well, all right. It isn't called a child caring institution until you reach the number seven. If you have less than seven children, it's not called a child caring institution. And he said when you reach seven, you must get a charter. Who said it, Brother Deaver? What did the State Office of Public Welfare say about it? They said, It is not mandatory that a separate corporation be formed and that a charter be granted in order for a person or an association to maintain or operate a child caring institution in the State of Texas. And therefore, they say you can have seven, it becomes a child caring institution then, and you can operate it without a charter, without an incorporation. That no person or association is required to get it. Not only is a religious congregation not required to do it. Nobody is required to do it. It just isn't so. And when I said there were no such legal demands, I wasn't talking through my hat. I knew what I was talking about.

Now, we go on to the speech to which you have just listened. All right, he comes to chart 69 and brings up things he says Porter admitted: Funds can be sent to a private home and a private home can be incorporated and the home is not the church and it's not an integral part of the church and it's not under the elders of the church and the needs of the orphans can be supplied and the church can meet its obligation and there is no in between organization. And then he gave chart 72 which was a repetition of it in just a little variable form. And then declared that all of that admits the whole thing and all that he needs. And there's not a thing on earth in that that admits anything that he needs. When he is endeavoring to sustain the idea that a church may contribute to Boles Home, Quinlan, Texas, he is insisting that they can contribute to the sort of arrangement that provides Boles Home because you can't contribute to Boles Home without contributing to the corporation that sets it up and the arrangement by which it is provided. And I have not admitted the very heart for which his proposition contends and which must be given or must be proven before he gets anywhere with it. And he has made no progress whatsoever along that line.

He gave his definitions: "Scripture" means the Bible and "teach" means to impart information and "the church" is a local congregation and "may" means it has liberty and "to contribute" means to send funds to and he went on to say it means to make a donation to and then "Boles Home" is a kind of arrangement that has a board and stood in position of parents and so on. And then he said, some things I'm not affirming: I'm not affirming that the church is insufficient; I'm not affirming the missionary society or anything that is parallel to it; I'm not affirming that the church delegates its work to a benevolent organization; I'm not affirming that this is the only way. But you would think it was, wouldn't you? When brethren say that this is not the only way, it's only a matter of opinion, you can do it this way if you want to, if you don't—you can do it some other way and you mustn't make a law out of your opinion, and then they turn around and say you do it our way or out you go. Do it our way or out you go. Quarantine you and disfellowship you if you don't subscribe to the principles we have in Boles Home and similar arrangements and that is what is happening all over the United States today and everybody knows it. If that isn't making a law out of your opinion, I wonder how you go about doing it.

And then he came to his total situation and the total situation looks rather bad for him. Here he said, there are two questions regarding the total situation—he made his argument—he had a syllogism on his chart—that the total situation here proves Boles Home. And so he gave his major premise and his minor premise: The total situation of a thing that is scriptural is a scriptural situation and that the situation described in his proposition, that is the various parts of it, are scriptural, therefore the whole thing is scriptural and Boles Home can be contributed to by churches. That's the subject or substance of his argument. So he makes his total situation argument and he says you have to prove that it's not valid or the premises are not true. He wrote to some universities to find out about it and they said it was unquestionably valid. And then he went to prove his major premise and his minor premise and so on. And of course, if the premises are true, the conclusion follows—no doubt about that. But he has to prove his premises true and when that university professor said it's valid, of course, he made his conclusion based upon the idea that the premises were true. And if they were, then of course, the conclusion would follow. But I deny that the premises are true and that's what he has to prove. And he undertook to do it and so we will follow them as rapidly and yet as elaborately as we can as time allows.

He gave us something to prove an axiom, that the whole of anything is the sum of its parts, a self evident truth, he said. Psalms 139:17—Precious is thy thoughts unto me and how great is the sum of them, David said. 1 Corinthians 13:10—The perfect and that which is in part will be done away. And then he said, "When I met Mr. Hathaway in debate, I introduced an argument on the constituent elements along that line." And he did. And while we are at that particular point, I want you to see a statement from that debate that he had with Brother Hathaway. And I want chart J Brother Shaw. I want chart J just at this point before we go on. And if I don't get to all of these because I wanted to deal with some of those things we had last night that I wanted to get before you—we will still have more time to deal with them as we go. Here is a statement taken from that debate, made by Brother Roy Deaver. He says, "Because the denominational world has used the term Sunday School frequently and has applied it to an organization, that has its own president and that has its own secretary and that takes up its own contribution, I recognize and understand perfectly well and would criticize just as severely as does he that any organization other than the church of the living God is something the Bible never heard of. I am not upholding therefore nor defending a denominational Sunday School; I am not upholding nor defending anything that has its own president; that has its own secretary or that has its own contribution. I'll criticize that along with him and when he makes a speech of condemnation of that very thing, I will say amen to every word he says about it. *Hathaway-Deaver Debate*, page 32 and 33 and that statement was made on Nov. 26, 1951. All right, the lights please.

Now then, Brother Deaver, in this chart—statement taken from your debate with Brother Hathaway, you said that you were not defending anything that has its own president—any organization that has its own president, or its own secretary and matters of that kind. That you would oppose that and say amen to every word of condemnation he spoke against it. I want to know, do you still hold that tonight? Or has there been some shifting of positions? I just wonder about that. Are you defending something tonight that has its own president, its own secretary and so on? Are you?

Now then, getting on to the matters involved here. He came to James 1:25 the perfect law of liberty which he said would include the sum of its parts. And then he proceeded to prove that this is a valid way to introduce things and to prove things by introducing something relative to the plan of salvation, he worked it out on the board here, and I want to use some charts if I have time. And Brother Shaw, I want chart O followed by chart O-1, in rapid succession as I deal with them. And we want to look at his total situation. We are going to see just what the situation is in this matter and whether or not his situation is going to help him at all in defense of Boles Home as something to which churches may contribute their funds in the field of benevolence. Now here we have the plan of salvation—we have his total situation set up here—the constituent elements of the total situation. First, and this is what he said a while ago, The gospel must be preached (Rom. 10:14). Second, Man must believe (Heb. 11:6). Third, must repent of his sins (Luke 13:3-5; Acts 17:30). Fourth, he must confess Christ (Rom. 10:9, 10). Fifth, must be baptized (Acts 10:48). And this was the plan given in the *Hathaway-Deaver Debate*, page 123. So I copied it from his debate and the scriptures he gave to prove those points. Now here are the constituent elements in the situation he is describing here that he is going to prove to be total, and scriptural. And so he says here, the whole of a thing is the sum of its parts. All right, his major premise: If the constituent elements or component parts of a situation are scriptural, then the total situation is scriptural. Minor premise: The constituent elements or component parts of the plan of salvation described above are scriptural. And the conclusion :

The total situation of the plan of salvation described above is scriptural. Brother Deaver and I will agree upon that chart, and upon the proof submitted there. Now let us have the next one, chart 0-1. We have another one on the plan of salvation and this one represents his position on the Boles Home situation tonight. Now here we have the same thing. And here we have the constituent elements of the total situation: First, the gospel must be preached, second, men must believe; third, he must repent of his sins; fourth, must confess Christ, fifth, must offer animal sacrifice; and sixth, must be baptized. All right, the whole of a thing is the sum of its parts. The major premise: If the constituent elements or component parts of a situation is scriptural, the total situation is scriptural. Minor premise : The constituent elements or component parts of the plan of salvation described above are scriptural. Conclusion: The total situation of the plan of salvation as described is scriptural. Is it? What is wrong with it? Why doesn't this prove that plan up there? Because there is no scripture for number five. There is an element or component part in that situation described there that he cannot sustain by the scriptures. No one can and therefore, the conclusion does not follow. This is a valid—you will admit Brother Deaver, will you not, that this is a valid arrangement down here. You won't deny that. You will admit that this is a valid arrangement—that the premises are valid—that the conclusion necessarily follows. You will admit that. You won't deny that. Well, what's wrong? We have an element up here in the situation described that's not scriptural—you have no authority for it. Now then, let us get the next two following that, chart P and chart P-1. I will get to all of these if I have time as rapidly as I can and after that I want chart Q and Q-1.

Now here we have the total situation on worship. Now he said, you get the total situation of worship and so you have worship. Well, actually Brother Deaver, you have worship whether you have the total situation or not. In either of these, you have worship already whether you get them all together or not. But we will just let you have it that way and so we take it as you have it. First, he said, in worship there's teaching, we get that from some passage and singing from another passage and praying from another passage and the Lord's supper from another and the contribution from another. Therefore, we get the total situation and all the elements up here are scriptural. And so the axiom is that the whole of anything is the sum of its parts. The major premise: If the constituent elements or component parts of the situation is scriptural, the total situation is scriptural. Minor premise: the constituent elements or component parts of the worship described above is scriptural. All right, the next chart right after that. Here we have again the plan of salvation under the total situation arrangement. And the same thing: teaching, singing and praying, the Lord's supper and contribution, but in that, we also have playing an instrument. Now then, the whole of anything is the sum of its parts. So the major premise: If the constituent elements or component parts of a situation is scriptural, the total situation is scriptural. The minor premise: The constituent elements or component parts of the worship described above is scriptural. And the conclusion: The total situation of worship described above is scriptural. Brother Deaver, will you tell me, is this syllogism valid? I want to know, is it valid and does the conclusion necessarily follow? Well, what's wrong with it? Nothing wrong with the syllogism. Except you've got to prove some of the elements and then you've got to prove some of the premises first. And upon the basis that the premises are true why of course, the conclusion follows, but what's wrong with it? Well, there's no scripture for number 4. You can't find playing an instrument as part of the worship of the New Testament church. And so one element is lacking in scriptural authority and therefore, the whole situation is not scriptural. All right, let us have the next two. That's Q and Q-1. So here we have Bible classes. He gave us that on the board. I'm taking them just in the order he gave it. The constituent elements of the total situation of Bible classes. First, he said there's the recognition of the elders' authority. Second, dealing with men as they are able to receive and the passages given are those taken from his debate with Brother Hathaway. And third, teachers are authorized. And fourth, students are authorized. And five, simultaneous teaching. And six, a small group taken from a larger group. And seven, the religious gathering smaller than the whole church. And so then makes his major premise and his minor premise on the same basis as the other and reaches the conclusion that the whole situation is scriptural. Now then (moderator: time) Well, thank you.

Deaver's Second Affirmative

Brother Porter, Brethren Moderators, Brethren and Friends: I want to call your attention now to my chart No. 7 as we shall discuss some things that have been said with reference to incorporation. I would like to impress upon your minds that night after night, Brother Porter has discussed and complained about and criticized points in connection with incorporation. And yet it's a known fact to all of us that Brother Porter does not oppose incorporation. He recognizes perfectly well that a church, an incorporated church even, can send the funds to an incorporated private home. That private home might provide the needs of orphan children and that a church may use that method in meeting its obligation to orphan children. Now he has admitted every bit of that. And yet, in spite of all of that, will come back and spend minute after minute and even hour after hour in discussion of matters of the matters in connection with corporation as if he thought it were sinful. He thinks that some how, some way there is created an in between organization when you get down to the matter of a church's sending a contribution to Boles Home.

On my chart No. 7 which has been introduced previously, but so far as I can recall, Brother Porter has done absolutely nothing with it, I want you to notice this. Just how many organizations are there in between? When a church, an incorporated church, which Brother Porter allows, sends funds to a private home now, how many in between organizations are there here? He says that's all right. An incorporated church can do this, now how many organization are there in between? You will notice please, that if the fact of incorporation brings into existence an in between organization, then you have an in between organization in this case because this church is incorporated. If incorporation automatically brings into existence another organization, then you've got it whether it's over here on this side with the church or over here with the home. And according to that reasoning, if that's what brings it into existence, why you have one in between organization here and in this case where an incorporated church sends to a church, you have an organization in between or a church sending to an incorporated church, you have that in between, and an incorporated church, you would have two of them in between.

We have a continuation of that chart, chart No. 7 continued, and how many organizations do you have in between there? And yet Brother Porter says that it's all right for an incorporated church to send to an incorporated church. But if an incorporated church sends to an incorporated private home, or to an incorporated home, then you've got somehow, an in between organization. What brought it into existence? Well, he says it's not incorporation and yet will spend his time in discussion of incorporation. And if that's what brings it into existence, then when an incorporated church sends to an incorporated private home, which he says is all right, then you don't have one organization between, you've got two. And when an incorporated church sends to Boles Home down here, you wouldn't have one in between organization but two, if the fact of incorporation brings it in and if it doesn't bring it in, then it isn't there. And he knows it isn't there and he doesn't oppose incorporation and yet he spends his time in discussion of it, as if it were sin, when he admits it's all right.

Now then, my chart No. 70 right quickly and then get No. 71 ready. On my chart No. 70, notice the syllogism that is involved in my proposition: All total situations, the constituent elements of which are scriptural, are total situations which are scriptural. I want you to notice and I would like to impress upon your minds, especially you brethren who stand opposed to what I have to say tonight, that Brother Porter does not quibble about that Major premise. Now we know—when you think about—all over this country brethren have written article after article, page after page and book after book trying to destroy the effect of that major premise and Brother Porter knows it—can't deny it. There's not a way under the sun you can overthrow that major premise. There's a lot of difference in validity and proof. According to what Brother Porter had to say a while ago, he doesn't recognize the difference, but there is a great deal of difference. If you've got a valid syllogism, and that simply means, if you have the proper arrangement here and the conclusion is guaranteed, then it is valid; whether the premises are true or not, doesn't enter into it—the validity of it. We said, is it valid? Now then, we didn't ask Mr. Anderson whether or not it's true. We said, is it valid? Now then, Brother Porter won't quibble on that, he knows better than that. And I'm glad for that fact. Then my premise: the total situation described in my proposition is a total situation, the constituent elements of which are all scriptural. He does not quibble on this. His only attack is on the minor premise. And you notice what he had to say about my chart No. 71. Let's get it please.

No. 71, which is a listing of every point that's involved in my proposition and what did he have to say about which one of these things is wrong? Is it this? No, sir. According to what he had to say, every point up there is scriptural. There is only one point that he made an attack upon and it isn't up here. He said there is an additional element. And I told you that that's what he would say. Brother Porter knows that the church has an obligation to orphans. He knows the details of meeting that obligation are not specified. He knows the meaning of the word "orphan." He knows that God's love extends to all men. Brother Porter, you referred to what I had to say on that and then grinned in connection with it. Did you mean to leave the impression you didn't believe what I said about it? That God's love does not extend to all men? Now you deal with that. All right, he'll not question that. And a church cannot function as a home. I thought he would come back surely and deal with No. 5 there, but Brother Porter has made no attempt to deal with that point. And he recognizes the fact that the needs of orphans cannot be met without having a home. He recognizes that there is no inherent sin in a board; there is no inherent sin in having a charter. And we must meet legal requirements.

You know he read a statement a while ago, I had already read the statement before or one at least similar to it, and whether you call it a plan of operation or a charter, doesn't make me any difference. They call it both down at the State Department. And I told you that it doesn't make me any difference what you call it. It's still a charter or it's a plan of operation. And if you are just opposed to that word, I'll quit it. If that's all there is between us Brother Porter, thanks be unto God, I'll give it up. Whether it's a charter or plan of operation doesn't make any difference. The law says you've got to have it. All right, he recognizes that there is no inherent sin in having that plan of operation. And he knows that a home can't exist without it. You just try to set up one. Brother Porter, did you ever try to start one? You try to and see how far you get. All right, we must meet legal requirements then. And he knows that Romans 13 authorizes that. The arrangement at Quinlan is just a home and the church can send to a home and make possible care of orphans. What did he say about it? Did he call for the chart? He recognizes the truthfulness of my major premise. He didn't question a single point here.

He said there's an additional element. And it's that in between organization and it doesn't exist. If it does, it's brought into existence either by the board or incorporation or a charter or a combination of them and let him tell you whether or not that's so. And see the difficulty into which he gets himself. All right, now then, that chart stands untouched. It's unassailable. And the major premise has been granted. That when you prove the parts of a thing that is scriptural, you prove the whole thing to be scriptural. Why don't some of you brethren write him up? For agreeing to that major premise? It's been denied all over this country. I never was worried about it because anybody who knows a thing on earth about 1 Corinthians 13:10, and James 1:25 knows it couldn't be denied.

All right, now let's come to the other things Brother Porter had to say. The lights please. He says the missionary society does not control the churches. Brother Porter, it does if the church is a member of it. Now a church doesn't have to be a member of it. But if you are a member of it, you do what they say. And if you don't do what they say, out you go. Now your membership there is voluntary. That's the way it has been or was when it started too. All right, there is a missionary society which is a human arrangement operating in the field of the church and assuming unto itself prerogatives and authority which God has restricted to a congregation and in particular to its eldership. The church is its own missionary society. The church is its own benevolent society—be careful there Brother Porter—but the church is not its own orphan home. The church is not its own orphan home and the needs of an orphan require the home. So the church can provide that home but the church can't be that home and that's the little end of the tap-root of this entire thing. The church is sufficient. It's its own missionary society. It is its own benevolent society but in meeting its obligation to orphans, a home is necessary. And Brother Porter knows it's so and I know it's so that a church can send to a home.

All right, I'd like to have now—get ready Brother Porter's chart No. 25 just a moment. He discussed Boles Home and the missionary society and we referred last night somewhat in detail to Brother Porter's position there. Now you keep in mind that he does not believe that Boles Home is parallel to the missionary society—whatever you believe about it, he doesn't now. And if you believe it is, that's not his position. Brother Porter's position is that Boles Home is parallel to the evangelism provided by the missionary society. Here he has the churches sending down here to a superintendent's office over here in the orphan's home and he's got a board up here that hires and controls the superintendent and then the home is over here. And I suppose—according to that—being supervised by the superintendent. All right, the truth of the whole matter is: this board, this rectangle up here, belongs right down here Brother Porter. It's a part of that home just like a husband is a part of his home. But Brother Porter has the ridiculous notion that just because the charter says that incorporation provides a thing, that that which provides is no part of that provided. And according to his reasoning—because the husband provides a home for his family—he is no part of it. It belongs down here. And on the same reasoning remember Brother Porter says a church can incorporate. Brother Porter says that the home to which a church can send can incorporate. Now then, on the same reasoning, by which he arrives at the conclusion that the board stands on the outside, in connection with the home, I am going to argue that it stands on the outside in connection with the church. Either way you take it doesn't make any difference. If it's inside in connection with the church, it's inside here. If it's outside here—it's outside there. But Brother Porter said it's all right outside in connection with the church, but down here it's all wrong if it's outside. This board belongs down here. In fact, all of this belongs on the inside. They are integral parts of the home.

Now my chart No. 59. In this chart he was attempting to show the similarity or the fact that parallel with the idea that Boles Home is parallel with the evangelism of the missionary society. I raised the question last night along that line: Brother Porter, do you really believe that they are parallel? Does Boles Home have a right to exist? You know what he said? And you brethren, some of you, were disappointed in that. Because article after article has been written on the point that Boles Home does have a right to exist. Brother Porter said, No Sir. Brother Porter says Boles Homes does not have a right to exist. On that point he says they are parallel. Will you fellowship those who support Boles Home, and will you fellowship those who support the evangelism of the missionary society? Do you know what he said about that? You are right. He said my position on that is just what Brother Deaver says and that helped me tremendously. That just helped a whole lot. Brother Porter, you come back and answer that. Will you fellowship those who support Boles Home and will you fellowship those who support the evangelism of the missionary society? You say they are parallel. Can an individual support Boles Home? Brother Porter, you said last night, I believe that they couldn't. Now if I misunderstood you, you correct me. Individuals cannot support Boles Home. Individuals cannot support the evangelism of the missionary society. And yet many of the brethren who stand identified with him, have argued for the last two or three years that individuals could support Boles Home. And can a church buy service from Boles Home? He'd have to say no, they can't—parallel to the evangelism up here. I'm simply raising the question, what about this? Will you fellowship those of us who support Boles Home? And will you fellowship those who support the evangelism of the missionary society.

My chart No. 68 please and get No. 40 ready. This is all in connection with Brother Porter's chart No. 25. My chart No. 68. Notice carefully, in the care of orphans a church may send funds to a home. Brother Porter said that's all right and this home can be incorporated. And the reason that a church sends funds to a home is because the church is not a home. It needs a home and a home's authorized. Who said so? I say so now. Brother Porter says so. Brother Porter won't deny that a home is authorized. It's there and it can be incorporated and a church can send to it. And he admits that and believes that the church can send to it because it's needed and it's authorized. It's there and it can be incorporated and a church can send to it. And he admits that and believes that the church can send to it because it's needed and it's authorized. Now in preaching the gospel, why can't a church send to the missionary society. The church is not its own orphan home. That's the reason why Brother Porter knows that a home must be provided. He makes the mistake of saying that this home can come over here and become a part of the church. But whether he is right or wrong, he still admits my proposition. Brother Porter if you could succeed in establishing the point that elders could oversee a home, you still have to admit and you have admitted my proposition, and you still have a church sending to Boles Home. You still have a church sending funds to a home that's incorporated to meet the needs of orphan children. And if you could succeed in doing that, you still have admitted my proposition. All my proposition says is that a church can make a contribution to Boles Home, Quinlan, Texas. Now if you could prove by the Bible, that this home is over here, you still have admitted that it doesn't have to be over there.

All right, No. 40 please. And in connection with this, we have already called attention to the fact that there's the parts of the missionary society—what makes it a missionary society—it's assumed to itself authority here that God has restricted to churches. Churches send delegates over here to this missionary society which makes decisions which are bound on the churches. Now they can get out of it. But as long as they are a part of that society, they are bound by its decision. Boles Home is not parallel to that thing. And it is parallel to the private home or the foster home down here which Brother Porter and I both know can exist and is right. It's parallel to the private home. Churches can send to a private home. Churches can send to a foster home and that home can be incorporated and the needs of children and orphans can thus be supplied and that's a way by which a church can meet its obligation and these are points admitted by Brother Porter. In connection with his chart 25, lights please.

Brother Porter, referred to what I had to say about the check. I make the statement I think the first night, and repeated last night, that if there is an in between organization, and that's all he has said tonight now, if there is that organization, standing between the church and Boles Home, will you kindly tell me the name of it and the address of it, how I can get in contact with it, and if you can tell me where it is—now remember, since it's standing between, it's no part of Boles Home—Brother Porter, that's where you slipped up a while ago—if it's in between, then it's not a part of it. All right, I asked you to give me that in between organization, the name of it and where it's located so that I can mail it a twenty-five dollar check with the assurance that Boles Home won't get it. And he talked about that in connection with chart 25, complaining about it, made several remarks about it and you know that he never did tell me where to send it. He never did. He never did tell me where to send that check so that I could have assurance that Boles Home wouldn't get it and that there was an organization in between that would get it. He tried to discuss the board down there but the very arguments that he made showed that they are connected with Boles Home. I asked him about that in between organization, which he says exists and exists only in his imagination.

All right, then he referred to Boles Charter and had somewhat to say about the charter there. And of course, we have Boles Charter. They have it simply because the law demanded a statement of this—of their plans and policies. Sometimes they speak of it as a plan of operation. Over at the Lubbock home, theirs is written up as a plan of operation. The Boles Home affair happens to be called a charter. And there's nothing inherently wrong with a charter and Brother Porter knows it. And even the churches, many of them, have to have their charter to incorporate if they do and that's a part of it. Brother Porter said last night, you don't get the charter without incorporation and he is right. That's what they tell you about it at the State Department of Public Welfare.

All right, then the in between organization. He said that the element that Brother Deaver left out is this in between matter and that's all he had to say about my proposition. Now he discussed in his chart No. X, in home duties—we will not call for it right now because of time—but he discussed some home duties here and he discussed some church duties here and if the home does this, it's invading the field of the church and if the church does this it's invading the field of the home. Brother Porter ought to know—the audience knows whether he does or not—that there are some duties which overlap. Certainly so. But does the fact that there are some duties which overlap mean that the church and the home are the same thing? The Bible outlines a distinction between these. And there are some things which elders are not authorized to do as elders. Now the same men who are elders may also be the legal board of trustees and stand *en loco parentis* in connection with orphan children. But in that capacity, they are not functioning as elders. Just exactly as the same men who hold this property in trust, may be the elders of this church—they don't have to be—but if they are, in this capacity they are not serving as elders but as legal trustees because the law says you have to have it.

All right, then no divine home. Brother Porter took a position last night for which I'm sincerely sorry. He made the statement and came back to repeat it tonight, that unless you have a husband-wife relationship, there is no divine home. And we mentioned last night and mention again, if that's true, if you've got to have a husband and wife relationship to have a divine home, that means Mary, Martha and Lazarus didn't have a home. That means a widow with six children doesn't have a divine home. And I'm ashamed of it, Brother Porter.

He referred to my statements regarding God's law of love and we mentioned a while ago and I ask him now: Do you believe what I had to say about it? Brother Porter, did you mean to deny that God's law of love extends to the just and the unjust? Then Buckner Home—my chart No. 67 right quickly. All right, my chart No. 63. And in this connection now, he had discussed Buckner Home. I mentioned to you last night that the churches—churches send to—this is 67 Brother Porter—churches or here you have a Baptist Church and that Baptist Church would be incorporated, sending over here to the Southern Baptist Convention and the Southern Baptist Convention is incorporated. And the Southern Baptist Convention provides Buckner Home. The Baptist Church here is an integral part of the Southern Baptist Convention. Buckner Home is an integral part of the Southern Baptist

Convention but you've got three different separate incorporations in connection with each. Now, in connection with the church of Christ, sending over here to Boles Home, that thing is conspicuously absent. And yet that's the very thing and that's the only thing that Brother Porter has emphasized. That you've got something in here that's just like the missionary society of the Christian Church or it's just like the Southern Baptist Convention to the Baptist Churches. Now Brother Porter, where is it and what brought it into existence? It wasn't incorporation. It wasn't a board. It wasn't a charter. It wasn't anything. It just isn't there. And there's nothing there like that. That church simply sends to Boles Home. And Brother Porter says a church can send to a home that's incorporated that the needs of orphans might be supplied but they just can't send to Boles Home. He has something against Boles Home and to dearly save my life I don't know what it is. In view of all the admissions he has made, he simply has in mind there's an in between something that just doesn't exist.

All right, he said that there is no charter demanded. The lights please. I want to read to you now. Whether you call it a manual of operation or a charter doesn't make me any difference. But I'm reading to you and I'd like for you to keep in mind that these read somewhat differently depending upon what organization or institution that you are dealing with. Now a foster care home is one thing and a child care agency is another thing and a child placing agency is something else and therefore the standards don't all read the same. I'm reading right here regarding the child caring institution now, and here's what you have to say: The agency or institution shall be legally organized and its objects and purposes shall be expressly stated in its charters, articles of incorporation and statutes, constitutions and other published material. The agency shall be—I have a note here, see page 21—and here's the note—in the footnote here—"should" as used herein indicates the standard recommended. "Shall" and "must" as used herein indicates that the standard is mandatory. The law says, you've got to have it Brother Porter. And if you want to quibble with them, go to it. But I'll tell you this, you won't start a home without it. We tried it, down in Fort Worth. You try it. Go down there and get acquainted with those people and see what they tell you to do. A man can live out in the mountains somewhere, have twelve children of his own, deal with them as he cares to do so but Brother Porter, when you set up a home to take care of them, you are going to walk the line. And thanks be unto God that's so. That the laws of our land recognize the need for the protection of innocent children. All right.

Now he says that a church doesn't have to have another corporation. He was dealing with the matter of incorporation here answering and was trying to leave the impression that you didn't have to have a corporation in connection with a home and he read to you the statements there that a church doesn't have to have another corporation. Nobody said that Brother Porter. That very statement shows that there's got to be a corporation. Why—even over in Lubbock they know perfectly well that they can use the same corporation for the church and for the home and that's what they do. Nobody said you've got here to have two of them. But you've got to have one for both of them, if you've got both of them. And that's what they tell you down at the State Department. Up in Lubbock, the church is incorporated. We use the same corporation for both of them. That's right.

He said, Brother Deaver's position is: Do it our way or out you go. Brother Porter, weren't you listening a while ago? When I said to you plainly, I am not affirming that this is the only way that a church can meet its obligation to orphans but I am affirming that it's one way and that it's a good way and that it's a scriptural way. And yet he says, Brother Deaver said, "If you don't do it our way, out you go." Where did you get that information? Nobody has ever said you've got to do it like this. And if a church doesn't want to do it like that, that's their business. And I respect their rights and defend their rights to refuse and not do it that way. But any time they get to the point of saying, "Brother Deaver, you sin if you do it and you can't do it" and if they draw the line I'm going to respect the line. Nobody's ever said you have to do it like this. But when they—or you—say you can't do it, then you've made a law that God didn't make and your practice comes under question.

Then Brother Porter did not question the validity of the syllogism. I appreciate that, and it speaks highly in my opinion of Brother Porter because he knows that that major premise cannot be overthrown. And he knows that the syllogism is valid. He knows that if the premises are true, the conclusion is inevitable. He recognizes that and admits the validity of it. Brother Porter's chart No. J. He had something there, quoted from the book: The *Deaver-Hathaway Debate* and he says that Brother Deaver says here that he will oppose something that has to do with—put it on there if you want to—Brother Deaver said that he would oppose anything that had a secretary, its own treasury and such like. Brother Porter, you know perfectly well what was being talked about in that discussion. And you know perfectly well that we were not discussing orphan homes and we were talking about the churches' teaching program—the churches' teaching work and in connection with that I said, I will oppose an organized Sunday school like the sectarian world had that has its own president, secretary, etc. just like Brother Hathaway would and just like you would. We don't have any such thing as that. But I do defend the right for the church to have Bible classes. Brother Porter, you said that a church can send to an incorporated private home. May that incorporation have a president, secretary, treasurer? Now you answer that. Would you oppose it? We were talking about the Bible Class work, when these statements were made and not about orphan homes. And every one of these points were made with reference to that Bible Class work.

All right, lights please. Brother Porter, you keep in mind, if that home that you say is all right and can incorporate, had a president in that incorporation, would it still be all right? Is it the president where the sin is? That would help us a lot I think. All right, Brother Porter said, if the premises were true, the conclusion would follow. If the premises were true, the conclusion would follow. If the premises were true, the conclusion would follow. He knows that the syllogism is valid. And he admits that is what has been denied by brethren all over the country. And the very fact that they continue to write and to write and to write and to write about it shows the power of that syllogism, and the force of the argument. He does not deny my major premise and again I ask, what do you brethren think about that? He says there's nothing wrong with the syllogism. That's in quotation marks. Brother Porter recognizes there's nothing wrong with the syllogism. If there's anything wrong and if there's any attack to be made, it's got to be made on the minor premise. And the only thing that he had to say about that was—he may have somewhat to say later—when I have no opportunity to reply tonight—we will get it tomorrow—but he has said, all he has said tonight is that there's something else that Brother Deaver didn't put in there. And it's that in between organization and that's the thing that we have been discussing now every night. Brother Porter says there's an in between organization. I deny the existence of any such thing as that in between organization.

May I have my chart No. 71 again please. And you keep in mind now that I'm in the affirmative of this proposition: *The Bible teaches that a church may contribute to Boles Home, Quinlan, Texas.* All right, then we've given you the major premise which cannot be denied—the syllogism which is valid and we've proved to you that a church has an obligation to orphans. The details are not specified as to how that obligation is to be met. We've talked about and proved the meaning of the word "orphan"; that God's love extends to all men; the church cannot function as a home; the needs of an orphan cannot be met without a home; there is no sin in having a board; incorporation or charter; we must meet legal requirements; the arrangement down at Quinlan is just a home; and a church can send a contribution to a home that needs of orphans might be supplied. Brother Porter says yes, but Brother Deaver, you've got an in between organization. Where is it and what brought it into existence. Remember, we proved there's no sin in having a board; there's no sin in the incorporation; there's no sin in the charter; and there's no sin in meeting legal requirements. Now if there's any in between organization, where is it? Where is it located? What's it like—what's the nature of it? What brought it into existence?

All right now, I'd like to refer briefly, in the fine few remaining moments, to some of the absurdities—lights please—and ridiculous positions or statements that have been made by Brother Porter. Brother Porter argues there is this benevolent organization standing between a church and a home and yet he makes no attempt to give the name of it and the address of it so that I can send a check to it in such a way that Boles Home will not get it. He spends much of his time discussing incorporation and yet he admits the fact that incorporation does not bring into existence a separate organization. He argues that Boles Home is not a divine institution—yet he fails to recognize that it's just exactly like the home in his proposition which is all right and which can be incorporated and that whether it's human or divine doesn't make any difference. If his home is human, then it's all right with me if Boles Home is human if he says the church can send to it. Just like the church can send to the home that he's upheld. But if he says that his home is divine, the one that he has been discussing, then you will also conclude that Boles Home is divine. Either way you take it. All right.

Porter's Second Negative

Brethren Moderators, Brother Deaver, Ladies and Gentlemen: I appear before you now for the closing speech of this session of the discussion. I will pay my attention to the remarks that have been made by Brother Deaver in the speech that just preceded. However, there are a few other things I want to get to. I would like to get to the matters contained in the other speech because of dealing with matters uttered in the speech last night. I want to call attention at this time to another question or two which I gave Brother Deaver. Question No. 1 was: Do you know of any home known in the brotherhood that you do not endorse? He said, I endorse a church sending to Boles Home and every home which is also included in these principles. Well, do these principles include Lubbock Home and homes like that? They are certainly not under the same set-up; it's not the same arrangement whatsoever. And some of these claim they are operating under an eldership. And Brother Deaver claims that homes cannot operate under an eldership; that elders can't be over a home. And so either they are wrong or he is wrong or they don't know what they are doing or he doesn't know what he is doing or something. There's something wrong somewhere about the matter because they do not agree.

I also asked him, question No. 5: Have the operators of homes such as Lubbock, Maude Carpenter, Tipton and others been misrepresenting the facts when they have advertised to the brotherhood through their papers that those homes are under the supervision of the elders? Now I gave you a chart the other night, last night or night before I believe it was, in which I had some of the clippings taken from the masthead of some of the publications of these homes in which they stated definitely that the homes were under the supervision of the elders and actually gave the names of the elders. And so I'm asking him if they've been misrepresenting these things when they've been claiming through the papers that those homes are under elders when in fact they are not under the elders.

Brother Deaver says there is no intentional misrepresentations, so I guess the brethren are misrepresenting unintentionally. There is a misrepresentation then, isn't there, Brother Deaver? You say it's not intentional but it must be a misrepresentation then according to you. He said some actually hold that they are elders over a home; I believe they are mistaken on this matter. And so, here are some who claim they are operating with the home under the elders and Brother Deaver doesn't believe it can operate that way and if they do, he believes they are wrong. And those brethren are following a practice that's wrong, according to him, if they are doing what they claim they are doing. Last night you know, he said they ought to know, they think they have a charter and if they think they have, they must have. And so, if they think they are under the elders, they must be, according to that Brother Deaver. And so I suppose they are under the elders and you just didn't know about it so there's homes that you can't endorse and you must denounce them as unscriptural and departing from the truth and all of that because they are operating under the elders according to their claim. And if they are not operating under the elders, you ought to get them straightened out on it and let them know what the facts of the case are so they will quit misrepresenting those things to the brotherhood, and getting money under false pretense. Because brethren have sent to those homes believing that they were sending to homes operating under elders. And if they were not operating under elders, then according to the position that some brethren have taken, who stand with you upon these matters, they ought to send all that money back that they've received from, these churches who sent to them with the impression that they were being operated under elders. Have they been sending any of it back that you've heard of?

Now, I was dealing with the total situation proposition and I want to get the rest of that I had a while ago. I liked just a little of being through with chart Q, so we will take chart Q-1 and here we have a continuation of the total situation, according to Brother Deaver's argument on Bible classes. The recognition of elders' authority and dealing with men as they are able to receive and teachers authorized and students authorized and simultaneous teaching; No. 6 burning incense, and 7 a small group taken from a large group, and No. 8 a religious gathering smaller than the whole church. And the whole of a thing is the sum of its parts. And the major premise: If the constituent elements or component parts of this situation are scriptural, the total situation is scriptural. Minor premise: the constituent elements or component parts of Bible classes described above are scriptural. Conclusion: The total situation of Bible classes described above is scriptural. Now Brother Deaver, I asked you about some of those others a question. I wanted to ask you about this one and you didn't pay any attention to it. I wanted to know, is this syllogism valid? Brother Deaver, is that syllogism valid, according to your argument? Is it? Or is it not? I asked that on some of the others and you didn't say. If you say that is valid, then are you going to admit that all these things up here are true? The situation is valid if the statements are true. That's the point. If the elements are true; if the premises are true; then of course it would be valid. But you must prove your premise. That's the point and that's where his failure is, to prove his premises. And up here, what's wrong with this? Well, there's no scripture for No. 6. Burning incense as a part of that Bible class work. There's no scripture for it. And therefore, the total situation breaks down, and that's because of an element or the proposition or the minor premise is lacking in scriptural authority.

All right, let us have the next one now on located preacher. Chart R and chart R-1. We have here chart R. He brought up the located preacher and the matter of Leroy Garrett and so on. Here a preacher may be employed to preach; and they may preach to the saved and the lost; and he may preach to a church having elders; and may preach and stay for any length of time; and he may receive pay for his labor; he may be paid by a church with which he labors. Well, we have scripture for every one of those elements, don't we? All right, then since we have scripture for each one of them, then the conclusion follows from the syllogism given. All right, let us have the next one now. Now here, we have the same constituent elements with only one added and that's no. 7—that the preacher may exercise authority over the elders. Now then, will we reach this conclusion down here? The syllogism is valid. But are the premises true? No, over here is an element that is not scriptural: they may exercise authority over the elders; there's no scripture for that. Therefore, his premise breaks down; his conclusion does not follow. And that's the same thing with his regarding the situation tonight.

Now he simply has an organization in there that arranges and provides Boles Home, that he has no scriptures for. They are doing the very thing that God requires the church to do. And I asked what can they do that the church cannot do, that the elders cannot do. He has never told me what it is. And therefore, he lacks in scriptural authority for the elements of his proposition and his conclusion does not follow and therefore his proposition does not stand sustained. Let us have the lights now.

He said in the speech just made, that Brother Porter found no fault with the Major premise; that he agreed that the major premise was true. Well, I didn't say whether I agreed that the major premise was true or not. He said, "he said it's valid, I have it in quotation." Yes, and these others are valid too, but that doesn't prove the conclusion because the premises are not true. And I made the attack on the minor premise. Did I have to attack both of them? If I show that you lack the elements in the minor premise, must I attack the major premise too? Suppose I grant the major premise is true, that still wouldn't prove your conclusion if your minor premise is wrong. And I showed that your minor premise is wrong and therefore if I just agree that the major premise is all right, that doesn't reach your conclusion at all. Because your total situation breaks down when you find an element in the minor premise that is not so, and we certainly did that.

Now the major premise, whether or not it's true, would depend upon how those elements are arranged; if they have the proper arrangement in relationship to each other. Why I can get some major premises and put them like this: Now you take the word Bethel, there's a scriptural term. And you take the word Baptist, that's a scriptural term. All right, here we have elements, each of which is scriptural. You put them all together and we reach the conclusion, Bethel Baptist Church is a scriptural designation. Will that follow because each one of these elements is a scriptural term? That doesn't prove anything. But just grant that the major premise is so and made my attack on the minor premise and showed the minor premise does not stand, therefore it's conclusion does not follow. He endeavored to prove his minor premise by (1) there's a recognition of obligations to those in need. (2) He gave some scripture, Acts 20:35; James 1:27; Galatians 6:10 and so on and (3) the manner is specified, becomes a part of the obligation but if it's not, then the how is an incidental matter. And so we've used this, he said, on black boards and baptisteries and cups and song books and collection plates and all those things. And (4) the recognition of the meaning of the word "orphan" and he gave James 1:27 and John 14:18. And (5) a recognition of God's love to all men. Did that include Baptist children too? Did that include the Baptist people? He wanted to know a while ago; he said, you made that statement and grinned, do you mean that God didn't love all men? No, I didn't mean that. I meant you had made a bad misapplication of it according to your stand on these positions. Because you said last night, you can't help Baptist Homes; you can't help Buckner Home. You didn't say that? Can you? Will you? Will you recommend that churches send support to the Buckner Home and to Baptist homes? Will you? Will you Brother Deaver? You say you didn't say that; you didn't imply that last night in what you said? You said, why they are Baptist homes and certainly they are teaching their doctrine and we can't send to them. Do you know of any Baptist home that wouldn't teach its doctrine? Can you send to a Baptist home? They teach false doctrine. You say you can't send to a home that teaches false doctrine. You can't send to Baptist homes. Well, when God's love extended to all men, if that justifies the church giving to every orphan in the world and to every needy person in the world, does that include those in Buckner Home? If not, why not? That's what I was grinning about. It wasn't what the Lord said, it was what Deaver said.

Then No. 5 the church cannot function as a home. No. 6 the recognition that the need cannot be met unless it's a part of the home. No. 7—that there's no inherent sin in incorporation. He says it's an artificial intangible thing. And No. 9—the recognition that there's nothing inherently wrong in meeting the demands of the law or obtaining a charter. And No. 10—also meeting the demands of the law (Rom. 13). And No. 11—that's a recognition of the fact that it's simply a home. He said now on one chart he had here a while ago that it's just a home—that last chart he used, 69 I believe it was or 71, whichever it was. That Boles Home is just a home, that's all, it's simply a home. And that proves you can send to it. Well, is Buckner Home simply a home? Is Buckner Home just a home? You can put Buckner in the very same place you have Boles there and have your whole arrangement just like you have it on the chart. Take that chart and go over every item of it, just as you did, and supply Buckner where you've got Boles and you'll prove just as much by Buckner as you prove by Boles. And then 12. that the church can contribute to a home.

And then he came to chart 4 and wanted to know, "Is this a home?" And he gave husband and wife and three children and the husband dies and so on and the husband and wife and then some legal children and so on until they get down here to number seven and have to incorporate and wanted to know, is this a home? Is this a home? Well, is Buckner a home? Do you mean by that that you can send to any home just because it's a home? He is arguing that if you can send to one home, you can send to every home. If that's so then you can send to Buckner Home on the same basis that you can send to Boles Home or other homes operated among us today.

Now I want to use my chart G and G-1 in this particular connection. Now here we have the chart on the question: Is one human, the other divine? Over on one side I have Buckner Home and the other column, Boles Home. These statements on the chart are taken, not from something Porter said or something somebody who stands with him said, but they are taken from the charters of those homes. Now I want to know if one is human and the other is divine? Boles Home he says is a divine organization. Now I want to know, is Buckner Home a divine organization? All right, notice what the charters say: Under Buckner No. 1—the name of this corporation shall be Buckner Orphan Home. Sec. 1. Under Boles Home, No. 1. The name of this corporation shall be Boles Orphan Home, Art. 1. Under Buckner, No. 2. Purposes of this corporation are to procure control of destitute orphan children for the purpose of providing them with a comfortable home—(see, it is just a home)—Sec. 2. And over here under Boles, No. 2. The purposes of this corporation are to provide a home for destitute and dependent children. Art. 2. Under Buckner, No. 3. The principle place of business shall be in the city of Dallas, Texas. Sec. 3. Under Boles, No. 3. The principle place of business shall be near Quinlan in Hunt County, Texas. Art. 3. Under Buckner, No. 4. The term of its existence shall be fifty years, Art. 4. No. 5 under Buckner, the number of directors shall be nine. Sec. 5. No. 5 under Boles, Shall be operated by a board of seven directors. Art. 5. Now the next one following. This is a continuation. No. 6 under Buckner, The management may make suitable provision for any of them in a private home. Sec. 7. No. 6 under Boles, The right to adopt such children by complying with the laws of the state, Art. 2. No. 7 under Buckner, The institution is to be to them *en loco parentis*. (You've heard something about that, haven't you?) Sec. 2. And No. 7 under Boles, Such home is to stand *en loco parentis* to the children, Art. 2. No. 8 Buckner Orphan Home is strictly charitable and educational, Sec. 13. No. 8 under Boles, this corporation is for benevolent, charitable and educational purposes only. Art. 6. No. 9 under Buckner, The corporation has no capital stock. Sec. 6. No. 9 under Boles, This corporation shall have no capital stock, Art. 6. No. 10. The membership of this corporation shall consist of the deacons who are members of Baptist churches within the State of Texas, Sec. 8. No. 10 under Boles, Each shall be a loyal member of some congregation of the Church of Christ in the State of Texas. Art. 7. Now, I want to know what makes the one on the left hand side, Buckner Home, a human organization, unworthy of support, but the one on the right side, a divine organization and they must be supported by churches? Is one human and the other divine? Brother Deaver, I want you to tell us when you come to the stand tomorrow night, whether one is human and the other is divine.

And why one is human and the other divine, if you say so. Here we have parallel arrangements, ten parallel statements, taken from the charters of these two organizations. And I want to know, Brother Deaver, if Buckner Home or Buckner organization there that provides Buckner Home, is a separate organization; an in between organization, why isn't it true with Boles Home and the organization there in connection with it. Why is one an in between organization and the other not?

All right, let us have the lights again. He brought up his chart No. 7 and said that Porter does not oppose incorporation yet he discusses incorporation as if it were sinful. And he wants to know how the thing came into existence. He says there is no in between organization, in the matter. And I want my chart No. 25 again just here. We are going to see about this organization again. He hasn't told us anything about it. He talked about the chart and he looked at it and he said this and that about it, but he never did deal with what I said about it or tell me what I was trying to find out. Now then up here he said, you have here a board of directors, yes. But he said, you ought to move that down here. That it's a part of the home, that it's not an in between organization. Well, I want to know then Brother Deaver, Is this board here an in between organization between the churches and evangelism? Or shall we use the board down here and make it a part of evangelism? Will you? What do you have here, incorporated evangelism or do you have a corporation that provides evangelism? Just which is it? I want to know Brother Deaver, why this board here that provides evangelism for churches and the churches send, not to the board, but they send to the superintendent's office or some man designated by them, who spends it according to their directions, are operating through a human organization but up here, when they do the same thing in benevolence, are they not operating through an in between organization that doesn't exist only in Porter's imagination? Well, if this one up here exists in my imagination, this one exists in yours. What proves the reality of this but denies this one? What makes this imaginary up here but this a reality? Will he tell us? I have been asking him for three nights to give us something about that and he hasn't answered to this good hour. I want to know why one is in between and the other is not in between. And regarding Boles Home, he said—they don't come into existence—Porter said they don't come into existence when they incorporate. I said, not necessarily. Sometimes organizations do come into existence with the incorporation, Brother Deaver. I didn't say they never do. I said, not necessarily. Sometimes the organization exists first. And then in the case of Boles, it did exist first. They had an organization that provided for and operated the home, Boles Home, for a number of years before they ever took out a charter for it and the organization was already there. And when they incorporated, they incorporated the same board that was already operating. And the very same men that were incorporated, were already occupying the place of the board and directing the home. The organization was there, the group of men was already set up and the names given in the charter and the very same men were the men who were incorporated when they got a charter and that did not cone into existence with the charter—with the incorporation because it existed already. So I'm not opposing the mere fact of incorporation, I'm opposing the thing that's incorporated. I'm opposing that board of directors of it over there, that human organization set up to do the work that God gave the church to do. That's what I'm doing ; I'm opposing that human organization. Not the fact that it's incorporated or unincorporated. It's wrong regardless of whether it obtains a charter or not. You have a human organization doing the work of the church. I don't care whether you incorporate it or not, it's still there. And it's that human organization in between. And if this is in between down here, why isn't that up there?

All right, the lights again. Regarding the legal plans, he read from a statement there, the minimum requirements for child caring institutions, about the plan of operation. They must signify to the licensing board or the state agency that issues licenses for that sort of thing, a plan of their operation.

He said, well that's the same thing as a corporation—that's the same thing as a charter. They have to do that before they can get the charter don't they? Don't they do that before they get a charter? It's not the same thing that's there first. You said they have to do that before they can even start. You've got to give your plan to them before you start. If so, then your plan of operation is not your corporation and it's not the same thing as your charter. You are certainly wrong about that. And he said, you can't set up one without a charter and I'd like to see him try. Can't set up one without a charter. Well, the State Welfare Board at Austin, Texas said I could. And they defined a child caring institution that you said and they said included seven children. When it reaches the number seven, it becomes a child caring institution. And the statement I read from the State Welfare Board of Austin, that came direct in a letter to me, said that no person or association is required to obtain a charter or become incorporated in order to take care of orphans in the State of Texas. Brother Deaver says it is; there's a law to that effect. But the State Welfare Board did not know it. And it did not limit on this to religious organizations. He said they were talking about a congregation, a religious congregation. They mentioned that as one thing, then they went on and said that no person nor association, not only a religious congregation, but no person nor association is required to take a charter in the State of Texas to care for orphans. Didn't say just a religious congregation. No person nor association. And the Attorney General's office said that if there is any such law on the statute books of Texas, that they know nothing about it.

And he said the Lubbock Home (church) operates the children's home because it's incorporated and that serves for the home. And the lawyer who wrote the charter for Boles Home, says that that's a misconception of the Texas law. That when people think that the charter for the church authorizes them to operate a home like Boles Home and other homes like that, they have a misconception of the law—that that isn't so. The man who wrote the charter to the Boles Home is the man who made that statement.

Well, regarding the church corporation, he said, now we have to have a church incorporated. That you've got to have that and therefore that's just the same thing, a board of trustees. The purpose of that is to have a permanent trustee—just to hold the property in trust. They have no authority, at least they should have no authority to make any decisions or provisions for the church. They are simply set up as a trustee to hold property just as trustees hold property. And besides, I'm certain of the fact that there are some corporations and some charters for churches which are incorporated that I wouldn't endorse. I'm just sure of the fact if a corporation set up for a church is to provide for the church—to do for the church what Boles Corporation does and what missionary society corporations do in the work of benevolence and evangelism in the spiritual field and the work of the church, I would certainly oppose it just the same. I have a charter over here of a church out in California, in which that corporation sets up and actually removes elders whenever they wish and prescribes laws to govern the elders and set them aside when they want to. Will you endorse that Brother Deaver? Would you endorse that? The church out at Burlingame, California has a charter like that. That those men can actually set aside the elders; can remove any laws of the church at their pleasure. Now I wouldn't endorse that.

The missionary society, he said, does control churches if the church gets into it. They make decisions for them—they have to be—I gave you the chart of the C.R.A., the Christian Restoration Association. Which puts no pressure on churches whatsoever and it's parallel to what you have in Boles Home. And last night you said they are both missionary societies but they weren't, one of them was a benevolent society. And so they have the same arrangement. I'm wanting to know if the Southern Christian Association is not a human organization and is not an in between organization between the churches and benevolence, why is the Christian Restoration Association, set up for and on the same fashion, an in between organization between the churches and evangelism. Has he ever told us? No. He can see an in between organization when he thinks about mission work and evangelism but when he sees the same thing in the field of benevolence, he goes blind. It just doesn't exist; it's not there at all; it's only in your imagination. Well, if so, then the same thing with the other.

Well, he said, Brother Porter get this: The church is its own missionary society and the church is its own benevolent society but the church is not an orphan home. No, and I told you last night and give it to you again tonight that neither is the church a gospel meeting and neither is the church an automobile or a train. Did you have anything to say about it? The church is not an automobile. The church is not a bus. The church is not a train. But when the church buys or rents a bus to transport people to the worship and back home when the worship is over, whose work is it? Did the work of the church discontinue and cease when they bought the bus? Then the rest of it was the work of the bus and the bus driver and they took over and performed the function of the bus and the transportation agency? Is the church its own transportation agency? Is it? Well, why didn't he say something about it? Certainly the church is not an orphan home and the church is not a gospel meeting and the church is not a Bible class and the church is not a bus and the church is not an automobile and the church is not a train. But I believe that the church can make provision for a bus. That it can put a man on it, a gospel preacher, to send him over to catch a train to go to a place where a gospel meeting will be held. And that in doing that it becomes neither a bus nor a train for anything of that kind. So I'm just sure of the fact that the church can make provision for those who are in need and provide for their care without becoming a home.

His chart 59 that he put on the board last night, we might have that just now if you can give us his chart 59. We had something to say about that last night and I want to say something about it again. Now here he says: Does Porter believe that they are parallel? First item, right to exist, Boles Home and Missionary Society. Evangelism of the Missionary Society I suppose he means by the EA (?). All right, Boles Home and evangelism of the Missionary Society. Do they have a right to exist? Well, I said last night that neither of them has a right to exist to do the work of the church. He stated my answer like he states my answer on various other things. Even in writing, he has scarcely ever read the complete answer to the question I gave. He just reads to where he wants to and then he stops and leaves the rest of it off. He did that on the written answers I gave him last night. And then he wanted to know: Will you fellowship Boles Home? Yes or no. Fellowship the Missionary Society? Yes or no. If you believe they are parallel, you must fellowship both of them. Well, sauce for the goose is sauce for the gander, isn't it? Brother Deaver, didn't you say in the debate down there at Borger just a few weeks ago that the church is parallel to the Missionary Society? You didn't? Does somebody have the tape to that debate? If so, we might get the record played tomorrow somewhere. That the church is parallel to the Missionary Society. You said that the home which the church provides is parallel to the home which the Missionary Society provides. And that the church providing the home stands parallel to the Missionary Society that provides the home. And therefore, that being true, the homes are parallel and those and those which provide them parallel if you make the Missionary Society and the church parallel. Now, do you fellowship the church? If so, then you will have to fellowship the Missionary Society and that's why I said we stand together on it. All right, then in the third, individual support? Yes or no. I said not as under the present arrangement of it. If they continue as they are presently arranged and carried on, No. All right, then—can the church buy service? And I gave the same answer to that. I might put a clause in both of them if you want me to. I'll say yes and no to both of them. Does that satisfy you? Yes and no.

All right, lights again please. In chart 68 he gave this to show that the church may send to a home. Porter admits that a church may send to a home. Now he says, since the church sends to the home, then the church cannot be a home. The church and the home are not the same thing because the church sends to the home according to Porter. Well, the charter, you say, the corporation provides the home. Now when the church sends to the home, you say the church is one thing and the home is the other, then when the corporation provides the home, that proves the corporation one thing and the home the other. If not, why not, Brother Deaver? If it works in one case, why doesn't it in the other? The church sends to the home therefore the church is one thing and the home is something else if the church couldn't send to it. All right, the corporation provides the home therefore the corporation is one thing and the home is the other or the corporation couldn't provide it you see. Thanks Brother Deaver.

Now then, I want to look at that chart 68. Don't have time? Well, all right, we'll get to that in the speeches to follow. My time is up? All right, I thank you very kindly.

Fourth Night

Deaver's Third Affirmative

Brother Porter, Gentlemen Moderators, Brethren and Friends: While Brother Clements is getting my chart No. 72 ready, I'd like to remind you that I'm in the affirmative of the following proposition: *The scriptures teach that a church may contribute to Boles Home, Quinlan, Texas.* I don't know how a proposition could be more simply stated than is that. By the way of summarizing the things that have been discussed in the nights previous, I'd like to suggest to you that Brother Porter has made a number of vital admissions. Brother Porter has not made these admissions now mind you that I have on the chart with reference to Boles Home. But he has made them with reference to another home. He says that the church can send to an incorporated home that the home might provide the necessities and needs of orphan children and that this is one way that the church can meet its obligation. May I call your attention to the point here that Brother Porter made that was under this thought. He says you don't have to prove what your opponent does not deny. All right, in this connection, he has already admitted that a home can receive funds from a church and according to Brother Porter, then I don't have to prove that. He has admitted that the home can be incorporated. I don't have to prove it then according to his thinking. And he says the sending church can be incorporated. He recognizes in this case that the home is not a church; that the home is not an integral part of the church; the home is not managed by elders functioning as elders now, and the needs of an orphan child can thus adequately be met and that a church may thus meet its obligation to orphans by sending funds to this home. He recognizes that in this case where a church sends funds to an incorporated private home now, that there is no in between organization. And he says if your opponent admits a point, you don't have to prove it. He has made these admissions now with reference to my questions concerning a church sending to an incorporated private home. So far as I am concerned, those very admissions apply with equal force and value to Boles Home. And he denies it with reference to Boles Home. He has made all of these admissions and that's where we are so far then in the points of this discussion.

Now then, I need my chart No. 75 please. And this chart refers to what I have styled double talk or it's somewhat evasive in connection with Brother Porter's statements. And it proves out some things we said with reference to the previous charge now. In my answer to question number four, I believe it was on the second night, Brother Porter says that a church can arrange a home. A church can arrange a home and a church can send funds to this home which the church arranges and that the church selects this care of this home which is arranged by the church. Now then, here's the point that I'm after in this chart and Brother Porter will call for it when he comes before you. Is this home, Brother Porter which his church arranges now, a home? Do you recognize that it is a home? And is this home that's arranged here, an institution? Now as far as concerns the private home, we talked about a while ago, he has already admitted that that is a home. He has already admitted that that private home incorporated is an institution. And he has already admitted so far as concerns that private home incorporated, that the elders do not oversee that particular home. Now then, Brother Porter, with reference to this home which is arranged by the church here, I want to raise the question: Do the elders function as elders in overseeing that home? And may this home now, which is arranged by the church, be incorporated?

Brethren, here's the point in that, and you can see why I've called it the double talk here. If you press Brother Porter on the point that he has already admitted, that a church can send to a private home incorporated, he takes up the word private and he says yes, that's so. But we are discussing a home now that is arranged by the church. And so you can see the loop there, if you press him in connection with the incorporated private home, then he still has the liberty of going to "yes, but here's one arranged by the church." And so it's making a distinction between that private home incorporated and the home which the church can arrange. And so my questions are now directed to the point of drawing out that distinction in his mind. Just exactly, what is that distinction now, Brother Porter? Between the private home incorporated and this home now which the church may arrange? You say the church now, the elders there, can oversee this home. And they arranged that home and can that home be incorporated? All right, Brother Porter will deal with that; that's chart No. 75 Brother Porter.

Now my chart No. 66. And I want you to notice carefully here. These are points that have been developed thus far in the course of our discussion and I believe, show you that a great deal of good has been accomplished. Brother Porter's logic puts him actually in the position of upholding the Missionary Society. Brother Porter says the following two points are parallel. In No. 1—you have a church here, sending to or providing evangelism which involves the Missionary Society or a missionary corporation board. He says in this situation, that a board controls the evangelism. Now it's his position that when a church sends to Boles Home, since Boles Home is incorporated, that you have a benevolent corporation over that. But notice carefully, if you will, what Brother Porter upholds. He says that a church can send to a private home which is incorporated. And if the private home can be incorporated, and if the fact of the incorporation up here in case No. 2 produces a benevolent corporation, then it's certainly obvious that the corporation down here would do likewise. You would have the incorporation producing or bringing about a benevolent corporation board. If an incorporated home means here, a benevolent corporation board in control, then in the private home incorporated you'd have the same thing, a benevolent corporation board in control. And so he upholds this particular point however. He says this is parallel to the Missionary Society. No. 2 is parallel to No. 1 up here, but it's certainly obvious that this case is parallel to this. And if this is parallel to this, and this is apparently parallel to the Society, and if Brother Porter upholds this, then he is upholding the very thing that he says is parallel to the Society. And there's not a way under the sun around it. His logic puts him in the position of upholding the very thing that is parallel in his mind now, to the Missionary Society.

Now then, I'd like to have my chart No. 77. Brethren, I'd like to emphasize to you that this chart No. 77 is actually the very foundation of this entire discussion. Here is the entire debate so far as concerns what we've covered in it thus far. You have in this situation here, a Christian Church and the entire debate boils down to the point simply that Brother Porter refuses to admit an obvious fact. You have a Christian Church sending to a Missionary Society which is incorporated and the church over yonder incorporated, and then providing evangelism here. In the Baptist Church situation, Baptist Churches incorporated send to the Southern Baptist Convention which is incorporated and then which provides Buckner Home which is incorporated. Brother Porter contends this No. 1 case here and so do I. Brother Porter contends this No. 2 case and so do I. You've got the Missionary Society in this one. You've got the Southern Baptist Convention in this one. Both of them in between organizations. He condemns them and we stand together on that point. But Brother Porter upholds this case. He says a church of Christ incorporated can send to a private home incorporated and in that case you do not have an in between organization. When a church of Christ incorporated sends to a private home incorporated, so that the needs or orphan children might be adequately supplied, he says you don't have an in between organization there and that's perfectly all right. Brother Porter says that's all right now. But in the case down here, the church of Christ incorporated sending to Boles Home which is incorporated too, so that the needs of orphans might be adequately supplied, you don't have an in between organization there, but he condemns this. He condemns this. Notice carefully, he condemns this up here; he condemns this and both of us do that—standing together on that point. He upholds this particular point here and he condemns the church sending to Boles Home. He condemns No. 4 here on the ground that it's parallel to No. 1. He condemns No. 4 here on the ground that it's parallel to No. 2. When the truth of the matter is No. 4 is not parallel to 1 or 2 but it's parallel to No.3, the very thing that he upholds. And brethren, I'm here to tell you that if you can't see that, there's not a thing on earth I can do. Not one thing. That's the entire debate. That's all he has had to say. There's an in between organization. Well, you have it up here and you have it here but in the case which Brother Porter upholds, you don't have it. And in the case which he upholds and in which you don't have that in between organization, you have a situation to which the church sending to Boles Home is exactly parallel. He condemns this because he assumes it's parallel to 1 and 2, when actually it's parallel to No. 3. And it's not parallel to No. 1 and 2. That's the entire debate.

All right, now then please, my chart No. 74. Brother Porter has come to the ridiculous position of assuming that God has put elders in the position of overseeing two institutions. And that's a little bit surprising. Elders of the church of the Lord, the Bible says, have been put over the church. The Bible makes a distinction between a church and a home. But Brother Porter now is in the position of saying that elders can function as elders over a home. Will you notice please? God put elders over a church. All right, but he knows perfectly well that the needs of an orphan child cannot be adequately met without its having a home. But he says that if the church must provide a home or if a church has an obligation to orphan children, and if their needs involve a home, then that the church may direct or elders may oversee that home. These are all home matters, would you notice carefully, in connection with the needs of an orphan, these are home matters. An orphan child needs secular education. Well, that involves elementary school, high school, college and on the same principle as here would involve even a university inclusive of a law school, a medical school, engineering school and such like. Now why in the world criticize the church in its relationship to a college and then take a position that puts the elders in the oversight of that very thing? Over here a child needs medical care and according to his reasoning, you could put elders in charge of a clinic and a hospital because that's a need of an orphan. But again, a child needs recreation. And why criticize the church of the Lord in recreation matters, and then take a position that puts elders of the church in the position of providing recreation? These are home matters. And again, he takes the position that puts elders in oversight of providing food here. Why fuss about drinking a cup of coffee in the vestibule or the basement, and then take a position that puts elders in the position of providing food for the orphans? Then again, why criticize the church in business, and then come along and take the position that puts the elders in the business of running a farm and a dairy? These are home matters. And the Bible talks about a home and the Bible talks about a church. And the Bible says God put elders over the church and did not put elders over a home. These are needs of orphan children. The church has an obligation to orphans. What can it do? Well, it can't function as a home. It can provide a home and the elders oversee that provision. They can oversee the sending of that fund or the funds. But the Bible nowhere authorizes the elders to function as elders over a home.

Now I'd like to have my chart No. 64 please. As you notice this chart, I'd simply like to impress upon your mind the definite fact that there is not a home among us being provided by a church or by churches, which Brother Porter will endorse—orphan home I mean—which Brother Porter will endorse. Furthermore, he's not attempting to start one and in the third place he can't start one because when he does, it's going to have to meet the same legal objections that he is opposing now. There isn't one. He can't start one. And he is not trying to start one. And if he should try, he would run into the very same objections that he is making against Boles Home. And yet he knows that the needs of an orphan child cannot be met without having a home. Now that's the situation.

I'd like to have Brother Porter's chart No. C right quickly. In Brother Porter's affirmative, he had the position now that the church is all sufficient and definitely and certainly that's right. It is sufficient in evangelism, edification, and in benevolence. That's certainly true. But Brother Porter also had the position now that when a church sends funds, it delegates its work. Remember his proposition. When you send your money, you delegate your work. That's the very point that I was denying. But on this chart he has: The Jerusalem church can send to the Antioch church and the Antioch church sends to Philippi and Philippi to Thessalonica and Thessalonica to Achaia. Notice what you've got brethren. Jerusalem sends to Antioch. All right, that means Jerusalem delegates her work to Antioch, according to Brother Porter's logic now. That means that Antioch then sends to Philippi and her own work is delegated plus the work that Jerusalem delegated to her—she sent it on to Philippi. Philippi sends to Thessalonica. Thessalonica delegates her own work then by the sending of those funds plus the work that had been delegated to her by these churches and Philippi sent it on over here and on down the line until Achaia gets the shifting of the work all the way down the line. Anybody under the sun ought to be able to see that. If he is right, that a church delegates its work when it sends funds then he has established a super-cumulative sponsoring church. Look what you've got out of the case. My, my, that's worse than Brother Finley got into.

All right, notice this passage right here, by the way. I have listened time and time again as brethren used Philippians 4:15,16 to prove that a church sent directly to Paul. You notice Brother Porter uses it to show that Philippi sent to Thessalonica and he has a church here and a church here. I asked Brother Porter, where in the world is the orphan home then, which you say can exist and can be incorporated and to which the church can send? Where is it on this chart? The church is all sufficient but you say a home can be provided, now where is it? All right, Brother Porter has taken the position now that it belongs inside one of these circles. It will have to be inside one of the rectangles rather, in connection with the church. But a church can send to a home, mind you which is incorporated and not vitiate against the all sufficiency of the church in the field of benevolence if you'll let it be Brother Porter's home. But if a church sends to Boles Home for the same purpose, a home that meets the legal demands, then you're violating the all sufficiency of the church. It's just a matter of who does it. It's not a matter of what's done at all.

All right, now Brother Porter's chart No. T. I don't need to see it but let me mention a thing to you, a thing which Brother Porter knows. He's made a remark or two about it but if he'd actually thought that I said—admit what he knew that I said, he'd have been pressing me on it still. He knew perfectly well that I made a misstatement with reference to his chart No. 2 and that's the reason he hasn't pressed the matter and I knew that. When Brother Porter introduced this chart, he referred to two missionary societies, you remember he had them. And I thought that what he was referring to was two different societies in connection with the Christian Church. And hence, when I replied to it, I said there were two societies but I upheld no such society. And the fact of the matter is, these points which he used to establish the fact that these were different societies, didn't prove that they were societies or missionary societies at all. According to Brother Porter's reasoning along that line, I can prove—I can prove that an incorporated church is parallel to the Southern Baptist Convention. Brother Porter had a missionary society in connection with the Christian Church and then he had some points over here in connection with the Morrilton Home and he said they are both societies but his reasoning was: Here you've got a name and over here you've got a name; but over here you have a corporation and here you have a corporation; here you have a charter and here you have a charter. According to that reasoning, you can prove that an incorporated church is parallel to the Southern Baptist Convention. You've got a name over here and you've got a name over here; you've got a charter over here and you've got a charter over here; you've got bylaws here and you've got bylaws here; you've got incorporation here and you've got incorporation here. His reasoning is not worth a dime. That's not the thing that makes it a missionary society.

According to the same reasoning, you could prove that an incorporated church is parallel to the *Gospel Guardian*. According to that reasoning, you could prove that the *Gospel Guardian* is parallel to the Southern Baptist Convention. Over here you have a name and here you have a charter; here you have bylaws and here you've got bylaws; here you've got incorporation and here you've got incorporation—both of them; and according to that reasoning, if its any good at all,—and it's not—then the *Gospel Guardian* is parallel to the Southern Baptist Convention. That's not the thing that makes it a missionary society.

All right, Brother Porter referred to the differences between Boles home and the Lubbock home. And basically, there is no difference. In one case, the elders a church select themselves to constitute the legal board. In the other case, the elders of a church select men other than themselves the board. Both cases, you've got a charter; both cases you've got bylaws; both cases you've got boards; both cases, you've got incorporation. Basically, there is no difference. That is somewhat distressing to me to listen at brethren try to make that distinction between them. I know that in one case the men refer to themselves as elders when it's my firm conviction that they are not functioning in the capacity of elders and that's my only objection to what they are doing. He said, do you endorse a home under elders? Brother Porter, I endorse the organization; I endorse the work; I do not endorse the title by which the men are known. And then again, I want to ask Brother Porter do you endorse that? Do you endorse that home under the elders now? He quibbled regarding my statement that he agreed with the major premise of my syllogism, yet he never did tell you. Brother Porter is an artist at that kind of a thing. He quibbled about the fact that I said that he agreed with my major premise. He never did deny it. He does agree with it but he sought to leave a doubt. He just quibbled a little bit about it but he doesn't disagree with it. He knows the premise is right—the major premise. But he raised that question: I didn't say that Brother Deaver.

All right, in an attempt to deal with my argument on the constituent elements, he referred to Bethel Baptist Church, and you can give Brother Porter credit for being original. Down at Lufkin, Abilene, and Houston, it's all Tabernacle Baptist Church. Now it's Bethel here. He was referring to my argument on constituent elements and I'd like for you to notice carefully here. He says the word Bethel is a scriptural term, that's right. But it's not a scriptural term with reference to the total situation he was trying to establish. Is it a scriptural term with reference to a scriptural designation for a church? That's what he came out with. Now is Baptist a scriptural designation with reference to a church or is that scriptural part of a scriptural designation of a total situation, of a scriptural designation for a church? Baptist is a scriptural term. But with reference to a church? These don't even touch his total situation. But in my proposition, every one of the component parts has a direct bearing upon the totality of my situation.

All right, he referred to Buckner Home now and may I say to you, I don't know how in the world Brother Porter would make a speech or would have made one in this debate if it hadn't have been for Buckner Home and the Missionary Society. Brother Porter, if you would just simply make the same arguments against Boles Home that you are making against them or that you would make against them, I'd appreciate it a whole lot more. You don't have to tell me this is parallel to that. Just tell me what's wrong with it. Make the same argument against Boles Home that you would make against those things. Just to say it's parallel to something doesn't mean an argument. All right, and then again, he says do you—he said that I said a church couldn't send to a Baptist Home. Brother Porter, I didn't make that statement. I'd say that it would certainly depend on the situation. But I've never said that a church could not under any circumstances send to a Baptist Home—A Baptist private home. All right, there are some homes that involve members of the church, to which a church cannot send.

My position is that all the homes which properly let—or supply the needs of orphan children, are homes to which a church may make a donation. That's my position exactly. And then he said, concerning Buckner Home and Boles Home, why is one right and the other wrong? Simply because the Buckner Home is an integral part of the Southern Baptist Convention and in connection with Boles Home you don't have any such thing. And he says, in connection with his chart No. 25, if the Missionary Society is in between, why isn't the board in between? Well the home which the Missionary Society would provide would have to have a board, and if the board means an in between organization, then in that situation would you—or rather, you would have two in between organizations—the society itself and the one brought into being by the board there. You'd have two of them. The Missionary Society is separate and apart. It's a distinct thing of itself. The board of Boles Home is a parent factor—it's a part of the home. And that's the exact difference. It is not the fact of having a board that brings into existence a separate organization and that point Brother Porter admits. He said Boles Home operated for a while without being incorporated. Brother Porter, you said Boles Home operated for a while without being incorporated. And yet you continue to argue that it's the corporation that provides it. It operated for a while without the corporation but it's the corporation that provides it. Brother Porter, when it operated without that incorporation, did you endorse it then? He said I'm opposing that board of directors. That's the statement last night, I'm opposing that board of directors. He has already made the statement that in order to have a divine home, you've got to have a husband and wife. I asked him the question the other night—the third night—if the board of trustees at Boles Home consisted of a husband and wife, would you still object? And he said, a husband and wife as a board of directors to do a brotherhood work would not change the arrangements. That's not his objection. At least, that's not the only one. You can put a husband and wife down there and he is still going to oppose it and he jumped the gun here and went back to cooperation. It's a brotherhood work there. I oppose it, you can't have a divine home unless you've got a husband and wife. Well, if we put a husband and wife down there, will you still oppose it? Yes sir. There's no way under the sun to fix it so Brother Porter won't oppose it.

All right, he criticized the idea that the same corporation could be used for both the church and the Home at Lubbock. Here's the statement from Brother John White along that line. He says the church itself is a corporate body—this was effective several years ago. Since the church already is a corporate body, it is not necessary that the home be separately incorporated. And that's the very thing that they told me down at the Department of Public Welfare. That they can use the incorporation for both purposes. He can criticize it if he wishes. He admits that it's all right for a church to have trustees to hold property and he's right. He admits that it's all right for a church to be incorporated and he's right. He said a church is not an orphan home and he's right on that and that's the very thing I've been trying my very best to get him to see. The church is not an orphan home but an orphan needs a home. And the church can provide that home but the church can't be that home.

Then on my chart No. 59, I said Brother Porter, are they really parallel? You've taken the position now that Boles Home is parallel to the evangelism that is provided by the Missionary Society. If they are, this question: Do you fellowship those of us who support Boles Home? And do you fellowship those who support the evangelism of the Missionary Society? Do you know what his answer was? Yes and no. That didn't help me one bit. Yes and no. But if they are parallel and if he can say yes in any sense, then he's got to say yes in both senses. And so there's a sense then in which he would fellowship those who support the Missionary Society or there's a sense in which he doesn't fellowship those who support Boles Home, one or the other. That's the reason Brother Porter wouldn't here answer that question.

All right, just a word or two about Brother Porter on automobiles, trains and buses. Brother Porter has argued that elders can function as elders over a home. I call his attention to the fact that God put elders over the church. And that, since the church and the home are separate institutions, for him to say that elders could oversee a home is to make a home an integral part of the church and to attempt to put elders over something other than the church. His argument tends to make a home out of the church. His reply was that a church could provide an automobile, a bus or a train without becoming an automobile, bus or a train. Well, when a church provides an automobile, a bus or a train, it's functioning as a teaching organization.

And which function is authorized by the Bible. The church, in this case, hasn't become an automobile or a bus or a train but has become a teaching organization which is authorized. But if God placed elders over the church and if elders have been placed as elders over a home, they are engaged in a function which is not authorized. The command to go teach authorizes the use of an automobile and a bus and a train. But the command to visit the fatherless does not authorize elders to function over something other than the church. Brother Porter would have to conclude that because the church is authorized to teach, and that since an automobile can be used in teaching, that elders can oversee an automobile industry, and that since a bus can be used in teaching, that therefore elders can oversee a bus company, and that since a train can be used in teaching, that therefore elders could operate a railroad. That's exactly his conclusion—that would have to be it. Elders could operate a railroad since the command to go authorizes the use of a train. Elders are over the church, Brother Porter. The church has souls to save. This involves teaching. And elders can oversee the church. And the church must visit the fatherless. This involves a home for orphans. Elders can provide a home just like they can provide a bus but they cannot function as a home just like they cannot oversee a bus company.

Then Brother Porter on the Bible class. He had somewhat to say along that line. And these points that I've dealt with now are simply dealing with what he had to say in his last speech on last evening. Brother Porter has taken the position that an orphan home is parallel to a Bible class. That elders oversee a Bible class and that elders can oversee a home. It should be pointed out that with reference to a Bible class, elders are overseeing a teaching situation, and not a Bible class as such. Let him make out of that what he will. Suppose a particular class is made up of six year olds. They are not Christians. Do elders oversee these persons? Or do they oversee a teaching situation? Now suppose a class is made up of two year olds. Are elders overseers of these persons or are elders in oversight of that teaching arrangement which is authorized by the Bible? Since elders are over the church, to say that elders oversee these persons—these two year olds, is to bring about infant membership in the church. Just to say that elders function as elders over a home, is to say that they have oversight of persons who are not Christians. Unless he takes the position that you can't have anybody in that home excepting a person who is a Christian. Brother Porter, as I said, you haven't told us that yet.

Elders oversee the church and can provide a home for orphans but there is no authority for elders to function as a home. Brethren and friends and neighbors, let me suggest to you that there are three basic errors, as I conceive the situation, upon which Brother Porter has been laboring. He labors upon the understanding—the assumption that there is an in between organization. He's built his entire case upon the assumption that when a church sends funds to Boles Home, that there is a benevolent organization standing between the church and the home. That's his assumption. That's all he has had to say in the entire discussion. Any such organization as that does not exist. He cannot give you the name and address of it. I told him the first night, and I've told him every night since, Brother Porter, if you'll just tell me where that in between oorganization is, the name of it and the address of it, I'll send it a check—a $25.00 check, if you'll just give me the assurance that Boles Home would never get it. I just want to prove to you that it will come back and that there is no such thing as that in between organization which you imagine.

He fails to recognize the distinction the Bible makes between the church and the home. He says now there's an in between organization. And that's a basic error. I'd like for Brother Clements to get my chart No. 44 ready please. And I would like to suggest to you briefly in the closing moments of this first speech, the Bible distinction between the church and the home. Brother Porter simply needs to recognize that. He's in the position now of having elders oversee a home—function in the capacity in which God placed parents. All right, notice carefully now. Answer these questions: Are these particular matters functions of a home or a church, Brother Porter? No. 1, to provide food, clothing, shelter, discipline and education and medical care—is that a church function or then is it a home function? If it's a church function, give the scriptures please. Over here, is it a home function or a church function to secure possession and control of children? Church function or home? And so far as concerns this matter—to adopt children—is that the function of a church or of a home? And so plan for custody of these children—is that the function of a church or home? They give such care and guidance as expected of natural parents—is that a function of a church or a home? And then to acquire property and other things necessary to meet the needs of those children.

Fourth Night

Porter's Third Negative

Brethren Moderators, Brother Deaver, Ladies and Gentlemen: I appreciate the privilege of appearing before you again to make a further investigation of the things before us in this discussion as they concern the work of benevolence for the church. I appreciate the speech that Brother Deaver has just made and the effort that he put forth to sustain his proposition that it is scriptural or the scriptures teach that a church may contribute to Boles Home, Quinlan, Texas. Now to a number of things I want to call you attention—a few things regarding some matters I didn't quite get to last night because I had to deal somewhat with the last negative speech the night before, so I shall get to those and then go on with the speech to which you've just listened. But in the first place, I want to use my chart Y as we had this up last night regarding the matter of church sending to a home and the thing that Brother Deaver said about that.

We have here, as we had last night, the idea of a church sending to a home. And Brother Deaver said, now since a church sends to a home, then this proves that the church is not the home. All right, so notice that now, the church sends to a home; if the church sends to a home, then the church is one thing and the home is something else. Otherwise the church could not send to it. So Brother Deaver says this proves the church is not the home. All right, in the second place, a corporation provides a home. All right, if a church sends to a home, and it means the church is one thing and the home is something else, if a corporation provides a home, then would the corporation and the home be the same thing? How could a corporation provide a home if the corporation is the home any more than a church could send to a home if the church is the home and so on. Now then, does this prove a corporation is not the home and if not, why not?

All right, we'll pass on then from that to some other matters. And let us have the lights for just a little while again. And he brought this up again in his closing moments of the speech he has just made. He is wanting to know where to send to the corporation so that Boles Home would not get it. He wants to send a check for $25.00 over there to the corporation and wants their address so he can send it to them so the home won't get it. Well, I suppose you would do that Brother Deaver just like you would send to the corporation for Buckner Home so Buckner Home wouldn't get it. Do you think you could send a check to Buckner Home so Buckner Home won't get it? To Buckner Corporation? If you send a check to the Buckner Corporation, why of course, the check is going to go from the corporation on to the home just like it would if you sent it to Boles Corporation. But he is arguing all the time that Buckner Corporation reaches back the other way to the Southern Baptist Convention and not to the home at all. According to him, if you send it to the Boles Corporation, it goes to the home because it's an integral part of the Southern Baptist Convention (sic). Therefore, if you send a check to Buckner Corporation, instead of it going to the home it would go to the Southern Baptist Convention. Because it is an integral part of that Convention you see according to Brother Deaver. And everybody knows it won't go that direction at all, it will go to Buckner Home.

And now I want my chart X Brother Shaw, regarding the matter of the function of the church and the home. You know Brother Deaver has been claiming, of course, the function of the church is one thing and the function of the home is another and so we had this up last night; the function of the church is to provide the money and the function of the home is to provide the care. Therefore, he says the church cannot provide the care; the church cannot do this; it cannot feed, clothe, bathe or spank the children and so on. And it cannot do this because if so, it invades the function of the home and therefore the church becomes the home. And since he says the function of the church is to provide the money, the pennies, the nickels, the dimes and the dollars, then the home cannot do this without invading the function of the church and therefore, the home would become the church. According to his reasoning, in this case the church becomes the home if it performs something that's function of the home, then if the home performs something that's a function of the church, then the home becomes a church according to that. What did he say about it? All right, he said their functions overlap, I thought you ought to know that. I did. That's what I was trying to get you to say. And that's what I was hoping you would find out; that their functions overlap. Now then, I want to know Brother Deaver: Can they overlap both ways or doesn't this overlap here? And he says the home can do this because their duties and their functions overlap. Well, when their functions overlap does it include this down here or is it limited unto the dimes, dollars, pennies and nickels? Just where and how far can they overlap?

All right, now then the lights back please. Regarding the divine home established by marriage, he said, according to that, Martha and Mary and Lazarus had no home. Certainly they had a place where they lived and they were at home as used in two different senses: a place where one dwells and oftentimes used in the other sense referring to a divine organization that God ordained—the marriage relationship by which the home was established originally. And he said, upon that basis, a widow with six children couldn't have a home. Well now, suppose that there's a widow and she has six children and that very likely there was a marriage relationship back there and that she had a husband, and that a home evidently was established by reason of the marriage relationship and the children are the product of that marriage. At least that would be true if she were a widow. All right.

Again he said, regarding Buckner Home, that the Southern Baptist Convention stands between the Buckner Home and the—rather between the church and the home—that you have in their Southern Baptist convention that you don't have with Boles. But it just so happens that Buckner Home was not established by the Southern Baptist Convention. And furthermore, that the home was operated a good long while and is still operated under its own charter—it has a charter of its own—and the charter says not one word about the Southern Baptist Convention. It was set up by a group of men, members of a Baptist Church, they set it up originally by Mr. Buckner himself, and later was taken over by members of the Baptist Church just as Boles Home was set up. When it became incorporated, at least when it was incorporated, when it became a corporation, and therefore occupies exactly the same place. And you don't have to send to the Southern Baptist Convention to get a donation to Buckner Home. That absolutely is not necessary, they can send to the Buckner Corporation and reach the home. And all he has had to say about the Southern Baptist Convention being in there just doesn't do him any good whatsoever.

And he said last night, now Deaver does not say, "Out you go." I said in view of what he said about being only one way you can do it, we don't require you to do it this way; you can do it some other way if you want to. And I said, yes, but if we don't do it your way, you'll say, "Out you go." And he said, "Well, Deaver doesn't say that." Brother Deaver, didn't you say over at Buena Vista just a few days ago, that those elders over there ought to repent and confess to the congregation or resign because they had stopped their contributions to Boles Home? And that they had sinned and they ought to repent of it? What does that mean but "out you go"? And if you don't believe it means "out you go," just take a look at what's happening over the brotherhood. Why are men being disfellowship and quarantined? Because they are not doing it his way. If they are not saying "out you go," we don't have to worry about the fellowship matter. He had that chart up there again a while ago, and we've dealt with it two or three times, that whether you will fellowship us and fellowship the Missionary Society or not. We don't have to worry about the fellowship question. Brethren who stand with him have already taken care of it. We don't have to worry about that. They've taken care of it already and we've been disfellowship all over the nation. So we don't have to worry about that situation at all.

And regarding what he said on the chart as I used from the debate with Hathaway, he said, we were not discussing orphan homes when he said he would not endorse something with a president and a secretary and so on, we were discussing Bible classes. Yet, you also said, I will not endorse "anything." Not only the Bible class; you said, I will not endorse anything or uphold anything that has its own president, and its own secretary. That's what he said. He didn't say just the Bible class, he said "anything."

Now I want Deaver's chart No. 72. He used it last night and again to-night. I didn't quite get to it last night so he brought it up again tonight. We want to look at this chart No. 72 of Brother Deaver's. Here he says there is nothing left for him to do; you don't have to prove what the opponent does not demand. And so he has a lot of things here he says Porter admits. And some of them have been matters twisted around but we will just let it go at that and just suppose that Porter does admit it. And there on No. 9, he says Porter admits that there's no in between organization. He said he didn't admit that about Boles Home but he admitted that about some other home. Well then, you are putting Porter here as admitting the very thing that we are contending for and the very thing that's the very center of this debate. Porter does not admit that there is no in between organization where Boles Home is concerned and that's where we're debating and that's what the issue is tonight. He said that there is no such thing and I've been proving that there is. I admit no such thing. Now let us have the lights again.

Concerning those legal demands that we had last night. He referred to them again a while ago, that legal demands are such that Porter hasn't any home and he couldn't set up one if he wanted to because if he started one, he would find out he would have to set up the very same thing we have at Boles. And so he said last night that you can't operate a home without getting an incorporation and getting a charter. And I showed that the Attorney General's office said that it's not true and that the Welfare Department down at Austin, Texas, said that no person or association, much less a religious organization, just no kind of association or not any person wishing to establish or operate a child caring agency in the State of Texas is required to get a charter, or to be incorporated. And yet he comes back and tries to prove that it is after they said it's not. And so he read a statement from the minimum standards for child caring institutions and that statement was this: The agency or institutions shall be legally organized and its objects and purposes shall be stated in its charter's articles of incorporation. So he is saying now that shall means it must have because they defined the word "shall" to mean that its mandatory. And so it's mandatory—they must have these matters and the matter of charters and incorporation. But that isn't all it said. It said that purposes and plans or objects and purposes shall be expressly stated in its charter's articles of incorporation, statutes, constitutions, or other published material. Does that say they have to have a charter and incorporation? No. No, either charters or articles of incorporation or statutes or constitutions or other published material. Why didn't you tell us about that Brother Deaver? The very last expression shows they don't have to have the charter and don't have to have the articles of incorporation, they don't have to have statutes, they don't have to have a constitution; just any published material that states their purposes and plans. That's all they require. And so he misrepresented and misapplied all of the very thing he quoted from the Minimum Standards for a Child Caring Agency in the State of Texas.

Now then, I want to use my chart No. Z. And you might get chart I ready. Here we have some comparisons and this at the top of this chart is Brother Deaver's chart that he used last night, chart No. 68. And in care of orphans, he has there the church sending to a home and he says, first the home is needed and second, it is authorized. Then in preaching the gospel, the church sending to a missionary society and he says that first, it is not needed and second, it's unauthorized. Well, whether Brother Deaver realized it or not, he paralleled the home and the missionary society on that chart. He has there the church parallel to the church; the church sending to the home;

the church sending to the missionary society and makes the home and the missionary society parallel in the chart. I don't believe he believes that but he has it pictured that way on his chart. And so the home is needed and the home is authorized. And I'll certainly agree with him on that. I agree that sometimes the home is needed and sometimes we need a home in which to be cared for ourselves. And that such is authorized and I agree with him that a missionary society is not needed and it's not authorized—is unauthorized. That doesn't represent the issue in this debate at all. Here's the picture down here in the care of orphans and the preaching of the gospel. Let us look at the one down at the bottom first. The church sends to a missionary society and the missionary society does the work of evangelism. And up there the church sends to a benevolent society and the benevolent society performs the work of benevolence to the home. Now then, we have church parallel to church, we have home parallel to evangelism, we have benevolent society parallel to the missionary society. And here we have: the home is needed and the home is authorized, but the benevolent society is not needed and evangelism is authorized, but the missionary society is not needed and the missionary society is unauthorized. Therefore, let's have the things which are needed and the things which are authorized and abolish those things that are not needed and are not authorized. The evangelism is needed just as much as the home. The evangelism is authorized just as much as the home. The missionary society is authorized just as much as the benevolent society. Neither of them is authorized so blot them both out and leave what we have authority for and what we need. Thank you.

And now then, the next chart I. Here I ask the question: Are all these divine? Over on the left hand, two Christians form the home by reason of the God ordained marriage relationship. And over here we have two Baptists forming a home by the same process. And in such we have a husband and wife, and a child. And for some reason the home is destroyed in both cases. And then over here on the left hand where two Christians have formed a home and the home has been destroyed and the child has been left. Seven Christians set up a corporation to operate Boles Home. And over here this home is destroyed by reason of death and the child is left. And nine Baptists decide to restore that home and they form Buckner Corporation to provide Buckner Home. Now then, we have on the one hand a corporation providing Boles Home and the other hand a corporation providing Buckner Home. And I ask the question: Now are these divine and are churches of Christ obligated to support both? Now he tries to put the Southern Baptist

Convention in between here but that isn't so. Southern Baptist Convention had surely nothing to do with setting up Buckner Home. Buckner Home was established and in operation under its own charter, and therefore, the Southern Baptist Convention did not set it up. And the corporation provided the home and provides the home now just as the corporation does the same at the Boles Home. Now I want to know if they are all divine organizations or if they are all divine. Let him tell us about it.

Now I want chart 32—No. 32. Here the Christian is. Where is the end? Down here Christians hold a mass meeting and decide to build an institutional orphan home, set up, an institutional home, under a board of directors from various congregations, for the care of the needy. And this is to be supported by the churches. And then suppose another group of Christians hold another mass meeting to decide to build these organizations: A Christian college under a board of directors from various congregations to teach the Bible; a Gospel Press under a board of directors from various congregations to advertise the church; a grocery company under a board of directors from various congregations to feed the hungry, and a hospital under a board of directors from the various congregations to take care of the sick; and a drug company with a board of directors from various congregations to supply the remedies. Now then, if this over here can be supported by the church, then why not this and this and this and this and this? And where is the end? Where would there be a stopping place? All right thank you.

Let us have the lights again. On chart 72, which I have already dealt with, was the first that he gave us. And then he brought up chart 75, double talk, that the church arranges the home. And so he had some double talk here about the matter he said. Chart 75. And he put that chart up and said, Is this the home? Is this home an institution? Is the private home, which you uphold a home? Is the private home incorporated, which you uphold an institution? Do the elders function as elders and oversee the private home which you uphold? Do elders functioning as elders, oversee this home? May this home be incorporated? Well, he has the church here sending funds to the home which arranges and directs its care. And he says, is this the home? Yes, this is the home. Is this home an institution? Not if you mean by that an organization, a body of men set up as a group to govern it. No not that, if that's what you had reference to as an institution. And third, is the private home incorporated, which you uphold a home? I don't know of any private home that is incorporated and if it were to become incorporated, it might cease to be private. I do not know what the law would require in a case of that kind, I never heard of one. But at any rate, it would be a home but at the same time, you might have a corporation to provide a home like you have in the case of Boles. And fourth, is the private home which you uphold an institution. I certainly would not uphold any institution set up by man. Now if the private home you mean is the private home that God ordained—an institution—yes, it's a divine organization. And certainly we recognize the fact that God ordained that marriage relationship and that brought it into being. But Boles doesn't have that. That isn't the situation down at Boles at all, although he says the board stands *en loco parentis* to the home. I don't know where the *en loco* mother part of it comes in. They are all men. And again, do elders functioning as elders oversee the private home which you uphold? No, I've never said that elders could oversee a private home—an organization that God ordained. Elders are over one organization. But when they make an arrangement for a place to feed and clothe somebody, that's not an organization set up at all, any more than you have an organization when they teach a Bible class or conduct a gospel meeting. And, may this home be incorporated? There would certainly be no need of any home of that kind being incorporated because it's not an institution in the first place. It's not an organization and I don't suppose you could incorporate something that didn't have something set up in the form of an organization or had become an organization of some kind.

Now then, chart 66 he gave, the Missionary Society, in connection with chart 25. And chart 66—I think I have it here somewhere—I may have left it over there. Anyway, was it 76? Then I made the notation wrong—chart 76. All right, chart 76. And Porter's logic puts him in the position of upholding the Missionary Society. Porter says the following is parallel: The church sends to evangelism—let us have that on the screen please, his chart No. 76. This is made in the contemplation of a reply to my chart No. 25. We have this here: The church sending to evangelism under a missionary corporation or board that controls the evangelism. And a church sending to an orphan home under the control of a board or benevolent corporation that controls and directs that. So, I had that pictured on my chart and I said, "Now if this is an in between organization when the church sends to evangelism, why wouldn't this be?" And Brother Deaver admitted last night, if the church sends to the place of evangelism or the field of evangelism, to some person that had been selected by the board to spend the money under their direction, they would be doing the work through a Missionary Society. All right, on the same basis, the church sends the money to an orphan home—he says it doesn't go to the board; it goes to the home—but he admits that the home or the superintendent of the home, whoever has charge of it, must spend it under the direction of the board. And that being true, they work through the board just as much as they do up there, and so you have the same organization in between. And I said the same thing if it's a private home. If you have a private home down here in which orphans are to be cared for and the church sends to that home and that's controlled by a benevolent corporation or board over there that provides and controls that, you would have the same situation. Yes, I suppose so, but I'm not defending that sort of thing at all. Not at all. So, if you send the same thing up here—and I want to know Brother Deaver, if this is parallel to this, as you say it is, then why isn't this parallel to both of them? You have the same sort of arrangement; if these two are parallel, what's wrong with that one up there that it's not parallel also?

All right, let us have the lights again. Now the questions which I gave Brother Deaver a while ago: 1. Is the money spent in the operation of Boles Home, spent without the approval of the board of directors or under their direction with their approval? You know, he has been arguing that it doesn't go to the board, it goes to the home you see and therefore it's not through a board. Well, his answer is: The money is spent under their direction and with their approval. There you are, the very thing that I had pictured on the chart. He admits now that it's so. Even though it doesn't go directly to them, that they cannot spend it in the home except under their direction and with their approval. That's exactly what the charter says. 2. What makes Boles Home a divine organization and Buckner Home a human organization? He said, "You assume my position regarding Buckner. Keep in mind that it is an integral part of the Southern Baptist Convention. Then when you send a contribution to the Buckner Corporation, it goes to the Southern Baptist Convention instead of going to the home, you see."

Now isn't that something? Isn't that something? He said, You assume my position regarding Buckner. Well, I assumed that you thought it was a human organization. Was I wrong? Am I wrong in my assumption? If I am, tell me so. 3. Which is the corporation in connection with Boles Home: the board of directors that provides the home or the matron, cook, janitor, children, and other personnel that live there? He says, "The corporation extends to all within its benefits." The seven men of the board stand in the parent relationship to the children legally. And so he has the children incorporated; he has the cook incorporated; he has the janitor incorporated; and I suppose everything out there incorporated; they all make up the corporation. And if you are working for the Chrysler Motor Company, why you are incorporated.

All right, 4. In the incorporation of Broadway church, only five of the elders compose the board of directors, but there are seventeen elders of the church. Do the other twelve elders have any oversight of the Lubbock Home? He says, "In the eyes of the State, the Board of Directors oversee the home." The scriptures authorize elders functioning as elders, to serve in the oversight of only one institution. All right, so then he is just saying that those other twelve elders have no oversight of the home. And they have been misrepresenting the thing to the brotherhood all these years because they've been saying that its under the direct supervision of the elders of the Broadway Church. And yet it isn't. The twelve of them would have nothing at all to do with it. Only five of them were involved and they compose the board in the corporation and the other twelve elders have no connection with it whatsoever, according to Brother Deaver. Let the Lubbock brethren explain this to the brotherhood from whom they've been soliciting contributions under the claim that it was being operated by the elders of the church.

5. Why is the Christian Restoration Association an organization that actually exists between the church and the work, but the Southern Christian Association is one that exists only in my imagination? He said, "The Christian Restoration Association is an ecclesiasticism." I suppose then a thing has to be an ecclesiasticism in order to exist. "And the Southern Christian Association is an incorporated home." So, in one case, the thing exists only in my imagination and in the other case, it actually exists. And the reason, it actually exists is, that it's an ecclesiasticism. If it's not that, it doesn't actually exist you say. Isn't that profound logic? A thing doesn't actually exist unless it becomes an ecclesiasticism in a way of a matter of this kind, and if it's not that, why then it's only an integral part of the home and it doesn't actually exist at all. It exists only in my imagination. Now the fact is, the C.R.A. the Christian Restoration Association is not an ecclesiasticism as he calls it. He can't think of a Missionary Society without thinking of the United Christian Missionary Society. And these men that operate the C.R.A. have repudiated the United Christian Missionary Society because of its control and ecclesiastical authority over the churches. And they set up one that does not operate that way. And that's the Christian Restoration Association that has no such authority over the churches. And that's why they set it up; getting away from the United Christian Missionary Society

that does thus exercise such control. And it's set up simply on the same parallel that the Southern Christian Association is. And he hasn't told me yet how or just why one organization is in between and the other isn't.

How much time do I have now? Three minutes, all right. On chart 77, he has said there is no in between organization—the missionary society—and Buckner—and I've already dealt with that. And on chart 74, he wanted to know if the elders were over two institutions. No, elders can oversee only one organization, and one institution, and that's the church. But remember this, that when they provide a home where there's food, clothing and shelter, there is no organization set up for them to oversee, any more than when they arrange a Bible class or conduct a gospel meeting. Now, he said in that connection, regarding the matter of the train, that the church doesn't become a home. I asked about it becoming a train or a bus or automobile or something of that kind. He said, it's merely a teaching agency or it's a teaching work that it's doing. It's a teaching situation, I believe that's the way he put it. He said that it is a teaching situation he's overseeing. Well, in this other case Brother Deaver, it's a feeding situation they are overseeing. And they are overseeing a clothing situation and a bathing situation and a spanking situation. Don't you see? That's about the total situation I suppose.

He denies that my chart C can be true because he said, he's delegating the work to the other congregations. When they sent relief to a congregation in need, they were delegating their work to another congregation. No, they were simply sending it to a congregation that was in need to do the work of the congregation that received it because it was in need. That isn't true with the situation he tries to defend in the field of sponsoring churches. And so matter of delegation is entirely out on that deal.

On Chart T, that was the one on the two missionary societies and of course, that's the reason I didn't press him on it. I was sure he made a slip on the matter. And Boles—and I think the basic difference was that one has the Southern Baptist Convention in between and the other one doesn't—and I've dealt with that already.

The constituent elements of the Bethel Baptist Church. He said now that Bethel and Baptist and church are terms that are scriptural but they have no reference to the church. But in the elements of your proposition, there's nothing in the scripture, much less something found in the scripture that doesn't apply to it, there's nothing in the scripture at all to authorize a separate organization such as you are defending, to do the work of the church. The element is missing in every form from the New Testament record, referring to anything, much less to the work that you are trying to apply it to.

Boles Home operated before the incorporation and how can the incorporation provide it then? Well, before it was incorporated, it was operated by a group of men set up as an organization that was not incorporation. And then when it became a corporation, they got a charter and it became an incorporated organization and now they provide it since that time. I think anybody can see that.

And he referred to Brother John White and what he said about the home being incorporated. But John White wrote me a letter and said that the work of the Lubbock Home is under the direct supervision of the elders of the church, just like their Bible class work. That's what he said. Will you endorse that kind of an arrangement for Bible class work? Will you endorse a board of directors with a president and a vice president to do Bible class work, Brother Deaver? Thank you very kindly.

Fourth Night

Deaver's Fourth Affirmative

Brother Porter, Brethren Moderators, Brethren and Friends: I'd like to call your attention to all my charts No. 40 and No. 77 which actually summarize everything that has been said in the speech to which you've just listened. Would you notice carefully in connection with No. 40, that we have the matter here of the Christian Churches sending to—sending delegates to the missionary society and the missionary society makes decisions which are binding upon the churches. The delegates simply carry back the information and as long as they are a member of the society, then the decisions have to be bound upon these churches. And we have insisted all along that there is absolutely no such thing in connection with the church of the Lord as is that. And yet, that is the very point that Brother Porter has insisted night after night and speech after speech that does exist. That is, he says there is something that is parallel to that.

The truth of the entire matter is: Churches send to Boles Home and simply for the purpose of making possible care for orphan children and that there is absolutely no situation like here such as you have up here. He admits and has many times admitted that a church can send to an incorporated private home that the needs of orphans might be supplied. And in that situation, the incorporation didn't bring into existence something separate and apart from the church. It didn't create the in between organization or any such thing. It's perfectly all right. The home is not a church. It's not an integral part of the church. It's not managed by elders. And so the situation is all right. And as we mentioned last evening, just suppose that Brother Porter could succeed in proving that it's right on this to have elders over a home, he's already admitted everything in the world that's involved in my proposition, and he would have simply succeeded in establishing the fact that there are two ways that it could be done. Even if he's right that elders can function over a home—I deny the point—but even if he's right, he still has admitted that elders can send funds to an incorporated private home for the purpose of enabling care to be given to orphan children. This situation here is not parallel to that but it is parallel to the private home or the foster home which Brother Porter here upholds. This foster home can be incorporated; churches can send to it. Now this situation is exactly parallel to that. We know this is not parallel to that. And that covers two thirds of everything that he had to say.

Now, let's get my chart No. 77 right quickly. And these points simply take care of—and if we have the time, we'll come back and deal more in detail with them—but you mark it down that these two charts cover everything that he had to say. Speech after speech and night after night, it's been that in between organization which does not exist excepting in his own imagination. Brother Porter is fighting a straw man just like Leroy Garrett was, fighting a thing that does not exist. And if he could prove that it did exist, I would oppose just like Garrett does. And in the same situation here you don't have that in between organization; you simply have a church sending to a home. It's a special kind of home. It's the kind the law says you've got to have when you don't have a husband and wife or mother. And Brother Porter has taken the ridiculous position that you have to have that husband and wife relationship in order to have a divine home. Or he has come tonight to say, that either you have to have or must have had it at some time, which is a vital point. And we'd like to get down to deal with that and perhaps we can. Here you have the Christian Church sending to a missionary society which then provides evangelism. Here, you have the Baptist Church sending to the Southern Baptist Convention and then that provides Buckner Home in spite of what he has to say about it. This has it's own charter; it has its own incorporation but at the same time, it's provided by the Southern Baptist Convention and even the churches are a part of the Southern Baptist Convention. And don't let him mislead you on that point. The Southern Baptist Convention stands between the Baptist Church and Buckner Home over here. Each of them is separate; each of them is chartered and each has its own charter and its own incorporation but just the same, it's a part of the Southern Baptist Convention and gets its support here and even the churches are a part of the Southern Baptist Convention.

All right, in this situation, No. 1 Brother Porter condemns that and so do I. Brother Porter condemns this and so do I but Brother Porter says a Church of Christ which is incorporated can send over here to a private home which is incorporated, so that the needs of an orphan child might be supplied and that in this case, there is no in between organization. Brother

Porter said that's all right. Brother Porter contends No. 4. here, as being parallel to No. 2. In the case of churches of Christ sending to Boles Home, he says you have a situation that's parallel to this up here, or it's parallel to this up here. The truth of the matter is: it's not parallel to this and it's not parallel to this; but up here it is parallel to this which Brother Porter upholds. That's the truth of the whole matter, and that's in this entire debate, night after night and speech after speech and that's all that has been said: there's an in between organization and that the in between organization is parallel to this and this. You don't have it down here. He talked about the check and never did tell me where to send it and he can't tell me where to send it. Now Brother Porter, I'll tell you where to send that check to that organization, between a Baptist Church and Buckner Home if you'll just write her out, I'll put it in the mail for you. But you tell me where to send my check now, to that in between organization in connection with a church's sending to Boles Home.

All right, now let's see about another matter. The lights please. May I suggest to you that in the course of this discussion, we've seen an entire reversal of positions, that is, so far as concerns positions occupied by the disputants here and the disputant over at the Borger debate. Over at Borger, Brother Finley argued night after night, that elders cannot function as elders over a home.(Time, how much time Brother Tom? Keep me posted all along please.) All right, Brother Finley took the position that elders cannot function as elders over a home. Over here, Brother Porter has taken the position that they can function as elders over a home. I want to read to you a statement here. It's too lengthy to read all of it but I'll get perhaps one paragraph, page 42, *Walking by Faith*, Brother Roy Cogdill. "When elders become directors, a board of trustees or officers in any other arrangement or organization than the church, they are acting in another capacity than as elders of the congregation. God did not intend them to oversee anything but his church." And in that statement, Brother Cogdill is exactly right. Brother Porter, you stand in direct opposition to him on that. All right—here's the book if you'd like to check it and there's two more paragraphs just like it. I'd like to correct this matter. Brother Porter said; that over at Borger the Buena Vista debate, that Brother Deaver asked the elders to resign because they stopped their contributions to a home. There never was a bigger lie told than that. And I know where he got it. And when the man put it in his bulletin he knew it wasn't so. Over at Borger, here's what I had to say: You brethren have changed your position. And on the ground that you do not occupy the position now that you did occupy when these brethren put you in as elders, you are duty bound to resign. Not because you stopped your contribution. No sir. If the church doesn't want to send money to Sunny Glenn, that's their business and I respect it. But when elders change their position, that's a different matter, a different matter entirely. If men are selected as elders, who are in favor of having Bible classes, and they reach the point where they come to oppose the Bible classes, I maintain they are morally bound to resign. All right. It's a misrepresentation.

Brother Porter's basic errors. We were dealing with that a while ago. And I'd like to have my chart No. 14 right now and chart No. 20 and I want to know, Brother Tom, when I have twenty minutes left. Chart No. 14. Notice carefully, here's another vital point in this discussion. Brother Porter said that elders can function over a home. Notice carefully, we've raised the question: Who is authorized to have oversight or manage a church? Brother Porter, who is it? Parents or elders? I maintain that God put elders over the church and that God put parents over the home. And upon the same ground that you could put elders over the home, you could put parents over a church. You violate God's will on that matter. Go to a passage here: Acts 20:28 and Ephesians 6:1 down here. Now over which institution did God authorize elders to function? But Brother Porter has the unique position, and I'll say if you put this thing under elders, it's no longer a home. It's something arranged by the church. He is in the predicament of having to say here's Brother Porter's predicament: he must say that God put elders over two institutions or else then say the needs of orphans can be supplied without their having a home, one or the other. That's his predicament.

Now my chart No. 17 right quickly. And get No. 19 ready. In this section, Brother Porter, you have these statements that are vital, that elders are to rule over the church. Here you have the oversight, subjection or relationship in connection with the church. Here you have the oversight, subjection or relationship in connection with the home. This is the right way. That's God's plan. And as we mentioned a while ago, if you can put elders over a home here, why can't you put parents over a church over there? God distinguishes them. God separates the home from the church. The church is one thing and the home is something else. Certainly they overlap in duties, but the fact of those overlapping duties does not mean that their spheres of work coincide. And that's all that Brother Porter needs to think about.

Now then, my chart No. 19. please. In this connection Brother Porter, is it the function of the church or the home? To supply secular education, medical care, to supply recreation, to supply legal custody, to supply discipline? Are these activities or are these church activities? Are these things over which parents are to exercise oversight or are these things over which elders are to exercise oversight?

No. 22 please. Twenty minutes? All right, keep in mind that these are fundamental errors of Brother Porter's position. Let's have the lights please. He's failed to recognize or his entire speeches have been built upon the idea that there's an in between organization. That's basic error No. 1. He fails to distinguish between the home and the church and that's basic error No. 2. And he fails to recognize what a home is. He simply takes the position that you've got to have a husband and wife relationship to have a home. And it's on that point we've made the statement that, according to that, Mary, Martha and Lazarus didn't have a home. That just isn't so. There can be a legal guardian, child relationship and that's a home. And you know that he never did one time call for my chart No. 4. I used it night after night to show you what a home is but what did he say about it? Now, in his next speech he can't call for it because I wouldn't have a chance to reply. He let it go the whole debate. And I used that very chart to show you what a home was. And even in my chart, you have the situation of there having been a husband–wife relationship. Then it comes down to the point, as I said it could be, being a legal parent–child relationship.

All right, some very significant points are these: In the course of this discussion, Brother Porter did not even attempt to make a real scriptural defense of his proposition. He said you don't have to prove what your opponent admits. He didn't make a single objection to a single argument which I've made on a single passage, not one. He has based his entire case upon the erroneous assumption that there is an in between organization. He said last night that Boles Home existed for a while before it was incorporated yet he continues to argue that it's the corporation that provides the home. According to Brother Porter, there could be no divine home without a husband and wife relationship. So in a home which a church may provide, there must be a husband and wife standing in the position of parents to those children. And according to that then, the elders would take the oversight of the parents there with the child and would be a violation of God's arrangement. God puts parents over the home; elders over the church. Just because a church sends funds to your home doesn't mean that the elders displace you as the managers of those homes, or that home.

I'd like to read to you now, and you perhaps, have a copy of this in your hand and I wanted you to keep it—Brother Porter's absurdities and inconsistencies. Brother Porter argues, No. 1—There is a benevolent organization standing between a church and Boles Home, and yet he makes no attempt to give the address and the name of this in between organization. He spends much of his time discussing incorporation and yet he admits that the fact of incorporation does not bring into existence a separate organization. He argues that Boles Home is not a divine institution yet he fails to recognize that it's just like the home of his proposition and that whether human or divine doesn't matter therefore. He says Boles Home is not incorporated. They say it is and the law says it is. Write to Austin and find out. He says there is no divine home without a husband and wife. He admits that an incorporated church may send funds to an incorporated private home that the needs of an orphan child might be supplied adequately and that a church may thus meet its obligations to orphans and yet he denies that a church may send funds to Boles Home. He admits that a church can send funds to an incorporated private home which is not a church, which is not an integral part of a church yet he denies that a church can send funds to Boles Home. He says a church can send funds to a home that the needs of orphans might be supplied yet he says Boles Home has no right to exist. There is not a home among us, now being provided by a church or by churches which he will endorse yet he is not trying to start one and he can't start one because he knows that when he does start one he'll meet the same objections that he's filing against Boles Home; and yet he knows that the needs of an orphan child cannot be supplied without a home. He's taken the position that the church can function as a home and that therefore elders can oversee something other than a home. (I want to know at fifteen minutes, Brother Tom.) He says that a church can send funds to an incorporated private home that the needs of orphans might be adequately supplied. And that in this case, there is no organization standing between the church and the home but that when a church sends funds to Boles Home, there is somehow that in between organization. He says that when a church sends funds, it delegates it work—yet in his chart No. C, he had Jerusalem sending to Antioch, Antioch to Philippi and Philippi to Thessalonica, Thessalonica down to Achaia. And then, No. 14, he says the church is all sufficient to meet its obligation in benevolence, his chart No. C, but that this does not rule out the churches sending funds to an incorporated private home. But that when a church sends funds to Boles Home, that it violates the all sufficiency of the church. He fails to recognize that a proposition is either true or false. The law excluded middle. And that if one signs the affirmative, he's obligated to prove every point in the proposition but that one may sign the negative if there is a single point which he denies. No. 16. He blundered in his argument that since a corporation provides a home, that the corporation is no part of the home. Since his argument would mean that since a husband provides a home, that he's no part of his home. He says the in between organization can exist chartered or unchartered, incorporated or unincorporated, yet refuses to tell what and where this organization is by saying that it can exist we mean there is a possibility of it. Not that he approves it but there's a possibility of its existence. Now, No. 18, when he says this in between organization can exist, chartered or unchartered, incorporated or unincorporated, he admits that its not the charter and not the fact of incorporation which brings that organization into existence. He says that when a church sends funds, it delegates its work yet he says a church can send funds to an incorporated private home, hence he upholds the idea that a church can delegate its work to an incorporated private home. No. 20, he says that a church can supply the funds and direct the care, yet he, with reference to my chart No. 14, he said elders were not authorized to have oversight of that home. On the first night, he said Boles Home was not in his proposition then on the second night, he said it was involved in his proposition. He worked on the ridiculous notion, that whatever we agree on, he does not have to prove. He knows the needs of an orphan child cannot be adequately met without its having a home, yet he attempts to put elders over the home. And yet he refuses to call it a home. It's an arrangement provided by the church. He admits that Boles Home existed for a time before it was incorporated, yet he continues to argue that it's the corporation which provides the home. Now then, I want to summarize for you briefly the points that we established last night in my affirmative.

I gave you a syllogism, my chart No. 70 I believe, that all total situations, the constituent elements of which are scriptural, are total situations which are scriptural. Minor premise: The total situation described in my proposition, is a total situation, the constituent elements of which are scriptural. Conclusion: It's certainly obvious therefore if these two premises are true, that the total situation described in my proposition is a total situation which is scriptural. That simply says that since the whole of a thing is the sum of its parts, when you prove the scripturalness of the parts, you prove the scripturalness of the whole thing. I read to you last night, a statement from Brother Foy Wallace Jr., *Bulwarks of the Faith*, page 38, Vol. I which says exactly that in different words, and he's right. And I've never heard anybody criticize him because of it. That's his argument. Any time you prove the scripturalness of the parts of a thing, you prove the scripturalness of the whole thing. That's the argument in 1 Corinthians 13:10. And so I give you—Brother Porter will not deny the scripturalness of that major premise. Any time you prove the scripturalness of the parts of a thing you prove the scripturalness of that total situation. There's no way under the sun to deny that.

If there's any attack made, it has to be made on that minor premise. Now then, it's my job then, to prove the component parts that are involved in that minor premise. And so we did that last evening. My minor premise of the situation in my proposition simply involves, first of all, recognition of the fact that God has given the church the obligation to orphans that is proved by James 1:27. And in the *Gospel Guardian*, July 25, 1957, Brother Porter says that that passage authorizes or teaches church responsibility to orphans. No. 2—my proposition recognizes the fact that God has given the obligation but has not specified the details as to how the church is to meet that obligation to orphans. It's a definite fact that, when God gives an obligation, but does not specify the details as to how that obligation is to be met, then the details involved in meeting that obligation fall in the realm of human judgment and expediency. And that's the principle upon which we build a baptistery, build a church building and have a Bible class, a located preacher and on down the line. Brother Porter will not attempt to deny the scripturalness of that point.

My proposition recognizes the true meaning of the word "orphan." The word occurs in James 1:27, John 14:18 and that's all. It simply means, one bereft of parental guidance and care. And a child may be bereft of parental guidance and care with one parent still living or two parents still living. It can be an orphan because of dereliction or desertion or disease or abandonment. He's still an orphan, none the less.

And my proposition involves the recognition of the fact that God's love extends to all men, Matthew 5:43-48. Some have taken the ridiculous position that a church can only help that orphan who is a member of the church or who had some parents who were members of the church. What about that one who is not a Christian? And its parents were not Christians? Brother Porter hasn't said where he stands on that. But my proposition recognizes that God's will and that God's love extends to the just and to the unjust, and we also gave the passage last night, Galatians 6:10, authorizing that point.

Then, my proposition recognizes or involves recognition of the fact that the church cannot function as a home. The church is one thing; the home is something else. God put elders over the church. God put parents over the home. The church is all sufficient to do the work that God gave it to do. The home is all sufficient to do the work that God gave it to do. And it's just as sinful to violate the Bible teaching on the all sufficiency of the home as it is to violate the Bible teaching on the all sufficiency of the church. Elders are over the church (Acts 20:28). Parents are over the home (Eph. 6:1).

My proposition involves recognizing or recognition of the fact that the needs of an orphan child cannot be met adequately without it's having or being a part of a home. A child needs food, clothing and shelter, education—secular and religious, and recreation, medical care and discipline and custody. And when you supply these things, you supply a home regardless of what it might be called. And the church of the Lord has the right to provide or supply the funds that a home might be made possible for an orphan child. That doesn't mean that elders function as elders over the home.

My proposition involves recognition of the fact that there is no inherent sin in having a board. (How much time, Brother Tom?) The legal board of trustees stands in the position of the parents and the children of that home. The law demands a recognized governing body. If the board is inherently sinful, then it's sinful to have a board of trustees in connection with our worship and in the building, the church building or in connection with our teaching in a Bible class or it would be sinful in providing a home for a preacher. And yet the law says you've got to have that board of trustees to hold the property in trust. All right, the proof of that point Brother Porter was Romans 13.

My proposition involves recognition of the fact that there is no inherent sin in incorporation. We mentioned last night that a corporation is simply an artificial being, invisible, intangible and existing only in contemplation of law. Incorporation insures perpetual existence and protection. Some states demand that even a church be incorporated in order to hold property. Now, if there is inherent sin in incorporation, then it's sinful to have a corporation in connection with the building in which we worship, in connection with the classes in which we teach and learn and in connection with a home for the preacher. The scriptural proof of that is Romans 13. Recognition of the fact then, that there is no inherent sin in having a charter. This simply is another legal requirement. The law says, the agency or institution shall be legally organized and it's objects and purposes shall be expressly stated in its charters, articles of incorporation, statutes, constitution, or other published material. Now here's Brother Porter's quibble on that: He said "or other published material." Therefore, if you simply have other published material, you don't have to have a charter. Brother Porter, that's not what that means. You go down to the State Department of Public Welfare and see. You've got to have a charter; you've got to have the articles of incorporation; and you've got to have the other published material. You cannot say "or" and therefore that eliminates the other. You can't start a home without a legal organization and they'll tell you can't have it legally organized until you have the charter and you can't have the charter without incorporation. That quibble on that "or" just won't work. And yet that's exactly what it was. All right, a child care agency must be legally organized and the State Department of Public Welfare tells you plainly—I have it in my notes and I got it directly from them and he can get it at the same place—that it is not legally organized until chartered. Can you get a charter without incorporation? No sir. They said that's what it is. That's a very part of what they mean by incorporation.

Now my proposition recognizes the fact that we must meet legal requirements. The board, the charter, the incorporation; these are legal requirements and the proof again, Romans 13. The law says you've got to have a license. You've got to have a recognized governing body, and in many states, incorporation. A thing that's right, doesn't become wrong, Brother Porter, simply because you make it legal.

Then in No. 11, my proposition involves recognition of the fact that the arrangement down at Quinlan—Get my chart No. 4 ready please—that arrangement down at Quinlan, Texas is just a home and nothing more and nothing less. If brethren could simply get this point in their minds, much of the confusion would forever be gone. That it's God's will that every child have a home. Many times because of tragic circumstances that natural home is destroyed. Boles Home is simply an effort on the part of Christian people to provide a home for that child. And Brother Porter simply needs to recognize that it is a home and that's all that it is.

Now before coming to this, let me suggest to you another point here. My proposition involves recognition of the fact that a church can contribute to a home to make possible care for orphan children. Now, that arrangement down at Quinlan in Texas is simply a home and I maintain that a church can send funds to a home in order to make possible care for orphan children. Notice carefully if you will. Here you have husband and wife and three natural children. Brother Porter, is that a home? And here, No. 2, a husband and wife and three natural children and they take in three foster children. Now, is that still a home? But they decide to take in four more. But when you cross the line of number six, the law steps in. You have become, according to them, a child caring institution. And the law steps in and tells you what to do and what you can't do. All right, you have seven legal children then. Is that a home? Husband and wife and three children of their own and seven foster children. Is that a home? In No. 4, a husband and wife, three natural children, seven legal children licensed and incorporated, because when you got seven here, the law says you've got to have a license, you've got to have a charter, you've got to incorporate. Brother Porter says the law doesn't demand it. But the law does demand it, but suppose it didn't. Would he approve it if it didn't have that incorporation?

He said the Lubbock Home is not incorporated. I'll accept. Do you approve it Brother Porter? You say it's under elders. Do you approve it? Do you endorse that home? Why make all that ado about that when you know good and well you don't endorse it? And if you didn't, you've still admitted that a church can send to a private home incorporated to provide for the needs of orphan children. All right, we have a husband and wife, three natural children, seven legal children, licensed and incorporated. Is that a home? No. 5, husband and wife, three natural children, seven legal children and licensed and incorporated. All right, the wife died right here. So you just have a husband, three natural children, seven legal children, licensed and incorporated. That's no longer a home, according to Brother Porter, up until tonight. Tonight it is. Last night it wasn't because we didn't have a husband and wife. But now he says they did have and so it's still a home right there. The wife died. Here, we just have the husband with these and I ask him: Is that a home? But the husband remarries. And so you have a husband and wife, three natural children so far as concerns the husband, seven legal children so far as concerns the husband, ten legal children so far as concerns the wife, licensed and incorporated. Brother Porter, is that a home? And the husband dies; that leaves the wife, ten legal children, licensed and incorporated. Is that a home? This wife remarries and you've got a husband and wife, ten legal children, licensed and incorporated. You've got a situation in which there has been a husband and wife relationship. Is that a home? Is that a home?

All right, my chart No. 5. I maintain that arrangement down in Quinlan is nothing more under the sun than just a home. I maintain that the church has a scriptural right to send to a home, in order that that home might provide the needs of orphan children. Here's the same situation now if you just had this husband and wife and three natural children. Could the church send to that? Suppose they take in three legal children—foster children. Can a church send to that? Suppose they take in four more and the law steps in. Can you still send to that? That's actually the way the home at Morrilton, Arkansas got started. It used to be at Ft. Smith. They didn't have that and they got too many children and the law came out and arrested the husband and wife because they weren't operating legally. So they had to get on the ball and operate legally. All right, notice carefully, can a church send to that? And in this situation, where you have the husband and wife, the seven children licensed and incorporated, could the church send to that? If the wife died, could the church still send to it? If the husband remarries here, could the church still send to that? And if the husband dies and you have the wife and ten legal children, could the church send to that? If the wife remarries here and you have ten legal children, licensed and incorporated, could the church send to that? And Brother, bless your heart, that's Boles Home. Let Brother Porter say the church can't send to this situation here. And that's Boles Home. That's all in the world you've got. That's Boles Home. And the church can send funds to it, that the needs of orphans might be supplied.

My chart No. 70 please then. And I'd like for you to notice simply by way of summary of this discussion. Brother Porter, there are the elements that I have established. A church has an obligation to orphans and the details of meeting that obligation are not specified. The meaning of the word "orphan," we've discussed that and proved it's meaning. God's love extends to all men.

A church cannot function as a home. The needs of orphans cannot be met without a home. There's no inherent sin in having a board or incorporation of a charter. We must meet legal requirements. The arrangement down at Quinlan is a home. And the church can send to a home. Now then, if Brother Porter objected to any of these points it would be such a simple matter for him to come up here and say, Brother Deaver, this point is wrong or this one's wrong or this one's wrong, but he'll not do it. He'll tell you, the thing that's wrong is, a missing element. That there's an in between organization. And the whole debate has been about that in between organization and until this good minute, he hasn't told me where to send my check.

All right, give me my chart No. 72, I believe—I thought the time was up. No. 70. This is the point we've referred to several times in connection with this in between idea. Brother Porter, if you would just admit a simple and obvious point. Here's the Christian Church incorporated sending to a missionary, society incorporated and then the evangelism out here is provided. In connection with the Baptist Church incorporated you have the Southern Baptist Convention here, to which the Baptist Church sends which in turn then provides the Buckner Home incorporated and here you have an in between organization and here you have one. Brother Porter condemns that and so do I. Brother Porter condemns this and so do I. In the situation No. 3, Brother Porter upholds this: A church of Christ incorporated can send to a private home incorporated so that the needs of an orphan child might be adequately supplied and he says there's no in between organization there. He approves of that but he condemns this situation down here : A church of Christ incorporated sending to Boles Home incorporated. He says there's an in between organization; this is parallel to that which he upholds.

Porter's Fourth Negative

Brethren Moderators, Brother Deaver, Respected Friends: I appear before you now for the closing speech of this discussion. Of course, when another thirty minutes shall have passed, the debate will be history. At this particular juncture, I want to express to you my appreciation for your coming from time to time and your very patient hearing and attention while we've discussed these matters. And for the fine order you've maintained from the beginning until now. I appreciate the privilege of having met Brother Deaver in this debate and the fine spirit he has manifested in the discussion of these issues. I am certain that you can go home believing that debates can be had without bloodshed, without somebody getting roughed up physically or anything of that kind. I appreciate greatly every kindness and courtesy that has been shown me since I've been here and the association I've had with you from time to time. I'm grateful to Brother Paul Lusby for his serving as my timekeeper or moderator, to Brother Darrell Shaw for operating my charts for me, and for Brother Lusby's son and for Brother Shropshire for operating the recording machine. And of course, for every other assistance that has been rendered in any way by anyone to make this the discussion that it ought to be.

Now I want to come to a consideration of a number of things here that Brother Deaver brought up in his closing speech. Of course, he passed out the little sheet in which he listed all of Brother Porter's inconsistencies. And they are amusing when you read through them, to see the inconsistence that he has tabulated. It will not be necessary for me to take time to go right through those one by one and show the absurdity in them. Because you can read them for yourselves and discover whether that represents the situation or not. He thinks I'm inconsistent because I say that funds may be sent to some home or the church may provide some kind of home to care for somebody and at the same time can't send to Boles Home; so that's an inconsistency. And so I suppose I'd be inconsistent if I said that a church can take care of an orphan but it can't send to Buckner Home to take care of an orphan. If you can take care of an orphan one place, you can take care of one anywhere. And therefore, they can send to Buckner Home or any other home just as well and if I can't send to all of them, then I'd be inconsistent if I say they can send to one. Now that takes care of all of his inconsistency he has listed on that sheet along that line.

And that chart that he had a while ago, that No. 4 was it? We want to look at that, chart No. 4. Here he has the husband and wife relationship with three natural children; the husband and wife with three natural children and three legal children; the husband and wife with three natural children and seven legal children. I believe this is the one he said that I hadn't referred to and I couldn't refer to it now. Well, I did refer to it and I showed that he was absolutely wrong in his claims about it—that the law did not demand what he claimed. Because, he says down here, when you get to seven, then the law steps in and says you must be incorporated and the law says no such thing. Now, then, let us have the lights back on and I'll show you why I said that and he has gone on and just kept repeating that the law says it; the law does say it, and although I showed from the very quotation he made, that it didn't say it; that it said they should have a charter or articles of incorporation, statutes or constitution or other printed material. And I suppose, since "or other printed material" doesn't mean they don't have to have all the former things, then you have to have all of them. Just what does the little word "or" indicate? Does that mean the same thing as "and"? That they must have a charter, articles of incorporation, statutes, constitution *and* other printed material? That's the way it would read according to his interpretation of it a while ago. But it says "or other printed material." Therefore, you could have one or the other. You don't have to have all of them. You can have a charter, articles of incorporation, you have a constitution, you can have statutes *or* other printed material. If you have other printed material, you don't have to have the ones going before, or there wouldn't be any "or" to it, it would have to be "and." Certainly Brother Deaver ought to know that.

But he said, now, "regardless of what he said about it, the law does demand that when you come to No. 7 here or have seven children, that you must be incorporated; you must obtain a charter; the law says so." Where's the law Brother Deaver? You haven't read it. You have it in your possession—you have the law in your possession, I'm sure, that governs child caring institutions. There's not a word in it that they have to have a charter, or the incorporation. I have it also. And I know that it's not there. If it had been there, you would have introduced it; you didn't do it. You've had four nights to introduce it in and you've been claiming all the time that the law demands it. And Porter can't set up one—if he does, he's got to have one like Boles because the law demands it. You've got to set up a human organization out there, and incorporate it or bring it into existence with the incorporation, one or the other, and you've got to have it there or you can't operate. Brother Deaver says so, and he keeps on making that statement over and over and over, and there's not a word in the law that says any such thing. If there had been, he would have introduced it. Brother Deaver, why didn't you introduce it? You have a copy of the law, don't you? If you don't have, I'll lend you mine. You have a copy of the law, don't you? If it did say it, why didn't you introduce it? Why didn't you show us where the law said that and that would have been an end to it? But did he? No, he didn't. He twisted the things around where it referred to the licensing and tried to make it mean charter one time. And the other time, he tried to make the word "or" have the significance of "and," and you've got to have all of them. And he never did introduce the passage that said you have to be incorporated or have a charter in order to maintain or establish a child caring institution in the State of Texas. Did he? No, he didn't. If you did, Brother Deaver, where was it?

Now, I read to you last night or night before, a letter which I had from the State Department of Public Welfare. And this comes, not from Fort Worth, nor from Lubbock nor Amarillo nor some other place like that. It comes from the state headquarters from Austin. And from the very man that is the very head of the situation, and here is what he says about it: "It is not mandatory that a separate corporation be formed and that a charter be granted in order for a person or an association to maintain or operate a child caring institution in the State of Texas." Who said that? The State Welfare Board of Austin, Texas. They say definitely that it is not mandatory—mandatory means required—it is not required, it is not necessary, is what they say about it. That a separate corporation be formed and that a charter be granted in order for a person or association to maintain or operate a child caring institution in the State of Texas. That is, a person or association can operate or maintain one child caring institution in the State of Texas without being chartered or incorporated. That's what the State Welfare Board said. He says it's not so, the law says they must have and he's never introduced the law. Now I believe they know as much about it as he does. And if I thought he knew more about it than they did, why at least I'd expect him to introduce the law and he hasn't done it.

Concerning the matter of his charts 77 and 40 in which he summarized the matter and all that Porter had said, he declared. And that, in the missionary society, there's delegates which make decisions that are binding on the churches. And he can't get away from the idea of the United Christian Missionary Society; I gave him one a number of times, I've called his attention to it over and over, the Christian Restoration Association of Cincinnati, Ohio, that was set up by a number of men in the Christian Church who had repudiated that ecclesiastical machine known as the United Christian Missionary Society. They would not go along with it. They threw off the shackles and set up the Christian Restoration Association with no such authority. And they have no high pressure methods and do not high pressure anybody to contribute to it or support it or anything of that kind. And yet, Brother Deaver, it's a missionary society and I ask you: will you endorse it? Will you endorse it—that kind? It's exactly what you have in Boles Home. Simply a corporation that provides it just like the corporation provides Boles Home. And if you can send a donation to Boles Home as the church, then you can send to the Christian Restoration Association because they are parallel. And you're coming along and saying they have delegates that make the decisions binding on the churches just won't work. Because we've called your attention to one that has no such authority over the churches. And you yet won't tell us whether you endorse it or not.

Then on chart 77, he also said, there's no in between organization, that it does not exist only in Porter's imagination. Well, does the Christian Restoration Association corporation exist except in my imagination? We have the same situation. I suppose that exists only in your imagination and the Christian Church men can say to you the very thing you are saying to me; you are fighting a straw man; it's not there, it just exists in your imagination. Well, if one exists in mine, the other exists in yours and if the other actually exists, then the one actually exists. Yet he says the law says you have to have it and the law doesn't say any such thing. Why didn't you produce the law, Brother Deaver? You've had four nights to do it and you haven't done it and this audience knows you haven't done it. What difference would it make?

He said, Porter admits that incorporation doesn't necessarily bring an organization into existence and he doesn't oppose incorporation. Well, then why are you trying to prove so much about incorporation, if I don't oppose it? Certainly, I'm not opposing incorporation, I'm opposing the thing you incorporate. You have a human organization set up there, a group of men, that I showed the other night on a chart I used, a group of men set up to do the work that God gave the church to do and whether you incorporate them or leave them unincorporated—whether they are chartered or not chartered, you still have a human organization doing the work of the church and I opposed it on higher ground. Whether incorporated or unincorporated, not because it's one or the other, but because it's a human organization doing the work that God designed the church to do.

He made here a rather amusing statement and maybe this was a slip of the tongue: He said, the Baptist Churches are a part of the Southern Baptist Convention. Yet you went right on in the next breath and said the Southern Baptist Convention stands between the Baptist Churches and the home. I don't know just how that happened. They are a part of it and yet it stands between the churches and the home. And I've showed you already that Baptist Churches do not have to send to the Southern Baptist Convention to support the Buckner Home. That is absolutely not required of them. They send to the Corporation and the corporation passes it on to the home. He is still wanting the address of where to send it. Well, I showed—he said they spend it under the direction of the corporation—and if you send it to the home, it just the same as sending it to the corporation. But he wants to send it to the corporation without it getting to the home. And I asked him how he would send down to the Buckner corporation without it getting to the home. He said he would tell me sometime maybe, but he didn't. He didn't tell me how to do it.

Of course, according to him, it must be sent to the corporation and instead of going to the home; it would go to the Southern Baptist Convention. Because Buckner Corporation is not an integral part of Buckner Home like Boles Corporation is with Boles Home but it's an integral part of the Southern Baptist Convention, so it goes the other direction you see. In one case, the corporation works one way and the other case, the corporation works the other way. In Boles Home, it goes away from the home and goes to the Southern Baptist Convention. I wonder what the total situation would be on that.

Again, then he comes about the private home incorporated, in his chart there, the private home incorporated. And he is insisting that Boles Home is nothing more than just a private home. Now, if you have a corporation to provide a private home like you have a corporation to provide Boles Home, it would stand parallel and I would oppose it. And then he comes again to sending the check to the corporation and I've dealt with that.

Then he talked about a reversal of positions. Oh, there's been such a reversal put up here of positions. He said Brother Finley, over at Buena Vista just a short time ago, declared that elders cannot be over a home. But Porter, in this case, says that elders can be over a home. And that Brother Cogdill, in his book, said that elders can be over only one organization and that's the church. And he said that you are in direct conflict with Roy Cogdill on it, and that isn't true. I agree wholeheartedly to what Roy Cogdill said. Elders can be only over one organization, and if you have an organization set up like you have in Boles Home to operate the home, the elders cannot be over it, because they would be over another organization over which they have no right to be. And they cannot be over a private home with parents because those parents comprise a divine organization and elders cannot be over it.

When I said they can direct the care in a home, I simply said they can rent or buy a building and simply put them in there and have somebody to take care of them and set up no organization; just furnish them food and clothing and shelter, just like they would furnish a Bible class or a gospel meeting and there's no organization to it. And when they are over a situation of that kind, they are not over any organization at all except the church. Because that is not an organization any more than the Bible class is an organization.

But that isn't true with him, he wouldn't tell you whether he would take the same arrangement for his Bible class, would he? Why didn't you tell me Brother Deaver? I asked you, would you accept the same arrangement for the Bible class that you accept for the orphan home? Would you? I just often wonder if you would. John B. White said the Lubbock Home was under the direct supervision of the elders. He said, will you endorse it? No, I didn't say I'd endorse it. You won't either Brother Deaver. You've been trying to twist around and make folks think you will but you don't. You don't endorse Lubbock Home because you don't believe they have any right to operate it. And you don't believe it's under the elders and you believe they've been misrepresenting the fact to the brotherhood by claiming that it is because at least twelve of those elders have no connection with the board whatsoever.

Yet they say it's under the elders. Why don't they advertise that it's under five men, a small portion of the elders, less than one third of them, who comprise the board, and they are the ones that are operating it.

Well, concerning a reversal of position, I wonder if anybody else ever reversed positions. He was making a reversal of positions between me and Brother Finley. I think there might be one where only one man is involved. Because, in the former debate, over at Buena Vista, Brother Deaver took the position and argued long and loud on it, that there is no limit to be placed upon your relief to orphans. That it's just as broad and extensive as God's eternal law of love. He sends the rain on the just and the unjust and makes the sun to rise on the good and evil. And no limit to it because Brother Finley was making some limitation on it and he was trying to keep him from making any limitation, and he said, here is God's law of love that extends to the just and the unjust. Where do Baptist children qualify, Brother Deaver? Are they among the just or the unjust? The good or the evil? And you've said that there has to be some limitation on that. You can't send it to people who teach a false doctrine. You can't send to people who are going to teach a false doctrine, so you can't send it to Baptist Homes because they are teaching a false doctrine. I asked him last night, do they have a right to restore the home the child lost? And he said, nobody has a right to if he is going to teach false doctrine. Now then, brethren, those who stand with me couldn't set up a home of that kind if we wanted to because we would be teaching false doctrine. And nobody can set up a home like that, as I showed you last night, except Brother Deaver and those who stand with him because they are the only people on earth who are teaching the truth. Don't you see? And therefore, Baptist children and Methodist children and other children will never get a home provided for them, according to God's will. Then brethren who stand with him will have to restore and provide it for them. Otherwise, it's ruled out because of the teaching of false doctrine. So it looks to me like somebody else has reversed positions.

Concerning the Buna vista situation, he said: I did not say that the elders should repent and make a confession to the church and resign because they quit sending to Boles Home. He said; that's the biggest lie that was ever told. Well, thanks for the compliment—whoever it belongs to. But nevertheless, he said: what I did say was, that the elders had changed positions and therefore they should repent and they should resign and so on, because they changed positions. Positions on what? Positions with respect to whether they should or would send to Boles Home or not. It wasn't because they had quit sending to Boles Home, it was just because they had changed positions, you see. Wouldn't that make a big difference? And wherein they believed one thing, they changed their position, therefore they should resign. I wonder if that would apply to preachers. Would that apply to preachers? If a preacher was preaching for a congregation and he believes one thing and he changed to something else, I wonder if the preacher should resign? Should he, Roy? I just wonder. Better be careful.

Well, he argued long and loud during that last speech that parents are over the home and elders are over the church. And that's exactly what I've contended all the time and I've been showing you from time to time that I do not believe that elders should be over any organization except the church. But he has admitted that their duties overlap. Yes, he said, their duties overlap but they're not identical; they don't go the same all the way. Well, I asked him how far did it go and he never did tell me. He admits that a home can provide the money without invading the function of the church and yet it's the function of the church to provide the money. But the church cannot provide the care—the food and the bathing and so on—without invading the function of the home and therefore it becomes a home. But if so, then the homes becomes a church when it invades the function of the church and provides the money. Where does the overlapping go and how far does it extend and where does it stop, Brother Deaver? Does it just reach one way and it doesn't over lap the other? It overlaps when it goes for the money. It's blocked, completely blocked, when it starts for the care.

And on his chart No. 19 and some other things that then were said in the former speech were, that the church would have to supply the education. And so, if they went on to school and then to a college and university, the same church would have to have control over the college and university. And if they sent them to the hospital, they would have to have control over that. Oh no, not at all. They would not have to control or oversee the hospital or the university or anything of that kind. They would simply be buying service from that. They wouldn't be making contributions to it.

And then he came back to his chart No. 4, the one that he said that I had not used but I had. And then: Boles Home existed before the corporation, and how in the world then can they provide the home now? Well, when the organization existed before the charter was taken out—was incorporated—it was the same organization that existed before, the very same men, as I told you last night, who formed the organization before the charter was taken out were the men who formed the board after it was taken out. And it was the same organization that had simply obtained a charter. And the same men who provided the home before the incorporation, continued to provide it after the incorporation, Brother Deaver. I thought you knew that.

And he says elders cannot displace the parents. Who said they could? I've never said that parents are overseen by the elders in their home; that they must oversee that organization. I said no such thing. And then he made a great play on the home again: that so and so cannot have a home and these cannot have a home and these cannot have a home; Porter says they can't have a home because the marriage relationship isn't there. You overlook completely the distinction between the meanings of the word "home." And I showed that the other night and so on—on my chart E, and I want to call that to your attention again; Let us have my chart E here and let you see about this matter. And actually, he has never referred to this chart any more than just to say that the idea of marriage relationship being necessary is absurd.

Now, here are two divine organizations, the church and the home. We refer to the church as a divine organization and the home as a divine organization. Why do they call the church a divine organization? Because of a divinely ordained relationship. There you have in the first place, the statement made by Jesus, "I will build my church" (Matt. 16:18). Second, "all baptized into one body" (1 Cor. 12:13). And third, "We being many, are one body in Christ" (Rom. 12:5). Fourth, "Christ is the head of the church" (Eph. 5:23). Now there is a divinely ordained relationship that constitutes or comprises the church. And without that divinely ordained relationship, existing, there could be no church; and yet, we know that the word "church" is sometimes used in a different sense. Down here, I have a definition, taken from a standard authority, that says: A church is a building, set apart for public worship. Is that what we mean when we say that the church is a divine organization? No. We don't mean the building where the church worships is a divine organization. Paul spoke about the church coming together in one place (1 Cor. 14:23), and come together in the church (1 Cor. 11:18), the church in their house, and so on. But the house or the place, we do not regard as a divine organization, though it is sometimes defined to mean church. But the divine organization we refer to is this that has become the divinely ordained relationship. And so it is with the home. There's a home that's a divine organization because of a divinely ordained relationship. First, "He which made them at the beginning, made them male and female"

(Matt. 19:4). And second, "they shall be one flesh" (Gen. 2:24). And third, "what God hath joined together, let no man put assunder" (Matt. 19:6). And fourth, "the husband is the head of the wife" (Eph. 5:23). Just as there is a divine organization called the church because of a divine relationship, that God ordained, so there is a divine organization called the home because of this divinely ordained relationship. And without that relationship, the home in that sense does not exist. But sometimes, the word home simply means a place where one lives. As for example, in Acts 21:6, "they returned home." 1 Corinthians 11:34, "let him eat at home." Matthew 8:6, "servant lieth at home sick." And often times we use the term "home" to mean the place where one lives. And in that sense, of course, anybody can have a home. But that place is not a divine organization any more than the church building is a divine organization. Here's your divine organization up here, that exists because of a marriage relationship, just as the church exists because of that divinely ordained relationship over there. He hasn't touched top, edge, side nor bottom of it and he never will. He can't and no other man can. Let us have the lights again.

On his total situation—how much time do I have?—thank you. On his total situation he said, I proved all my points, the elements in my proposition—named them, numbered them, one, two, three, four, five, six all the way down and wound up by saying that that sustains my proposition. But he said now, "What did Porter say about it?" Well, didn't he say there's one element missing and that is the benevolent organization in between? And that is exactly so, and that's the element that has—or his proposition and his chart fails to have. And that's where the issue is and that's where the fight is.

And I want you to keep in mind this fact, that these debates have accomplished a great deal. In the very recent past, men have affirmed in public debate, that churches have the scriptural right to build and maintain benevolent organizations through which to do the work of the church or the work of benevolence. But they back up on that now. They've found out that if they do that, they would have to defend the missionary society. And so, to get out of accepting the missionary society, they have resorted to another course. They'll just deny the thing exists. And so, that's where it's gone. No longer admitting that a benevolent organization exists; they are now denying that it exists. And so it exists only in your imagination. Better to do that then, than to accept the missionary society. Well, when you deny that it exists, you deny that the missionary society exists also, and so you are still where you were. You haven't made any progress whatsoever so far as your supporting the institutions is concerned.

Well, he repeated the fact—the idea that they must meet legal demands and so on. And at Morrilton, he said, there the husband and wife were arrested because they didn't meet legal demands. Do you mean they were arrested because they were not incorporated? Is that what you meant, Brother Deaver? Were they arrested because they were not incorporated or because they didn't have a license? Which was it? You know, he is confusing all the time the license with the incorporation. And I just wonder which it was? And that covers then—I have a little time left and if there is, I might look at another chart or so. How many? Four minutes.

All right, I want to use my chart—let me see here—chart G and chart G-1, I want these two in succession—chart G and chart G-1. To this chart, Brother Deaver has never made reference, so I want to call it to your attention here. Here we have: Is one human, the other divine? On the one hand we have Buckner Home; on the other hand, Boles Home. Now these statements are copied from their charters. They are not taken from something that some opponent to them has uttered, but is taken from their charters. All right. Under Buckner Home, (1) The name of this corporation shall be Buckner Orphan Home, Art. 1. (2) The purposes of this corporation are to procure control of destitute orphan children for the purpose of providing them with a comfortable home. Sec. 2. (2) Under Boles, The purposes of this corporation are to provide a home for destitute and dependent children. Art. 2. (3) Under Buckner, The principle place of business shall be in the city of Dallas, Texas. Sec. 33). Under Boles, The principle place of business shall be near Quinlan in Hunt County, Texas, Art. 3. (4) Under Buckner, The term of its existence shall be fifty years. Sec. 4. (4) Under Boles, This corporation shall exist for a period of fifty years. Art. 4. (5) Under Buckner, The number of directors shall be nine, Sec. 5. (5) Under Boles, Shall be incorporated by a board of seven directors, Art. 5. And the other is a continuation, beginning with No. 6 under Buckner, The management may make suitable provisions for any of them in a private home, Sec. 7. No. 6 under Boles, The right, by complying with the law of the State, to adopt such children, Art. 2. (7) Under Buckner, The institution is to be to them *en loco parentis*, Sec. 2. He says that means over here at Boles, that they stand for the parents and therefore take the place of the parents; but in the case of Buckner, it doesn't because it's not *en loco parentis*; it's *en loco* the Southern Baptist Convention. It goes back the other way, you see. And then (7) under Boles, Such home is to stand *en loco parentis* to children, Art. 2. (8) Under Buckner, Buckner Orphan Home is strictly charitable and educational purposes only, Sec. 13. (8) Under Boles, this corporation is for benevolent, charitable and educational purposes only. Art. 6. No. 9) under Buckner, The corporation has no capital stock, Sec. 6. (9) Under Boles, This corporation shall have no capital stock, Art. 6. No. (10) under Buckner, The membership of this corporation shall consist of the deacons who are members of Baptist churches within the State of Texas, Sec. 8. (10) Under Boles, Each shall be a loyal member of some congregation of the Church of Christ in the State of Texas. There, you have ten identical points in the two charters concerning these two homes or the corporations: one for Buckner and the other for Boles. And there's nothing in the charter of Buckner that says one word about anything relative to the Southern Baptist Convention. In fact, the Southern Baptist Convention did not set it up. It existed without their authority and had no connection with it and was set up by men, just as this one here, who formed themselves into a board and were incorporated and took over that which had been already existing under the provision and direction of someone else. And both of them came about in that way. And so, here we have two of them, and I'm wanting to know: and I've been asking and I've asked a number of times: Why on earth this is a divine organization and that one is not, and why this one exists only in my imagination but that one is a reality over there, and why Buckner Home or Buckner Corporation goes back the other way, away from the home, while Boles Corporation heads straight toward the home; and is a part of it while Buckner Corporation is no part of the home; it's a part of the Southern Baptist Convention, though the Southern Baptist Convention had nothing to do with setting it up, establishing it or anything of the kind.

Now keep that in mind; he paid no attention to that and why he let a chart like that, with all those points and parallels go, I don't know. Perhaps it was an oversight. I know it's difficult to keep up with all the charts we used. I know it's difficult to keep up with all the charts we are using. I find it so myself, and I am sure it is for him, but this fact stands, and here were parallels between the two homes—Buckner and Boles. He wound up a while ago on that chart and said, "Remember that this is just a home." "Boles Home is just a home." Remember, Brother Deaver, that Buckner Home is just a home. It has the same arrangements that Boles has. If Boles is just a home, then Buckner is just a home; and if a church can donate to Boles Home because it may help a private home, then a church can donate to Buckner Home because it may help a private home—that is, if it may help a private Baptist home. Can it? You know he said he didn't say that you can't help a private Baptist home. I thank you very kindly.

The End.

Note: This transcription was made verbatim from the tape recording of the debate.

(signed) Thomas F. Shropshire